W9-BRS-028

The YOUTH GROUP MEETING GUIDE

by Richard W. Bimler
& dozens of contributors

Group Books

P.O. Box 481 • Loveland, CO 80539

This resource book is dedicated to Hazel,
Diane, Bob and Mike—what a youth group!

THE YOUTH GROUP MEETING GUIDE

Copyright © 1984 by Thom Schultz Publications, Inc.

Second Printing

Library of Congress Catalog No. 83-82574
ISBN 0936-664-17-7

All rights reserved. No part of this book may be reproduced in any
manner whatsoever without written permission from the publisher, except in the case of brief quotations embodied in critical articles and
reviews. For information write Permissions, Group Books, P.O. Box
481, Loveland, CO 80539.

Credits
Designed by Jean Bruns
Illustrations by Rand Kruback—page 87

CONTENTS

PART 1: THE MEETING PLANNING GUIDE

PART 2: MEETING DESIGNS FOR YOUTH GROUPS

Part 1

THE MEETING PLANNING GUIDE

A "how-to" approach for your step-by-step meeting planning, execution and evaluation.

Introduction
WHY MEET AT ALL?

Some church youth groups are huge in number. Other churches have just a few youth in the entire congregation. Some churches have youth groups that take off on adventuresome summer trips across the country. Others do clown ministry, youth choirs and some even produce local radio shows. Yet every church youth group has one activity in common—the youth group meeting.

The youth group meeting is by far the most frequent event in youth ministry. Throughout the history of the Christian church, young people have gathered to study, enjoy each other, celebrate the Lord's presence and perform ministries that benefit other people.

Today's church continues in this ministry, and the common question of leaders remains the same: "What are new and creative ideas for studies, projects and meetings? What are we going to do at tomorrow's meeting?"

The following pages were written to guide you to stronger, more effective ministry with your youth group. **The Youth Group Meeting Guide** is to help you, the leader, review and evaluate your group meetings as well as to give you hundreds of ideas and suggestions for use in this vital ministry of the church.

For a youth group to function as a strong *part of* the congregation, rather than function *apart from* the congregation, we need to continue to check the relationship of our youth group to the rest of the church ministry. We need to make certain our goals are Christlike and our activities and events are timely, interesting and enjoyable.

This has become more essential as youth involvement has increased at the same time our world has become more complex and troubled. The youth group has the potential to meet many of the urgent needs of today's young people. Because of this opportunity and potential, you have a greater role—but as this book will show, your role need never be a burden. **The Youth Group Meeting Guide** will open to you a fun, wonderful world—youth group meetings.

Finally, this resource will perk up your energy, stimulate your creative urges and charge your group with enthusiasm, vitality and fun.

MEETINGS AS MINISTRY

Luke was wise to call his book the Acts of the Apostles, instead of the Meetings of the Apostles. Youth groups are, of course, more than meetings. The focal point of your group should be on activities, not on agendas. Meetings are necessary as a means to ministry and not as an end. So, take five minutes to write reasons why it is important for the young people in your congregation to meet at all. It is helpful to list the basic reasons for meeting.

Meetings provide a place for young people to:

● develop friendships. Young people need peers as friends and companions; youth groups provide opportunities for relationships.

● nurture faith and develop a church community. Meetings provide a place for young people to obtain a needed feeling of belonging, while nourishing belief.

● develop and use talents. The young people can use their talents to enrich the lives of others and at the same time meet their own creative needs.

Youth group meetings should be distinctively Christian in purpose, activities and programs. The meeting should enable youth to be nurtured in Christian faith and to serve one another.

Youth groups should not be:

● the singular youth ministry of the church.

● the exclusive training ground for future church leaders.

● a place to bide time until the members are old enough to enter the "real" church.

● baby sitters or police.

● a group of castes—cliques of popular or unpopular teenagers or elitist gatherings that exclude some young people.

● service groups to do the work and repairs about the church that no one else wants to do.

● adult-led and dictated with the young people merely attending meetings rather than taking control.

Think of other images your congregation has of youth groups and meetings. No doubt you can add to this list. Consider discussing these views with others in your church. With the help of **The Youth Group Meeting Guide**, you can change the negative attitudes and opinions to positive ones. A youth group *can* be a fun place to belong and meetings *can* be creative.

9

HOW DOES MINISTRY HAPPEN IN MEETINGS?

Ministry is what happens when God works through people as they share the love, joy and forgiveness of Christ.

Youth ministry is young people using their gifts to meet the needs of others as they allow the Lord to work through them.

Ministry Is
- worshiping our one God.
- proclaiming Jesus Christ as Lord and Savior.
- nurturing, serving and supporting one another.
- celebrating our relationship to one another in Christ.

Ministry happens as young people and adults worship, study, play, meet and care. Ministry happens during Sunday services, in Bible classes, at retreats and in the youth group meeting. It happens when God's spirit is present among his people and as we grow in the knowledge of our Lord, Jesus Christ.

Youth ministry needs to be recognized as an important aspect of the total ministry of the church. Too often young people are dissected and removed from the regular, on-going ministry of the church. The young people and their ministry often are not taken seriously. The teenagers are seen as a "junior" church, not yet ready to take up the church's "real" ministry.

As a teenager in a Chicago suburb, I had few opportunities to be involved in ministry through my church. I felt I had only two options—I could go to youth group meetings or else my mother would be mad at me. Sure, I could worship on Sundays or attend Bible classes, but everything else for young people was rigidly structured, including the youth group.

To fill this gap, youth groups should be structured to use teenagers' talents and abilities to meet their specific needs. This may sound overwhelming, but it's not. **The Youth Group Meeting Guide** has been designed to stretch your creative mind, give you ideas and better enable you to succeed in your efforts to meet needs of your young people.

Let the following pages speak to your needs and situations, then expand and adapt the ideas and resources to your specific ministry. Build on this resource. Consider these various thoughts and suggestions, and use this book to make ministry happen within your group.

Chapter One
ELEMENTS OF A GOOD MEETING

Here's the scene. Group members start arriving at 1:45 p.m. Sunday. They are not sure where the 2 p.m. meeting is to be conducted. A few guys are outside shooting baskets. The door is locked to the church. The cookies are in the kitchen, but no one has that key either. The youth counselors haven't arrived yet, possibly because the televised football game is just getting good. The youth group president arrives and unlocks the church. Teenagers amble into the meeting room. The president tries to talk someone into leading the opening prayer. He fails, so he leads the group in the Lord's Prayer. The group secretary calls and says he can't make the meeting because of too much homework. He asks if someone else can take the minutes. And so the meeting limps along.

Here's another scene. Teenagers start arriving at 1:45 p.m. The counselors and the two teenagers in charge of welcoming others have been at the church since 1:30 p.m. The meeting room is prepared with enough tables and chairs for each member. A sign on the front door tells the arrivals the meeting will be in Room 3. A youth group leader called the devotional leader that morning to make certain she was prepared. The refreshments were brought to church that morning and are ready to be served in the kitchen. The meeting and the planners are ready to begin.

If the first scene seems too familiar, don't despair. It is easy to change from poorly planned meetings to well-executed meetings. The following checklist includes elements to help avoid the meeting described in the first scene.

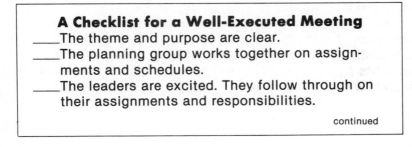

A Checklist for a Well-Executed Meeting
____The theme and purpose are clear.
____The planning group works together on assignments and schedules.
____The leaders are excited. They follow through on their assignments and responsibilities.

continued

continued from page 11

____The room is pleasant and properly prepared to meet the needs of the group.

____The adult leaders are present, not to act as "dictators," but to support and help the group.

____Care is taken to make certain all participants are welcomed and made to feel a part of the group. Group get-acquainted activities help make this happen.

____The meeting has a good mixture of social, spiritual, mental and emotional elements.

____The group is involved in the events, rather than being spectators.

____Any failures or disappointments are dealt with honestly and openly. Forgiveness is modeled by the group's leaders.

____An evaluation design is used to gather ideas and feelings from the participants.

____Plans for future meetings and events are clearly outlined.

The well-executed meeting is well-designed. The following suggested schedule is to help you best utilize the meeting time:

Suggested Meeting Schedule

Pre-meeting. An opportunity for people to arrive, welcome newcomers, have light refreshments and get acquainted (15 minutes).

Opening. Worship devotion, scripture reading, songs, prayers and sharing of faith (five to 10 minutes).

Agenda. Review of meeting plans and discussion of further agenda items (five minutes).

Content (Bible study or topic discussion). Should be the heart or "meat" of the meeting (30 to 45 minutes).

Bible study alternative. A special film, speaker or discussion relevant to the current theme (30 to 45 minutes).

Business items. Minutes, reports and roll call (10 minutes).

continued

continued from page 12

Announcements. Assignments for future events and schedules for projects (15 minutes).

Response (or closing). Thoughts and prayer (five minutes).

Refreshments. Further fellowship (30 minutes).

There are many variables in your situation that may require a somewhat different schedule. For example, the business items can be dealt with during the first 10 minutes of the Sunday morning Bible class rather than during the youth group meeting. Or groups can meet as they are involved in special projects.

The main point is to have a purpose for meeting, other than to meet and hear reports. Action, apostles, action! Stay out of the "let's-meet-to-say-we've-met" syndrome.

Good meetings don't just happen, they are planned. Following is an outline that shows the initial draft of a meeting. These thoughts then can be elaborated to create a more detailed meeting such as those found in the second part of this book.

TITLE: God's Grace

PURPOSE

To help the participants grow in their Lord and respond to others around them with God's love by looking at ways to use the gifts from God.

PREPARATION

Gather gift boxes, paper and pencils. Read Colossians 3:12-17 and Isaiah 43:1.

OPENING

Read and discuss: "You are mine. I have called you by name" (Isaiah 43:1). Lead the group members in a cheerful song of rejoicing. Structure this as the growth portion of the meeting.

THE "MEAT" OF THE MEETING

Do a Bible study based on Colossians 3:12-17. Distribute paper and pencils and ask all participants to list their gifts. Then have the young people put their favorite "gifts" in one of the boxes. Have the teenagers share the gifts with one another. The participants then should make another list of ways to use these gifts throughout the week.

RESPONSE (OR CLOSING)

The participants should share with one another what they plan to do. They should write a "contract" with the Lord outlining specific ways to use the gifts to enrich others. Close with a song of thanksgiving and a prayer.

The three *main* sections to a well-planned, effective and meaningful meeting are the opening, content (or "meat" of the meeting) and response. The following pages of this chapter will include more information on these three areas.

THE OPENING

Youth group members need to be reminded of the saying, "To make a friend, be a friend." Instead of waiting for someone else to make the friendship move, each individual needs to be encouraged to reach out to each other, taking special care to sincerely welcome newcomers. The leaders set the example by beginning each meeting with warm greetings.

The opening part of any meeting should set the tone and involve the group at once. Openings can vary so that the group does not get stuck in a routine. Here are some suggestions:

Open with a prayer and a brief devotion. In advance, suggest possible resource books and ideas to different youth group members, then help them prepare so they can lead the opening.

After the devotion, gather for 10 to 15 minutes of singing. Sing along with a cassette tape or record or invite a guitarist to lead the group. Music motivates us, brings us closer and allows us to share feelings. A youth group is blessed if it has members who are musically adept. If your group has such gifts, rejoice and use them. If you have not found that musical gift in your group, keep looking. Someone may be just about ready to volunteer.

As an alternative, turn to other members of the congregation for a change of pace in musical presentations at the youth group meeting. Encourage others in the congregation to share their musical gifts at the youth group meetings. In turn, the youth group can teach the congregation new songs.

A youth group meeting is an excellent place to learn new songs. Youth groups, however, shouldn't be limited to contemporary songs because young people continue to enjoy many traditional hymns.

If you expect your group to sing, provide the necessary song books. It is a calamity when a leader attempts to lead the group in song when no one knows the words.

A word of caution and concern needs to be expressed regarding misuse of copyright laws. Even though a youth group means well and is using and copying songs only for its own use, copyright laws state requirements and restrictions. Youth groups should check copyright laws and seek permission to use songs beforehand if necessary.

The Youth Group Meeting Guide contains excellent examples of incorporating music into the youth group meetings.

Another idea for an opening is to involve the group members as they arrive in a mixer or other community-building activities. **The Youth Group Meeting Guide** contains many ideas for opening games and mixers. Other useful books are listed in the Resource section at the end of each meeting design. Bookstores and libraries have numerous resource books that present get-acquainted ideas and activities.

Depending on the amount of time you have scheduled for your meeting, openings should not last more than 15 to 20 minutes. Show your excitement about being with the group, set the mood for the meeting, thank the Lord for your blessings and presence of the people, and then get on with the program.

CONTENT ("MEAT" OF THE MEETING)

The main reason for meeting is to study, plan, discuss issues or do action projects. The content, or "meat" of the meeting, needs to have substance.

The content needs to relate directly to the purpose of your meeting. Plan for up to one hour to discuss the issues and study the scriptures. Ask different leaders to develop this part of the program. Vary your approach—use a film, videotape, discussion group, panel of experts or debates.

It is helpful to print out any presentation of information, lists and concepts. It is easier for the participants to follow written information and they will retain more of it as well.

The "meat" of youth group meetings offers special opportunities for growth and nurturing. Following are a few suggestions to offer during this time. The meeting designs in the second part of this book offer many other excellent ideas.

Bible studies. Youth group meetings provide additional Bible study opportunities beyond the Sunday morning Bible classes. Studies can be conducted during the regular youth group meeting or held on another evening. Try to enlist an adult leader not already involved with youth studies—this will give participants new perspectives. (See Preparing a Bible Study, page 16.)

Topical presentations on major issues. Address contemporary concerns such as hunger, peace, justice, vocations, self-identity, death and dying, drugs, environment, politics, education, health care and family ties.

Self-help classes. Plan courses that can range from communication skills to diet and exercise.

Community concerns. Sponsor forums and debates to study main topics and controversies within your community. Topics include shoplifting, drunken drivers, sexual abuse or violence.

Adult-youth discussions. Your group can be the setting for helpful discussions and programs between young people and adults.

Special television programs. Television provides an excellent way to nurture. Call the television station to verify the schedule, then plan to meet in a member's home to watch the relevant telecast. Afterward, have fun discussing the program while enjoying popcorn and beverages.

Preparing a Bible Study

Writing Bible studies usually gets easier with practice, so don't be discouraged if at first you have difficulty putting your thoughts into easily understood terms. While practice might not make perfect, it certainly makes for better youth group meetings.

Following is a glance at the steps Dean Dammann took to write the "Be My Valentine" meeting design on page 202 of this book.

• **Step one**—Identify the theme you want to study, choose a scripture that applies to the topic and decide what you want your young people to gain from this study.

• **Step two**—Plan activities to encourage group members to interact with one another and to become acquainted.

• **Step three**—Choose activities that either help your young people identify with the topic or excite them about what they will be studying.

• **Step four**—Select activities to present the scripture so it relates to the personal life concerns of the participants.

• **Step five**—Plan group activities that encourage your group members to share their thoughts on the scripture and how it touches their lives.

• **Step six**—Plan an activity that helps your young people apply the Bible study to their lives.

RESPONSE (CLOSING)

To ensure that the content section of the meeting does not become an "end in itself," it is necessary to include a response time. Utilize this time for individuals to apply what was shared and to react to the needs that have been expressed.

Part of that response time should be spent in discussion.

Then encourage each person to answer questions such as, "How has this experience changed my life?" or "How could this presentation make a difference in my life?" Have each person write on a piece of paper what he or she plans to do with this new information. How will the young people put the information into practice in terms of daily life and ministry? Have each person share his or her plan with another person. Then ask for volunteers to share their ideas with the total group.

Another way to involve the group in the response is to brainstorm ways of responding as a group to what was presented in the content of the meeting. Perhaps the study will move the group members to change their behavior in their home life or at school. Or else they may want to volunteer their time in other church activities. Instead they may be motivated to visit the shut-ins, write to missionaries or just hug their parents.

It should be pointed out that responses need not always be as a group. God has given each of us different gifts and needs, so individuals should be encouraged to respond in their own unique ways.

So that the response will not be a one-time experience, plan to review what has happened at the next meeting. Give support and encouragement to those people who are living out their lives as the people of God.

Close briefly by reviewing the main points of the meeting, announcing the coming events and activities and reminding those who have assignments to follow through.

Make sure someone has been appointed to take care of cleaning up and getting everything back in order. Thank any new members for coming, making certain you have their correct names and addresses. Thank those who planned and prepared this meeting, and get ready for next week's meeting.

Chapter Two
PLANNING FOR MEETINGS

Successful planning for meetings includes tasks such as determining the needs of youth, developing goals to meet those needs, planning to meet those goals by creating specific purposes, preparation and publicity.

Successful planning is not as difficult as one might think. Simple guidelines are given for you to follow in this chapter.

HOW TO DETERMINE NEEDS OF YOUTH

Needs of young people should be checked and rechecked continually. It is too easy to assume that we know the needs of teenagers because we work with them, live with them and listen to them. But it is most helpful to keep abreast of each group's needs and desires.

One handy way of evaluating needs is to use the "Needs Assessment Kit" available from the Board for Youth Services, 1333 S. Kirkwood Road, St. Louis, MO 63122. This kit comes complete with easy-to-use instructions. **Five Cries of Youth**, (Harper and Row) available at libraries and bookstores, lists general "cries" or needs of/young people today.

Here is a list of other ways to keep in touch with the needs of your young people:

- Listen, observe and pay attention to them.
- Spend time with teenagers and their friends.
- Read the latest youth ministry books and magazines.
- Read reviews or see the current movies and television shows. Know what the advertisements, television, movies and records are saying and doing to young people.
- Prepare a schedule and visit the young people. Make the calls to become better acquainted with each teenager's family and to be seen as a friend.
- Ask other adults their views and opinions on young people. Regularly check what needs are important to other youth leaders in your community.
- Regularly invite two to three young people to your home for a meal. This helps to get to know them better and also keeps you in touch with their individual needs.

18

- Have the young people think of the "Top 10 Needs of Youth" at a meeting. Share these needs with other church leaders and use this list to help develop your youth group plans for the coming months.
- Do a youth survey. Ask the young people what they want to study, what they want to do and what their friends are talking about these days. Encourage input and involve as many young people as possible.

Here is an example of a youth survey (developed by Roger Dill):

Youth Survey

A. ☐ Male
   ☐ Female
   ☐ Freshman
   ☐ Sophomore
   ☐ Junior
   ☐ Senior
   How long have you been involved in the youth program?
   ☐ 0-3 months
   ☐ 3-6 months
   ☐ 6 months-1 year
   ☐ 1-2 years
   ☐ over 2 years

B. 1. Would you like to join a small group? ☐ yes ☐ no
   2. The one thing I like best about our group is . . .
   3. The one thing I dislike about our group is . . .
   4. If you could change two things about this group, what would they be?
   5. The three best activities that I have been to with our group are:
      1.
      2.
      3.

C. Complete the following sentences:
   1. God is . . .
   2. The Bible is . . .
   3. My family is . . .
   4. My looks are . . .
   5. My favorite sport or hobby is . . .
   6. My favorite music group is . . .
   7. My favorite movie is . . .
   8. A Christian is . . .

D. 1. If you could study any book in the Bible, what would you study and why?
   2. Circle five of the following topics that you would like to study:

- loneliness
- family
- anger
- guilt or forgiveness
- fear
- peer pressure
- prayer
- church
- self-esteem
- commitment
- friendship
- prejudice
- love
- sex and dating
- verbal cruelty
- happiness
- heaven
- drinking
- death and suicide
- Jesus
- marriage
- depression
- God
- honesty
- quiet time
- parents
- future
- resurrection
- music
- failure and success
- other (explain)

Other questions to consider are: What are church needs that your youth group can best fulfill? What needs are better handled by adult boards, elders or church staff? Even though all the listed needs are relevant, not all can be dealt with by the youth group. Leaders need to relinquish youth ministry to other bodies and agencies within the church. For example, young people often state the need to worship the Lord regularly and meaningfully. That is great, but often the youth leader must let that need be met in the regular Sunday worship services rather than trying to structure worship service during youth group meetings.

In developing needs, young people commonly list the same items, but you should conduct your own survey to find what is on the minds of your young people. Some of the most common needs are:

● loneliness
● self-identity
● vocational choices
● family troubles
● life issues such as abortion, dating, peace, justice, world hunger or war
● development of faith
● relationships with others and God

It is easy to generalize and assume that all young people have the same needs. Even though there are trends and similarities, it is important for leaders to keep aware of individual young people and the specific needs that each one is working through at various life stages.

DEVELOP GOALS TO MEET NEEDS

This moves us to an important aspect of the youth group meeting structure—setting long-range goals and objectives and specific meeting purposes. Remember the axiom, "If you don't know where you're going, any road will get you there."

The **SMART** approach to listing long-range objectives is:

Specific—Be concise in stating what the group hopes to achieve.

Measurable—Be able to evaluate objectives. To state, "Our youth group will grow closer to the Lord next year," is fine, but it will be difficult to measure. Instead, state, "Our youth group will have two Bible studies each month and will deal with three books of the New Testament."

Attainable—Be selective in what your group wants to do and can do. Keep in mind time available, dedication of members and church philosophy.

Realistic—A two-week retreat might be wonderful, but it might not be realistic for your group, especially if many members have jobs or school commitments.

Timely—Objectives need to be well-timed and well-planned to be workable.

However, the group need not spend hours writing formal meeting objectives. Involve the whole group in deciding needs and selecting the uppermost needs, but then let a small group of officers or interested group members write the specific objectives tentative on approval from the entire group.

Youth groups should continue to focus and be clear on what they are trying to do. If evangelism is a main objective, do it well, but then don't try to be a social ministry group at the same time.

The purpose of the meeting should be specifically stated and understood. When writing specific purposes, remember it is not enough to meet just because it is the first Sunday of the month. As you plan your meetings, write down in 50 words or less the concise purpose that you want to accomplish. For example: To meet together for two hours to plan for the fall retreat. To meet together to continue our discussion on sexuality and provide some helpful ideas to parents and youth in this area. To meet and to evaluate last week's bus trip and to plan for next month's Easter breakfast. Or, to meet together as a Bible study group to study the book of Ephesians and see how it applies to our daily lives.

Concentrate on expectations. Sometimes little happens during youth group meetings because little is expected. In a Midwestern church one Sunday, the pastor asked the 8 a.m. service participants what they expected from the morning worship. Ninety-eight percent replied they expected to get out at 9 a.m.

Even more perilous are unrealistic expectations. Youth groups cannot be all things to all people.

Don't automatically expect that all young people need to be a part of a youth group. All the young people of your church need to be encouraged and invited to participate. However, youth groups are not for all young people, just as men and women's groups are not for all adults. Teenagers can be at different levels, and that's fine—that's reality. Some people are joiners, others are not. Some teenagers have their peer relationships met in other ways—through school or community contacts. To expect all young people to attend every youth group meeting and every youth ministry event is setting yourself up for failure and disappointment.

My philosophy is that a church should provide so many

youth ministry events and activities that the youth cannot possibly get involved in everything.

This is one reason young people do well when encouraged to attend various church functions, rather than being limited to youth group meetings. In other words, keep as many doors open as possible. The door to the youth group meeting room is just one of many church portals—it should always be open and welcoming.

Common Questions About Group Meetings

Here is a list of questions you should raise concerning youth group meetings. These questions will allow you to plan better and be more specific in your objectives for each meeting.

● Why are we meeting in the first place? We meet to proclaim, relate and celebrate God's people. Everything else is secondary. We have a specific ministry—to share our faith.

● Whose meeting is it? The meeting is for the young people, not the counselors.

● Whose job is it to make sure everything is ready for the meeting? The adult leaders as well as the youth leaders need to take authority over the meeting and enable all the young people to have ownership in each activity.

● What happens when something goes wrong? We forgive each other, learn from the experience and move on. We do not wallow in our mistakes or blame anyone.

● Why meet so often? Weekly or biweekly meetings help develop a close group. Frequent meetings provide added opportunities to minister to each other and to the entire church.

● How many adults should be at youth group meetings? As many as possible. The more adults involved, the more opportunity for good relationships to develop between young people and adults. Encourage adult counselors and friends to attend. Just be careful not to overpower the young people.

● Who cleans up after the meetings? Everyone takes turns. Have a rotating system assigning young people and adults to teams. As a reminder, list these cleanup teams on a bulletin board. Encourage the group members to be kind and considerate through-

continued

---

continued from page 22

out each meeting, so little cleanup is necessary.

● Should the church staff be invited to attend all meetings? Sure, why not? And encourage your pastor to drop in at any time. Let the pastor know he or she is wanted and respected. Occasionally involve the pastor in the meeting itself as a leader or presenter.

● Are youth group meetings worth the effort? You bet they are. The Lord continues to bless and work through youth groups. Watch for the power of the Spirit. He's alive and well and living in and through your youth group.

PLANNING TO MEET GOALS

Every organization needs to take the time to plan well, and youth groups are no exception. At a set time each year, have youth group leaders gather for a day or weekend to make plans and set directions for the coming year's meetings. Some youth groups find it more helpful to plan from September of one year through August of the following year, rather than from January to December. In this way, school activities are kept in mind and the flow of the group members' schedules seems to tie in better.

Once a Year

Have the youth group officers and counselors meet for a day or weekend to develop tentative plans. At this point, they should write themes and objectives to share at the next general youth group meeting.

Take the entire youth group on a planning retreat. Develop a theme, objectives and activities for the upcoming year. Publish all plans in a neat notebook or calendar. Make assignments and do as much of the planning as possible during that weekend.

Host a general brainstorming session. Ask for five to seven volunteers to develop the ideas into a year's meeting plan. Present the proposals at the next youth group meeting.

Ask for adult volunteers to work with the youth leaders in the planning process. After the planning session, the adults' responsibilities also end, except for individual interests.

The yearly theme of the church can be used as a guide for the youth group. Invite church staff and adult board members to meet with a few group members and design programs to supplement overall church commitments.

In the preceding suggestions, begin by ascertaining the needs of the young people as well as the needs of the church and community. Brainstorm for activities to meet these needs.

It is important that the whole youth group feels an ownership in the meeting plans that are developed. That is why it is necessary to encourage everyone to join in the planning process. Do not expect teenagers and adults to get over excited about programs that have been developed without their individual and group consensus.

I learned that the hard way. At my first parish, I would develop what I thought were stupendous youth meeting programs. Using the mimeograph, I would prepare handsome booklets that outlined activities for that month. I had all topics developed and projects ready to go. On paper it was a winner. The only problem was that few people attended the meetings. That was the young people's way of saying that they did not have any ownership in the process.

Finally, I learned that the teenagers themselves needed to do their own planning and use their own ideas, so I let them take control. Other adults and I remained important to the process as idea people and helpful advisers, and we also had adequate opportunity to suggest ideas and programs. And this time the activities were a success, because we were working together with the young people, not working for them.

To actually put the young people in charge, enlist a few group members to act as a committee and assign them the responsibility of planning by utilizing this chart (developed by Roger Dill).

Planning Form for a Youth Group Event

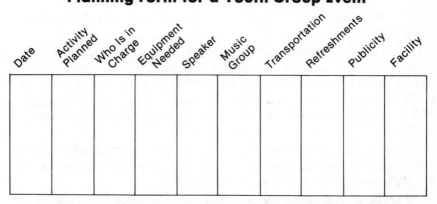

Date	Activity Planned	Who Is in Charge	Equipment Needed	Speaker	Music Group	Transportation	Refreshments	Publicity	Facility

Good meetings take young people and adults who have energy for their responsibilities, who know their roles and who can follow through. Good meetings are planned meetings.

PREPARATION AND PUBLICITY

"Be prepared" is more than the Boy Scout motto. It is a must to develop healthy and effective meetings. Just because a meeting went quite well a few months ago even though you were not well-prepared does not mean that you can continue that way. To prepare means, first of all, to pray. Ask for the power and strength from our Lord as you and your leaders develop the plans. Preparation should begin immediately after your last meeting. Begin by writing notes and ideas that come to you at any time during the day or night.

After you have your purpose in mind, devise ways to best meet that purpose. Brainstorm with other youth and adult leaders. How best can you develop what you want to happen? Search the resources you have available. Ask other teenagers and adults to be involved as presenters.

Make sure the room where you meet is prepared. Arrive 30 minutes early to make certain everything is ready—doors open chairs set, refreshments prepared, tables handy.

"Good meetings don't just happen," someone once said. How right that person was. Preparation is the key to a successful meeting.

An exciting aspect of a youth group is the promotion of the activities. Promote your group loudly and clearly. Proclaim the many events that are happening through God's people. The first message to share is, "Jesus Christ is Lord and Savior and this is what God's people are doing because of it."

Youth groups are a visible part of church ministry; therefore, care must be taken that your youth group is genuinely positive and energetic. Be certain that feeling is communicated accurately—it is important that the youth group is respected by the congregation.

Group publicity needs to happen on several levels. First, group members always should be informed. Second, make a special effort to inform the congregation and community of youth group meetings and events. Present regular youth group and youth ministry reports to your church council and church staff.

Inform neighboring churches and friends about youth group meetings and events. Welcome outside interest and support through their prayers and well-wishes.

To achieve this publicity, appoint the responsibility to a group member or willing adult with interest and expertise in public relations, advertising or promotion. Provide limited funding for printing and advertising costs.

Promotion

● The best way to let people know what is happening is to tell them personally. Show the teenagers that you are interested in them and also want them to know what is happening. This can be done through brief conversations after church, visits to homes or telephone calls.

● To further promote events, utilize bulletin boards, posters and banners. For special events, print buttons or balloons that state the theme.

● Do not assume that because you publicized a retreat in the church bulletin last week that everyone will be informed. Repetition is necessary to make certain the word is getting out and being absorbed.

● Repeat youth group meeting publicity through the church newsletter and bulletin, community newspapers and denominational literature.

● Continue to seek ways to publicize and promote the youth group to show that the group sees itself in ministry to all people—it is not a closed society or social club.

● Remember, "And whatever you do, in word or deed, do everything in the name of the Lord Jesus, giving thanks to God the Father through him" (Colossians 3:17).

HOW TO PLAN A MEETING—A SUMMARY

By now you're probably thinking, "Okay, enough of this philosophical stuff. What specific steps are involved?" Following are helpful aspects to planning an effective meeting; be ready to add your own ideas:

Aspects of Planning

Have a specific purpose to meet. This usually is assumed, but it is helpful to regularly check your motives. If you have no reason to meet—don't.

Prepare for the meeting weeks in advance. Driving to the church a half-hour before the meeting is not the best time to prepare. Work on your thoughts and ideas throughout the week, in your spare time, your quiet time and as you have an opportunity to reflect on what needs to happen at the meeting.

Publicize the meeting. The group members need to know the details in advance.

Include a good mixture in meeting plans. Effective leaders are ready to go to Plan B if Plan A doesn't work. If the special speaker gets lost, the leader has a film ready. If the speaker doesn't show and the film projector breaks down, the leader is ready with an alternative activity.

Print a step-by-step schedule for all leaders. This helps to keep the meeting organized. Only when a meeting is well-planned can it appear to be spontaneous and flexible. The leaders should have specific plans to reach objectives, but also be flexible enough to go to another plan when necessary.

Involve as many adults as possible. Ask adults to prepare and serve refreshments, serve on special committees, drive to the service project, play basketball before the meeting, or study with the teenagers at specific times.

Share leadership responsibilities. Group members should have been involved in leading and planning meeting events.

Brief the leaders so they know what is to be expected. They are ready to follow through on assignments. Capable leaders check and double-check their areas of responsibility. The leaders are concerned, not only about the agenda, but also about the people who will attend the meeting and how they will interact and relate.

Prepare the meeting room according to plans. It is important to have a comfortable and inviting place to meet. Sitting around the stove in the church kitchen probably is not the best place—unless there are a lot of "burning issues."

Pray. Take your concerns to the Lord. Ask him regularly for his guidance, direction and blessing.

As the meeting gets under way, watch how people are being involved. Involve those who are not yet a part of the group. Be sensitive.

Have fun! A leader who is having fun is modeling for others. Enjoy the event. Shout "hooray" for those attending. Thank God for the opportunity to serve.

Checklist of Things to Do
Prior to a Youth Group Meeting

Three weeks:

_____Clarify the specific purpose of your meeting. What are you trying to accomplish?

_____Deal with the needs for the meeting such as materials to order, special publicity posters or equipment.

_____Double-check with the main presenter or leader, making sure of the dates and times.

_____Visit the location of the meeting if you are meeting in a special place.

continued

---

continued from page 27

Two weeks:

_____Finalize the meeting schedule. List who is do-
ing what and when. Prepare a detailed schedule and share it with the other leaders.

_____Publicize the meeting.

_____Send materials needed for the meeting to the
group members—a special Bible study, a pro-
posal or a schedule of events.

One week:

_____Call the meeting leaders to answer any ques-
tions and to see if their materials are ready.

_____Have the calling committee telephone all group
members to remind them of the meeting.

_____Make final plans for refreshments, recreation
and meeting room preparation.

_____Double-check the need for transportation for
members, guests or presenters.

_____Assign young people and adults to arrive early
to set up the meeting room and greet the members as they arrive.

The meeting day:

_____Make sure Bibles, songbooks, chairs, evalua-
tion forms, other equipment and materials are
ready and available.

_____Call special speakers or guests to see if they
need last-minute directions or materials.

_____Arrive at the meeting at least 30 minutes be-
fore it starts to make certain everything is in
order.

_____If you see group members during the day, re-
mind them of the meeting.

_____Pray for the Lord's guidance and blessings on
your meeting.

The next day:

_____Study the evaluation forms from the meeting.
Find out what went well and what could have
been better.

_____Plan for your next meeting. Make a list of
things to do and people to do them.

continued

continued from page 28

_____Follow up on guests and new members who attended the meeting. Visit with them, call them, invite them to the next meeting.

_____Follow up on your guest speaker with a thank-you letter or honorarium.

_____Follow through on other assignments which were given to group members at the meeting—refreshments for the next meeting, thank-you letters, Bible study leaders.

_____Think of ways to begin publicizing upcoming meetings and activities.

Chapter Three
MEETING ACTIVITIES

Meetings can include a wide spectrum of elements that range from getting to know one another to growing in faith. Community-building activities are important to help the young people grow closer to each other. Discussion time is an opportunity for the young people to share. Worship helps strengthen the Christian faith. And business meetings are necessary to keep the youth group functioning smoothly and to teach administration. Even the refreshment time is full of opportunities, in that it offers a chance for youth to visit and informally share their ideas.

COMMUNITY-BUILDING

One of the more powerful and positive parts of an effective youth group is the development of close friendships. Relationships help young people draw closer to the Lord, the church and to others. Relationships also make the young people feel that they belong to a caring community. Young people do not drop out of church because the sermons are too long or the pews are too hard. Young people drift away because they feel they don't belong. Youth groups can be extremely helpful in providing a sense of belonging.

Youth groups rise and fall on relationships. Meetings thrive when a warm, caring atmosphere has been created. If a distrustful, skeptical, competitive feeling has developed, be prepared for added tension and struggle. Attitudes begin with the adult youth counselors as well as with the youth leaders. Adults need to constantly invoke feelings of openness, trust and acceptance. Adults also must be willing to share of themselves. If adults expect young people to share joys, fears, frustrations and hopes, they first must model that it is okay to do so. Youth groups should continue to work at affirming and supporting one another.

How does your youth group support one another? Sure, you do a lot of activities together, but how can you love one another? Consider these suggestions and then add a few of your own:

To Show Love

● Develop a prayer chain. When someone is in need of prayer, youth group members call one another and spread the prayer.

● Visit newcomers. Constantly encourage all members to welcome new youth.

● Send survival kits to college students. Include cookies, other snacks, paper, pencils and a stamped envelope addressed to your church—a hint to write to your group. Visit the former group members, especially if the college is within driving distance.

● Host a surprise Counselor Appreciation Day or other honor ceremony.

● Support and affirm your pastor and church staff members through words of appreciation, gifts and special thoughts.

● Say thanks to the parents of your members. Sponsor a yearly brunch, print certificates stating that each parent is "in good standing" with young people, or make the parents "honorary young people."

● Remember each member's birthday with a card from the group or start a tradition that each birthday person brings snackfood to the meeting.

● Include, as a regular part of your meetings, a time for people to share with one another specific joys, concerns or fears. Call this the "sharing faith time" or "time to share."

A support community as part of a youth group is not accomplished only at meetings. Support and affirmation come through the regular activities and programs of worship, service and fellowship. Caring for people takes time. A youth group can do tremendous things for one another by reaching out with love.

Common-sense ways to build a close community of believers include:

Support and Affirmation

Spend time together to get to know one another. Don't expect relationships to happen if the youth see each other for only one hour a month. Relationships take time.

Discuss the importance of accepting one another in the manner Christ accepted us. If conflicts arise, encourage the young people to deal with the concern openly and honestly. The entire group needs to have ownership in the struggles and solutions to build a caring community.

Realize members of a group never will relate to one another in the same way. There will be closer friendships developing between certain members. Be careful, however, so that friendships do not pull young people away from the group.

Work together on projects. People who work together tend to grow together. Give each member an opportunity to work with others in the group.

Be concerned about divisive cliques; yet also be aware of the positive nature of cliques. Certain youth want to do things together and be together—and to an extent, that is healthy.

Develop a concept that all of what the youth group does is spiritual—the group members are the people of God. Then encourage a good balance of activities including Bible study, recreation, trips, social functions, parties and worship events. Youth groups sometimes worry that more youth attend social events than attend religious events. In response, attempt to keep a solid balance of activities. Offer a variety of choices and continue to develop relationships with those who attend any of the events. Do not force young people to attend Bible study as a prerequisite to attending social events.

When to Do Community-Building

Do some get-acquainted activities as people are arriving. This helps to start the meeting on a peppy note. It also helps to involve the early-arrivers, before the whole mob gets there.

Do community-building activities as part of the closing. After the "formal" meeting, take time to play, have fun and laugh together.

Use these activities as a way to break up the meeting and provide for stretches. If you have been sitting still for a long time, play games to get the "juices" flowing again. If you are working with a junior high age group, do more active and energetic activities than with an older group. The attention span of many people is less than 20 minutes—teenagers and adults included.

What NOT to Do in Community-Building

Community-building has many advantages, but there are also a few things to watch out for:

Competition. As a rule, do not develop strong competition between people in your group. Volleyball and basketball games are fine, as long as they stay friendly. Recreation should build up the total group, rather than tear it down.

The winner/loser syndrome. Never play a game within your group that will make some people winners and others losers. More often than not, there are more losers than winners. Don't become involved in recreation that embarrasses or forces people into the limelight, especially if they are the backstage kind of people. Games that only encourage the strong athletic types do not do much for the other types of people.

At a youth group meeting, play a friendly volleyball game with every person rotating back and forth from both sides of the net. That way the competition of winning is kept to a minimum.

A good rule is to not play any kind of games that eliminate people within your group. Elimination destroys the community-building purpose. Anything from musical chairs to tag should be evaluated before playing again.

For those who enjoy competition, form a team from your church and play other area teams in a church league. Group cohesiveness will remain high, because all the youth members are striving for the same team goal.

Wastefulness. Don't waste food and others' gifts from God. Some community-building can get messy and wasteful such as Marshmallow Stuff (youngsters compete to see who can stuff the most marshmallows into their mouths at one time) or Shaving-Cream Sundaes (shaving cream is sprayed over people when certain questions are not answered). Some of these games are fun, but they also tend to take lightly the gifts that God has given us. Evaluate the kinds of games you play in terms of ways they can be helpful to your group and at the same time provide good models for a positive lifestyle and thankfulness to God.

Use food as part of your refreshments. Try to build the "world's biggest pizza" or make the "church's biggest ice cream float." That way the food will not be wasted.

Recreational Games

To some people, youth groups still are seen as the "place where kids play, stay off the streets, and have a lot of fun and games together." Although this thought is not totally wrong, it does give a narrow and limited view of the typical youth group. Youth groups are a strong part of a congregation's total ministry. But youth groups also need opportunities for fun and games, which, at times, can be more productive than heavy discussions or debilitating debates.

Games, community-building, get-acquainted times,

recreation, or whatever you call them, are important to the development and mood of any group. Group members need to grow closer together, let off steam, play together and work diligently at maintaining a close group feeling.

Every youth group meeting should have a time for such sharing. Sometimes let the games be loud and energetic, other times keep the activity low-key and subdued. But provide a recreation time. Do not see this part of a meeting as something extra you do "if there is time." You will find the group members' energy level much higher for other parts of the meeting such as devotions, studies, topics and discussions, because the group also has built a closer community.

DISCUSSIONS

Sharing is at the heart of youth group meetings. One of the most valued ways to share is through discussion.

The discussion leader should plan for three steps in preparing various learning designs. First, focus on the topic. How do you feel about it? What are the important points to share with the group? Then research the topic. Learn as much as possible. Think of ways to present the topic.

The planning stage is second. Put yourself into the mind of the youth group. What would make the discussion interesting? Rehearse the presentation with your friends or family. Use their comments to improve the presentation.

The third step is presentation of the topic. As you present the discussion at the meeting, believe in it. Know that the Lord will bless it. Be confident. Tell the group members that they will find the topic interesting. Do not apologize. Relax and enjoy the interaction.

Afterward, evaluate. Identify strengths and weaknesses in the design and in your method of presentation. Revise the discussion if you plan to use it again. Learn from the experience. And thank the Lord for the opportunity to share your faith.

To make the youth group meeting truly worthwhile, the leader should study various means of involving the young people in discussions.

Numerous books and other resources present common group methods and techniques. Following are more popular techniques for discussions:

Let's Talk
Share in large groups. Let each person think through the subject being discussed and respond voluntarily.

Small groups. Form dyads (groups of two), triads (threes) or larger subgroups to deal with specific assignments. For instance, a dyad might be asked to tell five significant facts about themselves and then to join another dyad with one person introducing his partner to the two new persons. A triad might be asked to engage in observation or dialogue in which two of the people would discuss a topic with the third person observing what is said and reporting the observations at a set time. Then the roles would be rotated. The small groups could be asked to report to the large group. Increase involvement by setting a time limit for discussion.

Talk face-to-face. Ask the participants to turn to the individuals seated next to them to share thoughts on the subject being discussed.

Use open-ended sentences. Each participant completes sentences such as:
- The world would be better if . . .
- I feel like crying when . . .
- The most worthwhile part of the film for me was . . .
- I wish people would . . .
- Ten years from now, I hope . . .

Prepare a handout. List the major points of the presentation topic or film. Often it is helpful to have visual material for the group. For example, list multiple choice thoughts such as: Which would be harder to do—turn in a friend for cheating, stop a fight, or tell a friend you disagree with him or her?

Use specific statements or questions. Concrete questions help the youth focus on specific discussion subjects, rather than talking in generalities. Specific questions also are less threatening than open discussion.

Read together. In doing a Bible study, for example, it is helpful to have the whole group read parts of the scriptures and respond accordingly.

Do dramatical readings. Involve the group by using drama and skits to make various points. Ask for volunteers ahead of time so they can prepare.

Use body movements. Have the group members relate feelings by standing up, using hand motions or making non-verbal expressions.

Utilize the written word. Distribute cards and pencils for the youngsters to write discussion questions. Or, distribute pre-printed cards that give each group a simulated situation to act out or discuss.

Don't overlook resources. Use films, records, videotapes, slides and posters in preparing discussion topics.

Incorporate music. Use music to set the mood as you discuss current events and issues.

Set up a panel discussion. Members of the group can serve on a panel to discuss the topic issue. Afterward, the entire group can discuss and react to the panel.

Fishbowl. Divide into two equal subgroups with one group in a circle for a discussion and the other group in the larger circle around the first group. The outside group observes how the first group reacts to the topic. Roles can be reversed after evaluating what took place during the discussion period.

Modified fishbowl. Put five to seven chairs in the middle of the meeting room, depending upon the size of the group. Ask volunteers to take seats and discuss the topic. Keep one of the chairs vacant. Whenever anyone from the group wants to share, he or she sits in the empty chair, expresses his or her thoughts, and then vacates the chair. Then those still seated respond to the questions and concerns. This also is called the open-chair design.

Observers. Plant observers in the discussion group who will look for specific activities. Did the group really deal with the subject? When was the group the most involved? The observer can help the group become more involved.

Case history. Explain a real-life drama stopping short at the solution point. Ask the group members how they would handle the crisis. After all have participated, conclude the drama by relating how the real-life participant dealt with the crisis.

Interviews. By recording or writing out the comments of others, you can add a number of stimulating opinions to your discussions. Use a cassette recorder to interview persons on the street, in the church, or any others who would be difficult to bring to your group for such contributions.

Remember the good old days. Have the group recall experiences in the past that connect with the subject being discussed. Help the young people identify with the issue by suggesting situations.

Use storytelling. Encourage each person to tell a story from his or her life that ties into the subject being discussed. Or, have the young people imagine stories concerning the topic.

As we work with young people at their meetings, we need to remember there are three learning aspects involved:
- The mind and cognitive learning.
- Feelings and emotions.
- Body movements (psychomotor).

An ideal discussion technique keeps all learning components in mind. For example, in the *continuum discussion method*, ask the teenagers to stand along an invisible line according to their feelings about an issue—opposite ends of the line represent extremes and the middle "undecided" or "don't care." To the statement, "I think the drinking age in every state should be raised to 21," those totally agreeing would stand on one end of the line, and those totally disagreeing would stand at the other end. Those having mixed feelings or uncertainty would group in the middle. The youth then would discuss their opinions with those standing in their proximity.

Another alternative to this is the *four-corner approach* in which four choices are given for a question and the participants walk to one of the corners to "vote" their opinion.

Guidelines for Leading Youth Discussions

● Scan the group's emotional environment for clues such as behavior, small talk, clothing and seating patterns.

● Probe for contact points between the chosen subject (film, reading, play) and the group's feelings (laughter, sadness, expressions of boredom).

● Utilize means by which students can make comparisons between the topic and an immediate experience. For example, read 1 Corinthians 13 and hand each person a spoon. "As you look into the reflection in the spoon, what do you see about God which is only viewed vaguely?"

● Draw on the resources of the whole group. Even the giggles in the corner are a contribution.

● Let unresolved points remain in the minds of the group. The mature discussion leader will refrain from forcing his or her opinion on the group. The leader's role is to moderate, not debate. His or her opinions should be expressed gingerly.

● Don't be afraid to pursue aspects of the topic you don't know.

● Be patient when silence reigns after your invitation to share. Silence allows the group members to think about the question or remark. Don't give in to the temptation to "rescue" the group all the time by answering your own questions. If you handle silence with confidence, you will find it an effective teaching resource.

● Affirm those who contribute their opinions.

—Dennis C. Benson and Bill Wolfe

WORSHIP

Worship within the youth group meeting in no way should try to take the place of Sunday morning worship. The regular Sunday worship still is the time and place for God's people of all ages to come together and be strengthened in the faith and to celebrate the love and forgiveness of Jesus Christ. Youth groups need to be aware of this and see the Sunday morning experience as a part of their total ministry.

Devotional and worship times are important parts of a youth group meeting. Opportunities are provided for young people to lead others, share their faith and experience a more informal worship setting.

Meeting devotions should not be considered the "making" of a Christian group. As God's people, all life is sacred. Christ bridged the gap between the secular and the sacred. Devotions need not always be at the beginning or end of a meeting. You can vary the schedule and have a worship in the middle of your business session or the closing prayer during refreshments. Variation shows worship is not tied to any special place in the Christian life.

If worship is a priority for your group, elect or appoint a co-ordinator to schedule youngsters and adults to lead worship. The coordinator should seek volunteers and encourage those who seem willing but shy; however, no person should be forced into leading worship.

Have both young people and adults act as worship leaders. As an alternative, ask teams of two or three teenagers and adults to plan and lead worship services. Guest speakers, the pastor or lay leaders of the church also can be devotion leaders.

Innumerable resources are available to guide worship in youth group meetings. Check with the church library, publishing companies, bookstores and the congregation for these resources.

For variety, devotions can include a skit or drama, hymn, prayer chain (each person joins in praying his or her own special prayers), short devotional film, filmstrip, tape recording or album.

A possible format for a youth group meeting devotion is:

Devotion

● Open with prayer asking the Lord for his blessing and guidance.

● If the group enjoys music, lead several songs. Be certain songbooks are available.

● Present a scripture reading that is tied to a theme, lesson or holiday.

● In your own way, share your faith. Connect your life and faith to the activities and events being planned and carried out by the youth group.

● Ask for prayer requests, then have a closing prayer.

Youth group worship can be meaningful, as God speaks to his people through the leader. Keep the elements for effective worship in mind as you plan to lead a devotion:

Worship Elements

Wonder, as we rejoice in the awesomeness of God. Worship is wonderful, as we share the excitement of Christ's love for us.

Opportunity to witness and share the faith, to speak of what God in Christ has done and is doing.

Resurrection-centered, as we rejoice in the empty tomb and the symbol of the cross.

Spiritual, as we grow closer to God and to one another.

Humanness, everyone has sinned but each of us has been called by God to be saints. Let worship be human in that it rejoices, not in our sin, but in the fact that we are people of worth in Christ.

Intrinsic in nature because our faith should not depend upon external circumstances.

Personal in relationship between God and us, but also a relationship among people.

Worship is a way that God helps us keep our lives in a balanced perspective. It reminds us of who we are and keeps us in touch with our Lord.

BUSINESS

The business meeting continues to be seen as a necessary evil. How can a group make decisions yet keep a business meeting short so that it doesn't get boring?

Groups need to keep their purpose and objectives in mind. There is no reason that formal business meetings need to be long or boring. Youth leaders should do much of the business part of the meeting ahead of time. This is not to suggest that only a few people make the decisions, but it is to say that once the general needs and objectives of a group are agreed upon, the officers can utilize their skills in making certain decisions.

Youth group officers should meet regularly to work out the nitty-gritty details. The officers can report to the membership through telephone calls, newsletters, church bulletins and personal conversations. If the total group has been involved in sharing its needs and offering its priorities in the regular planning times together, the youth group does not need to spend additional time going over this at the meeting.

One way to involve different teenagers in the decision-making process is to rotate officers every four months or appoint different young people to work on various projects. As this style continues, the young people develop a feeling of ownership and a better understanding of the group and its meetings.

Make a practice of publishing much of the business ahead of time in the youth group newsletter or church newspaper. Post information in a display area. Therefore, instead of using youth group meeting time for business reports, the group can concentrate on its main Bible study or theme emphasis.

If your group is following these suggestions but the business part of the meeting continues to lag, set a time limit. Follow the above guidelines to avoid long and boring business meetings.

REFRESHMENTS

"Okay, Ralph, we'll eat as soon as we finish watching this movie."

"What? Butter cookies again? That's all we ever have around this place."

"No, I didn't bring anything for snacks tonight. I wasn't hungry."

Perhaps you have heard these statements during a youth group meeting. For some group members, refreshment time ranks close to the top of meeting priorities.

Here are a few ideas to avoid these statements and make refreshment a time of fun and sharing:

Let's Eat

● Let refreshment time be a positive experience and an opportunity for group members to visit informally.

● Relate the snackfood to the major meeting theme. For example, if your topic is on hunger, serve bread and water. If you're talking about health care, serve fruits and fruit juices. If a missionary is speaking about his or her work in a foreign land, serve food common to that country.

● Serve refreshments at various times during meetings. Sometimes begin with the snack, other times take a break in the middle of the meeting.

● Plan a full meal as part of the meeting instead of the usual snacks. Or, have a progressive dinner, traveling to different homes for different courses. Conduct the business and topics as you travel.

● Plan a box lunch. Have each person bring a sack lunch. Auction the lunches to the highest bidder. Donate the proceeds to the needy.

● Ask a youth to coordinate refreshments; volunteers can be signed up for certain meetings. Encourage members to make treats, rather than purchase junkfood.

Refreshment time is more than a break from the content of the meeting. Refreshment time offers an opportunity for the group members to have fun, share and build relationships.

Are your group meeting snacks loaded with empty calories? **The Whole Thing: An Alternative Snackfood Cookbook** (Herald Press, 610 Walnut Ave., Scottdale, PA 15683) offers 50 recipes for nutritious drinks, entrees and fast snacks.

Chapter Four
OTHER CONSIDERATIONS FOR MEETINGS

When planning meetings, there are always extenuating circumstances to consider. Items that require attention include meeting frequency and continuity, meeting settings, leadership qualities, group size, combination of junior and senior high ages and discipline problems.

This chapter explains the various aspects of meetings and gives you ideas on dealing with each area.

FREQUENCY AND CONTINUITY OF MEETINGS

Groups often wrestle with the issue of deciding on meeting frequency. Whether your group meets once a week or once a month should be decided on the basis of the group's needs and objectives. The following list gives you guidelines for this issue:

When to Meet and What to Do

● Keep the individual needs of the young people in mind. Some youth groups reduce activities during the fall when there are many school functions. Other groups increase activity during the fall because the interest is high. Again, it depends on the individuals in the group.

● Do regular business and specific objectives in small work groups, thus freeing the large group from frequent business meetings.

● In large churches, various age groups can meet separately for weekly Bible studies and discussions. Then plan a monthly gathering of all ages for a "Super Sunday" meeting with special speakers, music, films, outings or other attractions.

● Youth group leaders should meet often between meetings to make special plans and to make certain future projects are on schedule.

● Conduct weekly or biweekly meetings of the youth counselors and the group's officers.

● Involve the pastor and other church staff. The pastor does not need to be present every time the youth group meets, but he or she and the staff should be invited and welcomed.

● Publicize all meetings and keep the group informed of special and officer's meetings.

● Do not schedule activities in conflict with other church events.

● Meeting frequency also should be coordinated with the overall church schedule.

● Some groups prefer to meet on Sunday afternoons, others on Sunday evenings, some on weeknights, although weekends seem to be preferred. The general rule is to meet at a time that is most convenient for the majority of members. It also is helpful to stay with a regular schedule as much as possible. Develop a pattern, keep the needs of the young people in mind, and consider what else is happening in the church, school and community.

● A few studies have indicated the more effective youth groups meet once a week or every other week. The high interest is attributed to broadened opportunities for young people to get together. A problem with monthly meetings is that if a person misses a meeting, he or she is cut off for actually two months of activities.

● A brief, to-the-point business meeting easily can be handled once a month. However, it is effective to provide at least two to four other activities and events for the youth group during every month. This can be increased during the summer months.

● Don't cancel meetings. Meetings should only be canceled for extreme emergencies. To cancel one meeting always makes the next scheduled event suspect. "Will it, too, be canceled? Should we attend and be disappointed again? Well, let's just not plan on attending!" And then this mind-set is perpetuated throughout the group. It is far better to go according to your schedule than to cancel. So what if only a few attend? It will give you an enhanced opportunity to relate better with the handful than with a whole roomful.

● Leave room for surprises. To plan regular meetings and keep them continuous is important, but also plan a few surprises. Surprise the group and call an impromptu meeting right after a Sunday morning church service. Or change the site of your next meeting and have everyone head to a "mystery hiding place."

● Continuity is strengthened by helping your group follow through on specific assignments between meetings. The leader of the youth group is the key in encouraging and supporting young people as they do their assigned tasks. The more often your youth group meets, the more work will get done between meetings, since meetings usually generate more enthusiasm and interest in the various tasks.

● Vary the programs and meeting format. Continuity causes boredom if the meetings lack a fresh spirit, new twists, unique ideas or creative challenges. Provide a steady diet of group meetings and a chance for young people to gather with specific purposes in mind—but be creative with each meeting.

People need a structure and a routine. We need a regular way of ordering our lives to feel secure and comfortable.

This is also true of youth groups. Groups need a continual pattern of activity. Groups need continuity so that relationships continue to be built and strengthened.

MEETING SETTINGS

Let your agenda dictate your meeting site. If you are studying the topic of death and dying, meet at a hospital or funeral home. If you're planning to discuss the needs of the elderly, meet at the home of a shut-in or at a nursing home.

It also is productive to have the group meet in different homes of members. The parents are familiarized with the group, the young people see how others live, and it tends to build positive relationships. Be sensitive to teenagers who might be embarrassed by their home environment and thus not want to host meetings.

The church, of course, is an excellent meeting site. Sometimes it is more convenient to meet at the same site, especially if the church is centrally located. Having a predictable meeting site also sets a good pattern for your members. If you decide to vary your meeting sites, be sure that each young person has directions and transportation.

Suggestions for meeting sites include:
● Church sanctuary—to discuss worship.
● Pastor's house—for an informal discussion.
● Movie theater—to review and later discuss a film.
● Public park—to have a picnic and your version of the Olympic games.
● Police station—to discuss crime and delinquency.
● Shopping center—to witness to shoppers.
● Television studio—to discuss current programs and shows.
● Bus or van—to have a progressive meeting from one home to another.
● School—to discuss the role of the school custodian, superintendent or counselor.

- Business office or car dealership—to discuss career choices.
- College—to discuss campus life with the campus pastor and students from your congregation.
- Cafeteria or restaurant—to discuss world hunger.
- Doctor's office—to discuss disease, health and trends in lifesaving procedures.
- Courthouse—to discuss teenage driving, justice and the court system.
- ROTC or recruiting office—to discuss the draft, war and peace.

WHO LEADS THE MEETINGS?

Every group needs leaders, but not all people are leaders. Youth groups need to work at developing a core of committed people who are willing to give of their time and energies.

A youth group that has teams of adults working with it is fortunate. The team ministry concept for youth groups allows as many adults as possible to become involved in the planning and doing. Team ministry includes young or older couples, single adults and parents of group members.

Congregations sometimes hesitate to involve parents of youngsters who are a part of the youth group. The key question is how do the parents and youngsters feel about the situation? If it is not a problem for them, then it can be a great relationship. If, however, the young person or the parents are uncomfortable with the idea, then perhaps the parents should work with another youth group. Ideally, parents and youngsters working together is an excellent model of acceptance, understanding and love.

After the adults have been recruited, allow them to decide on responsibilities and then work together with the young people in making certain everything is being covered for the various activities and events.

In this way, adults grow more closely together and at the same time use their gifts to meet the needs of young people.

The adult role is crucial to youth groups. Adults need to be present and available as counselors, idea-givers, directors and as friends. No adult has all the gifts needed to be the perfect adult sponsor or counselor, but each adult has gifts to give the young people.

One of the best gifts that adults can give is friendship. Young people need friendly adults around as models and listeners. Young people do not want or need "old teenagers"— that is, adults trying to act like youngsters. Rather, teenagers need mature, stable role models.

Other characteristics of adults who are effective as youth group counselors include:

- Committed to the Lord.
- Willing to share his or her faith.
- Likes young people.
- Trusts young people and is trusted by them.
- Relates well with young people.
- Has leadership skills.
- Has a sense of humor.
- Has a good self-concept.
- Knows his or her limitations and weaknesses.
- Has the time to take the time.
- Listens well.
- Understands the young people.
- Is an advocate for youth.
- Has ideas for groups to consider.
- Is a positive model in terms of lifestyle.
- Works well with other adults and involves other adults in their lives.

These characteristics shouldn't surprise you, because the Apostle Paul gave us a list of traits, "The fruit of the Spirit is love, joy, peace, patience, kindness, goodness, faithfulness, gentleness and self-control" (Galatians 5:22-23).

It would be ideal if adult counselors and leaders had all these gifts, but we don't. But that is the joy of the church—we need each other because we have limitations and requirements. The key is to involve adults with many different kinds of gifts. Adults who work with youth groups are among the most powerful and effective people in the congregation. The adults are meaningful models to youth. They unselfishly give of their time and talents. They serve in so many quiet ways that no one will ever know of their full scope of ministry. These people are you—the adults interested and committed to young people. You are people of power and promise, because the Lord continues to bless and guide you in your work with young people. You continue to be God's strong instruments in his ministry with young people. Keep strong in the faith. The Lord loves and blesses. He is your source of power and hope.

For the adult leader to concentrate on ministry, it is necessary to know what is expected, from both the church staff as well as from the youth. This is done best by talking frankly and firmly before problems arise. For example, the youth counselor should not be seen by the pastor or congregation as the one totally responsible for all youth ministry. It should be understood the church is responsible for youth ministry, not the youth group nor the counselors.

To spread this responsibility, the youth counselors need to work with the youth group officers. Clarify who is doing what and when. Assumptions lead to problems. The cartoon that shows the youth group president and the youth counselor sitting together in a roomful of vacant chairs is indicative of false assumptions. The youth counselor is saying to the president, "But I thought you were going to send out the meeting announcements."

Another concern in the youth group-counselor relationship is the peril that the group will become an adult-led organization rather than a group for young people being assisted by adults.

To develop the best role for the adult leader, review the following approaches to leadership:

Team ministry. Two or three couples or young adults serve together as a counseling team. This approach involves more adults, provides a variety of talents, enables more variations in the program, provides more role models, and builds a support system between the adults and teenagers.

Short-term commitment. Rather than ask an adult couple to serve as youth counselors "forever and ever," ask a couple to serve for a short term or the duration of a special project.

Rotation system. Leaders are elected or appointed at regular intervals.

Leadership cooperative. Community congregations share group leaders and resources and in so doing, reduce duplication and expenses.

Leadership "Snags"

A serious problem at many churches is the inability to recruit adults into any kind of leadership role. If you find you are carrying too great a burden as a youth leader, turn to your pastor or church board for ideas. Encourage the young people to seek adults they think would be good counselors. Or, have the youth call together their parents and ask for help. Also, develop a schedule in which parents take turns leading the group.

Sometimes it's the pastor who lacks involvement with the youth group. One solution is to invite the pastor to the next meeting. Do not ask the pastor to lead or even to say anything, rather allow everyone to enjoy fellowship without pressure.

Another approach in this situation is to have a number of youth confront the pastor in a polite but firm way. It can be a positive experience for the pastor to realize that young people are asking him or her to become more involved.

The opposite problem arises in situations in which the pastor unknowingly is replaced in his or her relationship with the youth by a dedicated and overenthusiastic adult counselor. The pastor must be the spiritual shepherd.

A similar problem happens in groups in which the adult counselor unwisely takes the place of parents. The counselor's role is not to be a surrogate parent, but rather to build positive bridges between teenagers and parents.

Another common concern in youth groups is that no one wants to be president. Coax your members more enthusiastically or have a few youth and adults campaign for the office. If all else fails, appoint three or four youth to serve as a leadership cabinet to give the group direction for the next year. Review and evaluate the youth group to ascertain the lack of interest and then ask the youth what they plan to do to increase interest.

JUNIOR AND SENIOR HIGH TOGETHER?

A common question is whether there should be one group or separate groups for junior and senior high members.

There is no satisfying answer, but there are ways to decide what is best for your situation. First, junior and senior high teenagers need one another—they need to be together in certain situations. The church does too much dissecting of these groups.

People of these ages also need to be with their peers. Senior high people have different needs and levels of development, obviously, than do junior high people. The church needs to provide settings and activities to develop these relationships.

There are certain topical areas and studies that relate more to one group than to the other, and there are a different set of needs and questions for both age groups. For example, the topic of sexuality would be viewed differently by junior and senior high youth.

A viable alternative is to structure two distinct youth groups and have the officers plan monthly joint events and projects. If your congregation has few young people, contact other congregations in your area for mutual programs and events.

Group leaders sometimes are distressed as high school seniors lose interest. The seniors tend to move away from the youth group structure because of working hours, additional homework, new friends, and to a large degree, because they are making the emotional switch from high school to college

48

or career.

Older youth in groups can be a source of strength, and groups should do all that they can to keep the seniors active. Consider ways to more effectively involve and help the seniors meet their needs such as college trips, vocational workshops or a senior recognition banquet.

An equally perplexing situation arises when the seniors seem unwilling to break from the youth group, even after high school graduation. If so, form a young adults class and plan a few joint activities with the young adult and senior high groups.

WHERE TWO OR THREE ARE GATHERED

Have you ever read in a youth ministry resource that you should divide your group into smaller groups of five to discuss a certain issue? The only problem with that suggestion is that your group only totals four. That's fine, for sometimes more ministry happens with smaller groups than with larger masses.

In small groups it is possible to give more individual attention, to be more personal with each member. In small groups people are not apt to be lost or overlooked. A pastor once made the thought-provoking remark that when the Lord stated in the scriptures, "For where two or three are gathered in my name, there am I in the midst of them," the Lord perhaps was giving youth groups a maximum number with which to work, rather than a minimum number.

Try this experiment: Think to a time when you were ministered to; that is, when the Lord used people or a person or a situation to help you through a crisis, or to communicate with you his generous and unconditional love. Have an experience in mind? Now, how many people were involved in this situation? One, a few or many? Most tend to select an example from their lives where one or two people effectively ministered. Remember, the Lord works through small groups in many marvelous ways. Leaders sometimes believe smaller youth groups have advantages, because better personal relationships can develop, more gifts can be used and shared and people can become closer to one another. Youth groups with 15 or more participants should consider doing small group designs and experiences as much as possible, to develop these caring relationships.

Another helpful suggestion for small youth groups is to join in activities with another small youth group from a neighboring congregation. Although bigger is not necessarily better, a larger gathering is a positive experience.

DISCIPLINE

The word discipline comes from the word disciple. As followers of Christ, group leaders sometimes need to discipline disciples. Discipline can be warranted to slow down a hyperactive group member or to settle a dispute between two warring members. Discipline is necessary whenever people are together because everyone is sinful. Harmony turns into disharmony. Trust breaks down. People are threatened and tempers flare.

Involve the youth group in writing regulations and guidelines for the youth group members. Leaders should draw up guidelines to be suggested to the youth group members. After the rules have been agreed upon, print the regulations, for example:

Friendly Rules to Live By

Group consensus is to be followed.

Wait your turn to speak. Only one person talks at a time.

No alcohol, drugs or cigarettes at meeting sites.

Treat others as you like to be treated.

The entire group deals with discipline problems, being direct and kind.

Group participants will abide by the counsel and guidance of the leaders.

This certainly does not cover everything, but it does point out the importance of guidelines and the need to deal with concerns as a total group as much as possible.

Considerations for the adult leader include:

● Keep positive in your relationships with youth members.

● Build close relationships with as many members as possible.

● Give the young people "ownership" of their problems.

● The more adults involved in the youth group, the better to deal with problems.

● Sometimes troublesome teenagers need special attention, things to do or responsibilities to make them more a part of the group.

● Discipline should be a positive word to disciples of the Lord.

Youth group meetings should not become oppressed by hundreds of "don'ts." Instead, a positive, gentle atmosphere needs to prevail. Deal with problems as they occur. Handle problems fairly and in Christian love. Share forgiveness as members continue to live as disciples of the Lord.

There will be times, however, when problems are bigger than the members or adult leader. The youth counselor needs to decide which discipline problems can be handled within the group and which problems need to be taken to church staff or parents. Involve parents when problems become acute.

At times it is necessary for a group member to seek professional help. It is not wise to ignore a potential problem. Rather, it is better to deal individually with a person and make referrals to professional help. This is touchy, so be careful. Involve the pastor and parents when making referral decisions.

The Ten Youth Meeting Commandments

Rules are necessary for a good youth group, but regulations don't need to be a bore.

The following rules are an adaptation of rules used by one youth group for a retreat:

I. Thou shalt not trespass on thy neighbor's body or self-esteem.

II. Thou shalt be to the meeting on time.

III. Thou shalt observe all youth group rules.

IV. Thou shalt not puff a weed of any kind nor space out on any pills or drink.

V. Thou shalt try to work out any problems immediately and if unable to do so, thou shalt talk with the youth group leader.

VI. Thou shalt participate respectfully at all group events.

VII. Thou shalt not sneak off from a meeting nor goof off in the parking lot during meeting times.

VIII. Thou shalt attempt to add to the group through enthusiasm and joy rather than detract through gossip and bickering.

IX. Thou shalt love one another as thou likes to be loved.

X. Thou shalt be okay.
                                        —Larry Keefauver

RESOURCES

Many resources are available for youth groups such as books, magazines, records and films. Although these materials are helpful, the best resources are people.

To better see yourself as a "resource," do the following:

● List five gifts you have.

- List how you have been using these gifts in your ministry at youth group meetings.
- List gifts that you do not have but that are needed in youth group ministry.
- List the names of other people in your church or community who have the gifts that you do not have.
- The purpose of this activity is to affirm that you have gifts and to show that you need other people and their talents to make a successful meeting. Encourage members of your congregation to be involved in all aspects of the youth group meeting. Also encourage the sharing of plans and activities between community churches. Remember, people are the best resources.

Furthermore, congregations need to provide growth opportunities for youth groups and sponsors. These growth opportunities can be initiated by the congregation:
- Paying counselors to attend training events and conferences.
- Providing necessary resources.
- Regularly conducting pastoral staff meetings to give ideas, feedback and support.
- Volunteering to share gifts.
- Praying for successful meetings and events.

People and material resources are a means to an end. They enable you to be effective in your ministry. As you use the abundance of resources around you, keep in mind the best resources are adapted, not adopted. Rewrite the study guide, change the design, alter the resource materials to better fit the needs of your youth group. You know best what will work effectively at your youth group meeting.

The many meeting designs in the second section of this book are excellent resources and ideas. Adapt them whenever necessary to better fit the needs of your group.

Youth Ministry Resources Consumer Tips

Each day barrels of ink are used to print youth ministry books, curriculum and other literature. Cutting room floors are strewn with film clips from new youth films and filmstrips. Your group deserves the best of these resources. A few consumer strategies may help you choose resources:

Films—You needn't rent a film you have only read about in a catalog. Why gamble good money to rent

continued

continued from page 52

a film with which you are unfamiliar? Most religious motion picture library staffs are eager to help you and will send you film catalogs, news of upcoming releases and allow youth leaders to preview films at the library. Usually there is no charge.

Filmstrips—Some film libraries and Christian bookstores sell filmstrips. Again, these usually are available for preview before purchase. If you order directly from the filmstrip's producer, ask for a 10- to 15-day evaluation period before paying for the product.

Curriculum—Most curriculum publishers allow a 10- to 15-day evaluation period to check out their products. Most will send youth leaders a free sample. Shop around. There's no reason to order from only one or two curriculum publishers.

Chapter Five

EVALUATING MEETINGS

After you work through publicity, assignments and planning and the event has taken place, it is time to evaluate the meeting to learn from it. How was the meeting? Was it successful or unsuccessful? What could have been better? Did it meet the objectives? Was the timing right? What kind of follow-up activity is needed? These are just a few concerns that should be raised after each event.

But how can you use evaluation of youth group activities to learn from them, see what needs are not being met and then make the necessary alterations? There are many helpful styles of evaluation to consider:

Evaluation Styles

Verbal. After a youth meeting, spend 10 minutes as a group discussing its pros and cons.

Written. Have the youth complete the evaluations after each major youth group event. Include such statements as: What was the most helpful part of the meeting? What would you have changed about the presentation? What suggestions would you make for future presentations? Would you be willing to help plan the next event?

Positive. Keep the evaluation procedures as positive as possible. For example, instead of asking, "What was the worst part of the program?" ask, "What would you most likely change about the program?"

Rating. Hand out cards and ask each person to rate the program on a scale of 1 to 10, with 10 being the highest. Or, instruct each person to write a word that describes the program. Share those words together.

Open-ended sentences. Use sentences such as: The best part of the meeting was . . . , At the next meeting, I would add . . . , The length of the meeting was . . . .

Visual aids. Use a visual aid to accumulate the tallies. For each event draw a big target on newsprint and tape it to the wall. Give each participant a colored, self-adhesive, round sticker to place on the target indicating a rating of the event. A variation of the visual-aid approach is to draw a chart and have the group members adhere the dots to indicate interest in events. In both approaches, you have a quick, easy, visual evaluation tool.

The following is an example of a written evaluation to use after each meeting:

Evaluation Form

1. The best part of the youth group meeting was . . .
2. The part that could have been improved was . . .
3. If I could have added one thing to the meeting, it would have been . . .
4. I would suggest that at our next meeting we . . .
5. Comment on the parts of the meeting.
   - opening:
   - Bible study:
   - presentation:
   - recreation:
   - closing:
   - setting or facilities:
   - mood of the group:
   - other:
6. I would be interested in leading or helping with the following at a future meeting:

Whatever approach you use, obtain as many evaluation responses as possible. The more you receive, the more fully you can evaluate.

The adult counselor or another designated person should carry through on this responsibility. Evaluations do little good unless they are used in the planning of the next event. It should be pointed out, however, that it is not wise to share the evaluations of someone else's presentation if he or she is not interested nor has asked for it.

Continue to evaluate through formal written forms and informal conversation and discussion. Youth leaders need feedback.

The youth group should file evaluation results for future reference and planning.

Ongoing evaluations include asking the right questions. The following questions don't require thorough answers, but do need to be asked repeatedly:

Ongoing Evaluations

What do we want to accomplish as a youth group? Reflect

on objectives and priorities. Youth groups cannot do everything well, so choose those that can be done well.

What can our youth group do well? Be open and honest about your gifts as a group.

How are we accomplishing needs? Continue to check this through feedback and observations. The needs of young people are primary, but the group also has to be aware of meeting a few needs of the parents as well as the adults who work with the group.

How am I helping my church understand youth ministry? How am I helping the other adults around me see youth as a total part of the congregation and not as just a youth group? What will it take to win a few more "converts" to this way of looking at youth ministry? How can the youth group be helpful in this dilemma?

How can our group help unite the congregation? What events can be conducted to bring youth and adults together for mission and ministry?

Now add your own questions to the list. What are some of your needs and anxieties that have not yet been addressed?

Veteran youth workers come to realize that every youth group goes through periods of highs and lows. Easily frustrated leaders think they never will get to a peak again. They continue to sing "Down in the Valley, the Valley So Low." But relax, you valley people, the good news is that youth groups do bounce back. Much depends on the makeup and nature of the young people involved.

One way to deal with ups and downs is to be patient. "This too shall pass" is a type of philosophy that says, hang in there. There's still hope ahead.

Evaluate your youth group in its high or low state. Is the problem something the counselor is or is not doing? Are the youth officers lacking enthusiasm or commitment? Is the problem the attitude of the members? their parents? the pastor? Talk with others, both for their ideas as well as their support. This up and down feeling is common to most groups, youth or adult. Learn from these levels and learn more about yourself in the process.

Dissatisfaction can take place if the group puts too much emphasis on numbers rather than on what it is trying to accomplish. The group might work at holding quality events, but then evaluate by asking, "How many attended the event?" There is nothing wrong in asking that question, but there is a problem if that is the only way youth group activities and meetings are evaluated.

If, however, you only have three members coming consistently when you know that many more could attend, you need to recognize there is an overall lack of interest and a problem. A number of factors may be at play—non-attending youth may perceive the group as dull. That might suggest a public relations problem. Or the group members may have little exciting to say about the group, in which case new activities are needed. Even more realistically, the youth group could need a complete overhaul.

If a group continues to limp along and is only surviving because of the dedication of a few adults and three semi-active members, then perhaps the group should be allowed to die. Sometimes a youth group has to die to regain excitement and purpose. After death comes resurrection, and perhaps the group needs a death experience so that new life can begin. Trust the Lord that a helpful and meaningful change will take place. To start again can be a positive move. New purposes and objectives can be developed by a fresh group of teenagers and adults, and the interest that was not present may return.

The church, as a whole, needs to evaluate its youth ministry not only on how many young people attend youth group meetings, but rather on how many young people are involved in other church ministry, including worship, Bible study, interest groups, church committees and social ministry.

In finalizing evaluations, frustrated youth group leaders often cite a lack of involvement and energy from the members. This can be a legitimate and accurate frustration. The solution to that frustration is in the gospel of Jesus Christ, which assures us that through Christ's death and resurrection we have received eternal life.

This promise frees us to share the good news with others and be concerned about the needs of others at the same time. That's powerful motivation. Sometimes that motivation is not always present, but it remains the source of our power and hope. We continue to care for and attempt to meet the needs of young people around us, even those who seem not to be overly motivated at the time.

Leaders often end evaluation time thinking that a lack of money is the cause of disappointments. "How do we get money to do quality events if we can't have money-raising projects?" leaders ask.

It is a poor practice to require dues for youth group membership. Young people and adults are better encouraged to give their gifts to the Lord through Sunday morning offerings, with portions of the donations then funneled to youth ministry for resources, speakers, trips, conferences, equipment and other legitimate items for youth group ministry.

So, let's say you've finished your evaluation, and by everyone's standards, including your own, the event was one big flop.

Rather than dwell on failure, evaluate and then plan again. Focus on the small successes in your youth group. Maybe it's a good Bible study. Maybe it's new faces. Maybe it's a good feeling of accomplishment. Whatever the small success is, celebrate with the group.

Again, the bottom line is to strive to make your youth group the best possible group. Work closely with those who attend meetings. As the youth group continues to be aware of needs and reaches out to others, additional young people will be attracted to its programs.

All people fail and so do youth groups. Failure and forgiveness, however, should go together in the youth groups and meetings. Failure need not be the end. Failure need not stoke tensions. Through all the relationships, problems, failures and frustrations, the Lord continues to work through his people. Christ's forgiveness distinguishes Christian youth groups from other groups.

Look for the place to say the kind word to the failed person. Watch for the opportunity to announce verbally and through your actions God's forgiveness in Jesus Christ. Share that forgiveness through kind words, happy hugs, warm smiles. Christ has forgiven us. And he gives us—and youth groups—the power to start over.

Strong youth groups are based, not on programs, structures, materials or schedules, but on the power and promises of Jesus Christ.

Relationships with the Lord and with his people are the key to youth group meeting successes. Work hard, relate well and celebrate the forgiveness we have in Jesus Christ. We all have a strong need and desire to stay alert and in tune with the young people around us. Seek to do that as you continue to put your priorities on the word of the Lord.

It is my prayer and hope that many of the meeting designs on the following pages will trigger your creative energies so these resources will become exciting possibilities for your ministry.

Part 2

MEETING DESIGNS FOR YOUTH GROUPS

Eighty-eight helpful and "field-tested" meeting designs that meet your teenagers' diverse needs, interests and concerns.

CLAY POTS

by Dean Dammann

PURPOSE

To understand that human weakness is not a reflection of spiritual strength but rather an opportunity to greater faith. To encourage faith even though troubles and doubts seem to abound.

PREPARATION

Gather pencils, 3 x 5 cards or identical slips of paper, a box or basket (any size) and a Today's English Version of the Bible.

Make copies of the Doubts handout below:

Doubts

Rank the following troubles and doubts from 1 to 8. One is the most troublesome, 8 the least:

____serious illness of a relative or friend

____a relationship with a friend that is hurting or breaking

____lack of money

____problems with parents

____feeling left out or lonely

____concern about the future

____fear of failing in school

____other

Share your ranking with the other members of your group. Discuss the number one rankings. Are they similar? Share why you marked it number one.

OPENING

Distribute pencils, the paper and the Doubts handout.

Form groups of six to eight. Choose a discussion leader for each group and discuss the Doubts sheet.

THE "MEAT" OF THE MEETING

As an introduction, explain: It can be threatening to share our problems and troubles with others. We often are afraid that others might think less of us or even use the information to hurt us. Yet, if we are aware of others' problems we can be helpful and supportive. Instruct the youth to write a concern or doubt that is troubling them. When everyone has finished writing, collect the cards in a box, mix and re-distribute them. Each person in turn reads the card he or she drew from the box. The group does not discuss at this time. Also, individual members do not reveal the card that they wrote. If a youth receives the card he or she wrote, the youth should act as if it were written by someone else. After all doubts and concerns have been read, go to the next activity.

Refer to 2 Corinthians 4:7-18 in Today's English Version. Have each person read by taking turns or choose one person to read the entire section. One at a time, read the concerns raised in the previous activity. Encourage the group to make helpful comments and suggestions on each item. Specifically try to find words or ideas from 2 Corinthians 4:7-18 that might be helpful to the person with the problem. Allow adequate time for the youth to respond to each of the doubts or concerns.

RESPONSE (OR CLOSING)

Have each person write a short one- or two-sentence prayer relating to his or her concern. Again use identical slips of paper or 3 × 5 cards. Collect the cards in a box and again distribute them. In turn, each person orally reads one of the prayers. After all prayers have been read, the group can join hands for the Lord's Prayer or a familiar song.

TENSION AND WORRY

by Cindy S. Hansen

PURPOSE

To recognize some of the tense areas in life, to understand anxious feelings and to find ways to reduce stress.

PREPARATION

Gather enough Bibles, pens or pencils, scissors, crayons, glue, construction paper, balloons, slips of paper, large rubber bands for the entire group and two sheets of posterboard.

Collect several types of rope, such as macrame, string, yarn or thread. Be sure to get several different lengths, widths and textures. Cut enough for members of the group to have several pieces when they make their tension collages. Place the rope on the center of a table.

Make copies of the Tension Sheet. (Enough for each member of the group.)

OPENING

As people enter the room, give them a balloon and a small piece of paper. Instruct the youth members to write a problem source or a "tension area" in their lives on the piece of paper, then wad the paper and put it into the balloon. They then should blow up the balloon and knot it. Keep the balloons in a box or in the corner of the room until the close of the meeting.

Play Rubber Band Faces. Put

Tension Sheet

Rank the following areas of stress from 1 to 10. One is the most tension-producing, 10 is the least.

____Being assigned homework or a test with only a week's notice

____Telling a lie—hoping I don't get caught in the act

____Arguing with a parent, brother or sister

____Arguing with a friend

____Speaking in front of a group

____Overhearing gossip about a friend of mine and wondering what to do about it

____Being late to church

____Worrying about the future

____Wondering about my past and forgiveness

____Other (explain)

---

large rubber bands around the heads of several members. Place each band so that it squashes the nose and folds the ears. On a signal, all contestants try to get the bands around their necks. First one to do so wins. No hands allowed, only facial expressions, walls or other people can be used.[1]

Have the entire group sit and explain to them the subject of the meeting is tension. Hold a rubber band and ask, "How is tension like this rubber band? Think of the time you had the rubber band around your face. How does tension sometimes feel like that?"

THE "MEAT" OF THE MEETING

Show everybody the table with the different types of rope on it. Ask how tension is like the ropes. Are some things we worry about bigger than others? Are some worries easier to carry or hold than others? Do some tensions feel different than others?

Pass out the glue, construction paper and scissors to the youth. Let them pick their own pieces of rope to design a tension collage. Help the youth create designs. What color of paper will you use? What shape will it be? Which ropes will you use? How will you place the rope on your sheet? After each participant is finished with his or her collage, assemble in small groups for discussion.

Pass out copies of the Tension Sheet and pencils. Have everyone rank the items from 1 to 10. Discuss the areas that cause the most and the least tension. Are some answers different? What causes some people to worry about things that never worry others? What are some of the other causes of tension that were written? Were any of these similar in your small group? Gather as a large group and write several tension areas on a sheet of posterboard or on chalkboard.

Next, discuss each of these tension areas. How could you deal with the tensions or worries in each of these situations? What helps the most? least? How do you deal with the tensions of homework? Do you relieve tension by doing the homework? planning ahead? studying? What about arguments in the family. Do you deal with tension by "talking things out"? What about worrying over the future and the past? Are there other ways we can deal with stress, such as jogging, hot baths, exercising or reading a good book? How does faith enter this situation? Why is it a necessity to believe we are forgiven and loved by God? Write these tension relievers on a second sheet of posterboard.

Get volunteers to read each of the following Bible verses: Job 30:27; Psalm 39:6; John 14:27; 16:33; Philippians 4:7. What do these verses say about stress? Do the verses mention other ways to deal with tension or worry? Write these additional ways of dealing with stress on the other sheet of posterboard. No matter how much Jesus tells us not to worry—we still do! Since we need reminders, pass out paper to the group and have every member write down these ways of dealing with stress. Move to the closing activity for a fun way to reduce tension!

RESPONSE (OR CLOSING)

Have the youth take off their shoes and socks, sit in a circle and get a partner. Take a couple of minutes to give each other a foot massage—a sure way to reduce tension! Then bring out the balloons prepared at the first of the meeting. Hand one to each person. Instruct the group members to pass the balloons to the right of the circle, using only their feet—for 30 seconds. When the time is up, they pop the balloons (without the use of hands) and read the problem written on the piece of paper. One at a time share a way to deal with the tension area in each balloon. Consider the past discussion on ways to deal with tension.

For the closing prayer—each person prays silently for the problem or tension area on the piece of paper. End the prayer thanking God for his message of hope and peace in a world of tension. Ask God for help in reducing stress in other people as well as ourselves.

HELPFUL RESOURCES

Freedom of Simplicity, by Richard J. Foster, Harper and Row, 10 E. 53 St., New York, NY 10022.

Stress/Unstress, by Keith W. Sehnert, Augsburg, 426 S. Fifth St., Minneapolis, MN 55415.

1Thom Schultz, ed., **More . . . Try This One** (Loveland, Colo.: Group Books, 1980), p. 9.

BEATITUDE ATTITUDES

by Robert C. Crosby

PURPOSE

To use the Beatitudes as a guide for young people and to assist the youth in utilizing the characteristics as God desires.

PREPARATION

Acquire easels; posterboard or art pads; art chalk; felt-tip markers; giveaway items; a spotlight or single floodlight; **Sketch Books, Vol. IV**; **Never Say Die** album; and songbooks (See Resources).

Several months in advance, contact youth to perform a short play based on Christian attitudes. A suitable one-act play would be **Chameleon** from the Jeremiah People's **Sketch Books, Vol. IV**. Prepare and plan for several rehearsals and collect necessary props and costumes.

A few weeks before the meeting, begin your study of the Sermon on the Mount (Matthew 5-7) with a focus on the Beatitudes (5:1-11). See the Resource section for suggested study books and the "Meat" of the Meeting for an outline guide.

Prepare a brief, concise teaching on each of the Beatitudes and copies of the Attitude Review worksheet listed in the Closing section.

Assign a youth to prepare a banner that says "BeARTitudes."

Just before your meeting, help the youth set up the lighting and props for the play.

Set up the easels and art supplies.

OPENING

Several minutes before the meeting, play "Chameleon" on the **Never Say Die** album. As the song ends, seat the youth.

Dim the lights and turn on the spotlight. That will be the actors' cue to begin the play.

After the play, turn on the lights and introduce the focus of the evening—attitudes.

THE "MEAT" OF THE MEETING

Divide into groups of seven or eight and assign each group to a drawing board. Explain that for the next 1,800 seconds they will be tested on their "ARTitudes."

Call the name of one representative from each group and show them a word. They are to draw an image of the word on their artboards—non-verbally coaxing their group to guess the word first. Keep score on which team guesses the most words. Following each of the illustrations, give a brief message on the meaning of that Beatitude.

Following are illustration ideas for the Beatitudes and points you can use in your brief message:

● Verse 3: Draw a hobo to illustrate "poor in spirit." Humility, meekness and godliness.

● Verse 4: Draw a tear to

illustrate "mourn." Empathy and compassion.

- Verse 5: Draw a lamb to illustrate "meek." Gentleness, kindness and submission.
- Verse 6: Draw a hungry baby bird to illustrate "hunger and thirst after righteousness." Pursuit of Christlikeness and spiritual nourishment.
- Verse 7: Draw a judge to illustrate "merciful." Forgiveness and grace.
- Verse 8: Draw a bar of soap to show "pure in heart." Purity, holiness and innocence.
- Verse 9: Draw policemen to represent "peacemakers." Ministry of reconciliation, cooperation and winsomeness.
- Verse 10: Draw a soldier to show "patience through persecution." Long-suffering and perseverance.

Award the prizes to the winning team.

RESPONSE (OR CLOSING)

Choose a discussion leader for each group and give that person a copy of the Attitude Review sheet.

Allow the groups to separate, discuss the questions and record their observations. After 10 to 15 minutes, gather everyone to share the conclusions.

For the final minutes of the meeting, pair and read Matthew 18:20 and James 5:16. Ask the youth to admit to their partners a

---

Attitude Review

What attitude do you have that your parents most dislike?

What do you not like about your parents' attitudes?

In what ways can our friends affect our attitudes?

What attitudes need to be changed in your life for you to get in line with the attitudes Christ taught?

How do your attitudes affect your characteristics?

---

characteristic or an attitude they have that they know is wrong. Then, encourage them to pray for each other, asking God to impart the right attitudes and characteristics into their hearts and lives.

HELPFUL RESOURCES

Jeremiah People, Sketch Books, Vol. IV, Continental Ministries, P.O. Box 1996, Thousand Oaks, CA 91360.

Never Say Die, by Petra, Star-Song Records, Word, P.O. 1790, Waco, Texas 76796.

Scripture in Song, Benson, 365 Great Circle Road, Nashville, TN 37228.

Christian CounterCulture, by John R.W. Stott, InterVarsity Press, P.O. Box F, Downers Grove, IL 60515.

Improving Your Serve and **Strengthening Your Grip**, by Charles R. Swindoll, Word, 4800 W. Waco Drive, Waco, Texas 76710.

MAKE A JOYFUL NOISE

by Tammy Spigelmire

PURPOSE

To discuss the feeling of belonging and how this relates to Christ's church.

PREPARATION

Gather several songs of praise (either classical or contemporary), a Bible, 3 × 5 cards and pencils. Study and make copies of the Groupie Guide in the "Meat" of the Meeting section.

OPENING

Open with prayer, then sing several songs of praise.

Explain that this study will delve into the feeling of belonging.

Define the term clique. Are there cliques at school? Are there cliques at church? Do Christian youth mix in well with the "popular" youth at school? Why or why not?

Divide the group in half and label one half the "in-the-clique" group and the other the "out-of-the-clique" group.

Have the youth answer and discuss the appropriate questions for the "out" and "in" groups.

Combine the groups and discuss the answers. As a Christian, do you more often feel "in" than "out"? Are there specific settings where you definitely feel "out" as a professed Christian? If you are a Christian and your friends are not, is there pressure on you not to

Questions for the "Out" Group

1. How do you feel when you are left out? Insecure?
2. Do you find it difficult to share your faith in this situation?
3. How can you let others know you would like to belong?

Questions for the "In" Group

1. How do you feel when you are included in a group? Secure?
2. Do you find it difficult to share your faith under these circumstances?
3. How can you let others know you really care and allow them into the group?

share your faith? Why or why not?

Read Psalm 95. What is the message? Then discuss the lyrics of the praise song from the Opening. Are we to "make a joyful noise" to God all the time or part of the time? How should we feel being a Christian?

THE "MEAT" OF THE MEETING

Give copies of the following questions to each young person.

Groupie Guide

Read Psalm 100 and answer the following questions:

1. What group are you in at school?
   A. The "in" group.
   B. The "out" group.
   C. Don't care.
   D. Other.
2. How can you be sure?
   A. My friends tell me.
   B. People tease me.
   C. I'm not sure.
   D. Other.
3. Do you want to change this situation?
   A. No, I'm happy (explain).
   B. Yes, I'm unhappy (explain).
4. I feel the "in" group should be . . .
   A. My church friends.
   B. My school friends.
   C. There shouldn't be an "in" group.
   D. Other.
5. What is the message of Psalm 100?
6. How does Psalm 100 relate to your life?

Gather in a circle and discuss the Groupie Guide. Ask if Jesus belonged to any earthly groups. Did the disciples have a strong feeling of belonging? Did they ever have doubts and feel "out"? Is anyone denied an "in" with God?

RESPONSE (OR CLOSING)

Hand out 3 x 5 cards and pencils to the participants. Encourage them to write a goal for the upcoming week by completing this sentence: I will make a joyful noise to the Lord by_____.

Examples could include: being more accepting to all people at school, having a more positive outlook about each day, or bringing a friend to the next youth group meeting.

Refer to Psalm 100 and explain this can be used as a guide for group involvement. Have half of the young people read verse one, the other half read verse two, and so on.

Close in a prayer of praise and thanksgiving.

WE BELONG TOGETHER

by Joani Lillevold

PURPOSE

To experience and bring to mind feelings of "belonging." To explore relationships with God and people and to see the ways such ties fulfill a need to "belong."

PREPARATION

Gather Bibles, newsprint, felt-tip markers, pencils, paper and masking tape.

On a large newsprint banner write in colorful, bold letters, "I have called you by name, you are mine" (Isaiah 43:1). Affix the banner to the meeting room wall.

Make copies of the Bible study for each member of the group.

Note: This meeting could last 90 minutes to two hours depending on discussion.

OPENING

As the young people enter, encourage them to sign their names on the banner. For fun, have them add words and graffiti that express their uniqueness.

After everyone has written on the banner, gather the group in a circle. Ask a boy and a girl from the group to read the following "Me/Me, too" dialogue.

Me: I'm afraid.

Me, too: I want people to like me.

Me: I want to fit in, but I'm not sure what it takes.

Me, too: I need acceptance; what do I have to do to belong?

Me: Let me in.

Me, too: I don't want to be on the outside.

Me: I just want to be *me*.

Me, too: I'm looking for someone who'll say, "Just be yourself— that's enough!"

Introduce the theme "Belonging—A Longing to Be" and pray for God's blessing for the time together.

Have the youth firmly hold hands to form an interlocking circle. Choose one person to stand outside the circle and try to break in. The participants in the circle try to keep that youth out. Make certain no one gets hurt.

Have volunteers take turns being the outsider.

After the experience, have the group members talk about their feelings. Encourage discussion with incomplete sentences, for example:

As a member of the "in" group, I felt . . .

As the "outsider," I felt . . .

Doing this reminded me of . . .

THE "MEAT" OF THE MEETING

Use these activities to further explore the idea of belonging. These can be done individually or as a group:

Clues and Cues of Belonging

For each category, think of two examples that demonstrate acceptance and belonging. Use clues such as words, actions, rituals or traditions for these groups:

● Family
● Friends
● Youth group
● Church

Also think of one special way you can show care and acceptance to each of the above categories.

People Traits

List five qualities or traits in people that help give you a sense of belonging:

Reflect on Belonging

Describe a time you especially felt a sense of belonging . . .

Describe a time you felt you didn't belong . . .

Now compare the two times. What made them different? Was it you, the people, the circumstances or something else?

The Art of Belonging

An artist has been asked to paint a creative picture called "Belonging." The artist will draw and design it only if you'll provide the details such as:

● Where (place)
● With whom (people)
● What is happening (activity)
● A caption

Who

Name three people who accept you as you are:

Name three people you accept as they are:

More to Think About

A group I'd like to belong to is . . .

A place I always feel accepted is . . .

School is/isn't a place I feel accepted because . . .

Church is/isn't a place I feel accepted because . . .

One way our youth group can help people feel welcome is . . .

Form small groups of six to eight. Remind the groups that sharing is encouraged, but no one should feel forced to share anything that would make them feel uncomfortable.

Have each small group list reasons their families give them a feeling of belonging. Allow three to five minutes for the youth to write the list on newsprint. Tape the list onto the banner.

Have each individual complete these sentences on paper:

● For me, being connected with my family means . . .
● Three things I enjoy because of my family are . . .
● Three difficulties I experience because I'm a part of my family are . . .

Share answers.

Select one person to read Romans 8:15-17. Now have each person finish these sentences:

● To me, being one of God's children means . . .
● Three things I enjoy because I'm a child of God are . . .
● Three difficulties I encounter because I'm a part of God's family are . . .

Talk about the youth group representing the people God uses to touch the lives of others. Ask the youth for ideas that help people feel included in the group. Think of ways members can experience belonging to the family of God. Write ideas and then tape them onto the banner.

Following are four stories illustrating a variety of Jesus' experiences. Assign passages to the small groups.

Belonging Isn't Mere Child's Play

Read Mark 10:13-16.

From this passage, I'd describe Jesus as . . .

What does this passage say about belonging to the family of God?

To me, the kingdom of God is . . .

To receive the kingdom like a child means . . .

To be held in someone's arms makes me feel . . .

What a Welcome Mat Could Mean

Read Matthew 10:40-42.

What are ways people make you feel welcome?

To welcome someone means . . .

God welcomes us by . . .

What surprises do you find in these words?

What rewards are there in welcoming people and helping them feel included?

Read Luke 6:38. Does this add a new insight into your current relationships?

Jesus Isn't Sheepish About Loving Us

Read John 10:1-16.

The shepherd loves the sheep because . . .

God loves you because . . .

Does belonging also mean familiarity?

To give your life for someone means . . .

Being compared to a flock of sheep makes me feel . . .

Jesus told this story because . . .

One thing I can depend on the Good Shepherd to do for me is . . .

One thing the Good Shepherd can expect of me is . . .

A Family Affair

Read Matthew 12:49-50.

What strikes you as unusual about this passage, if anything?

To be someone's brother or sister means . . .

The good things about being in the same family are . . .

The responsibilities that come from being in the same family are . . .

As sisters and brothers in the family of God, our greatest concern should be to . . .

RESPONSE (OR CLOSING)

Form a large group. Allow discussion about the previous activity. Join hands and pray the Lord's Prayer. Remind the group that we begin with the words "Our Father"—a statement of our faith and family relationship with God.

As an "Amen" activity, keep hands joined. Have the person who was the "outsider" for the first activity let go of one hand and stand still. As the rest of the group gradually spirals around the person to form a tight circle, sing a song of unity such as "We Are One in the Spirit." After everyone has wrapped around the middle person, give a giant "you belong" hug!

BIBLE FEUD

by Donald W. Palmore

PURPOSE

By basing a biblical knowledge contest on the television show **Family Feud**, the youth have an opportunity to find how well they know the Bible and the youth leaders can see the areas that need improvement.

PREPARATION

Gather Bibles, 3 x 5 cards, refreshments and a blackboard (songbooks are optional).

Make a list of 20 biblical questions, all with more than one possible answer. Questions could include: Name a disciple, name one of the Ten Commandments or name a book Paul wrote.

Prepare five non-biblical questions such as: Name a fast-food restaurant or name a type of bird.

Type your list and make 100 copies. Survey the adult Sunday school class for answers to the questions.

The goal is to receive 100 completed forms, so that these answers can be turned into points. The survey is tabulated by taking one question at a time and recording each answer as one point. If you only receive 50 surveys, give each answer two points.

Review each question and keep five to nine of the most popular answers. Some questions may have to be discarded because of confusion or ambiguity.

Once the questions and answers have been established, write them on the 3 x 5 cards. Record the total number of points possible and the points for each individual answer.

The final five questions should be handled the same way, but these will be used for the winners as a bonus round.

Before the contest, write "Biblical Feud" on the blackboard. The blackboard also serves as a scoreboard.

OPENING

Begin the meeting with songs, then split into contest groups of seven each. Arrange the chairs so the teams face each other.

THE "MEAT" OF THE MEETING

To begin the game, two team captains come forward and stand before the "host" who reads a question. The first captain to raise his or her hand tries to answer the question.

If that player gives the number one answer, then his or her team must decide to pass or play the question. If he or she does not give the number one answer, play passes to the opponents. Play continues in the same manner as on the television program **Family Feud**.

Once a team gets the opening question, the second player is

asked another question. This process is continued until all the answers are revealed or three "strikes" occur. A strike is given when a team member gives an answer that is not on the survey.

If the team members get all the answers before three strikes, they receive all the points. However, should they receive three strikes first, the opposite team has a chance to take any earned points by giving one answer that appears on the survey.

Once the play is over, ask the group to guess the unrevealed answers. If no one can do so, give the relevant Bible verses to show the basis of the question.

Play continues until a certain point value is reached or until all the questions are used.

The team with the most points wins and chooses two of its players for the bonus round.

One of the two chosen for the bonus round is sent to a place where he or she cannot hear the others.

The other bonus player has 20 seconds to answer the five non-biblical questions. His or her point value is added and then the second player returns to the room. The second player is given 25 seconds to answer the questions. If any of the first player's answers are repeated, the second player will be asked to give another answer.

If the two players reach 175 points, their team is declared the bonus winner.

RESPONSE (OR CLOSING)

Close the meeting with the group forming a circle and holding hands for group prayer. The prayer may express thankfulness for fun and the endless knowledge that God provides.

Enjoy the refreshments with the winners going first.

HELPFUL RESOURCES

Sing 'n' Celebrate, Word, 4800 W. Waco Drive, Waco, TX 76703.

The most helpful resource for this activity is to watch the **Family Feud** game on television.

WHAT IS THE BIBLE ABOUT?

by James P. Reeves

PURPOSE

To emphasize the importance of Bible study.

PREPARATION

Gather Bibles, posterboard, newsprint, and felt-tip markers or crayons.

For each participant, prepare copies of the True/False Quiz and the Bible study in the "Meat" of the Meeting.

On separate posterboards write out these scriptures: Psalms 119:9; 119:105; Romans 10:17; Ephesians 6:16-17; James 1:23-25; and 1 Peter 1:23. Place the scriptures about the meeting room.

OPENING

Open by explaining the focus of the meeting is the Bible. Distribute the true-false quiz and have the youth complete it.

THE "MEAT" OF THE MEETING

Discuss the Quiz and ask for scriptural support of answers.

Distribute the newsprint and markers and instruct the youth to draw concepts of the scriptures written on the posterboards. Afterward, have each group explain its drawing.

Together read 2 Timothy 2:15. Explain that when God tells us to do something, it always is to our benefit.

Read 2 Timothy 3:16-17 then distribute the Bible Study.[1]

True/False Quiz

The Bible is a record of God's search for man.

The Bible records a factual history of the Jewish race.

The Bible is an answer book that gives us solutions to our problems.

Every book of the Bible is of equal importance to the others.

You can prove God's existence with the Bible.

The Bible is the only record of truth.

Throw away the Old Testament and you still can know all about God from reading the New Testament.

We can use the Bible as a scientific textbook to prove the creationist theory.

Bible Study

List any and all action verbs you can find.

What or who is being told to do the action?

What does the verse say about you personally?

Are there any promises or blessings for you?

How can your actions reflect the message of these verses?

RESPONSE (OR CLOSING)

Have each person discuss the final question of the Bible Study.

Pray that the hearts and minds of the participants will be opened to God's word.

HELPFUL RESOURCES

What's the Good Word?, by John Souter, Zondervan, 1420 Robinson Road, Grand Rapids, MI 49506.

[1]Adapted from: John C. Souter, "Personal Bible Study Notebook: Vol. 1," (Carol Stream, Ill.: Tyndale House, 1977).

TASTE AND SEE

by Michael Walcheski

PURPOSE

To help young people understand that God's word can be an active part of their lives and to give them an opportunity to share their favorite Bible scriptures.

PREPARATION

Gather Bibles, scissors, multi-colored construction paper, pencils, paper, newsprint and felt-tip markers.

Prepare copies of the Bible study for all (see the following page).

This Bible study is designed for small group interaction, so plan to meet in a comfortable room that is not so large it overwhelms the group.

OPENING

As the youth arrive, have them use the construction paper to make name tags. Tell the youth to design the tags in the shape of their favorite food and to write their name on the tag. It is important that their favorite food remain a secret until later.

Divide into groups of four and distribute the Bibles, pencils, paper, newsprint and markers.

The participants are to try to guess each other's favorite food. The youth can give clues, such as texture, ingredients, food category or color.

Have each group prepare a list of the favorite foods, then on the same paper, write foods the youth dislike. Have them compare the lists to see if there are any items on both lists. Next, have each group list foods that take time to learn to like. Have the participants name foods they did not like as a child, but now enjoy.

THE "MEAT" OF THE MEETING

Have each person silently read Psalm 34:7-10, then one person in each group should read it aloud. The same should be done with 1 Peter 2:2-3.

Distribute the Bible study sheets and have the youth answer the questions.

RESPONSE (OR CLOSING)

Everyone in the small groups should take a moment to find his or her favorite Bible passage. Share the passages in the small groups with each youth and explain why it is a favorite. As each shares a passage, he or she should write it on the newsprint. Decorate the meeting room with the favorite scriptures.

Close in the small groups with circle prayers and thank God for the bountiful food supplies he has given and for his ample blessings.

Bible Study

● When I read these passages, I felt that . . .

_____God wants me to eat the Bible.

_____My body needs more junk food.

_____I need to alter my diet.

_____Pass the milk.

_____I need to eat this until I like it.

● What do these passages have to do with my favorite food?

● How is reading the Bible like sampling new food?

● Does it take time to develop a taste for God's word? Why or why not?

● What does God promise if we make his word a part of our daily diet? (Psalm 34:7-10)

● How does that make you feel?

PEOPLE JESUS TOUCHED

by Gary Moran

PURPOSE

To better understand several biblical characters and their interaction with Jesus. Also, to make the Bible's message relevant to today's youth by allowing them to identify with individuals in the scriptures.

PREPARATION

Collect Bibles, pencils, paper and pictures of people in the Bible. Cut the pictures in half.

Familiarize yourself with the scripture passages listed in the "Meat" of the Meeting.

OPENING

Give each youth a half of a picture and have him or her find the participant who has the other half. These couples will be partners for the activity.

THE "MEAT" OF THE MEETING

After the participants have found their partners, assign each pair one of the following New Testament figures and the relevant scripture passage: The Roman centurion—Matthew 8:5-13; Peter—Matthew 26:69-75; Simon and the prostitute—Luke 7:36-47; Mary and Martha—Luke 10:38-42; the blind man—Luke 18:35-43; the crippled man—John 5:1-9; Thomas—John 20:19-29; Stephen—Acts 6:7—7:1 and Acts 7:51-60.

After the pairs have read their passage, have them discuss ways in which the biblical figures are alike or different. The pairs then can report their findings to the entire group.

Have the group discuss differences Jesus made in the lives of these biblical characters. Ask the youth which of the biblical characters they identified with most. Why?

Have the young people choose one of the Bible characters and answer the following questions as they think that person would have answered: Is what other people think of you important? What is important to you?

RESPONSE (OR CLOSING)

Close with a prayer about the Bible and its importance to us today.

HOW TO HANDLE BOREDOM

by Ben Sharpton

PURPOSE

To have youth recall times they were bored, to understand reasons of boredom and to challenge the young people to overcome boredom by committing themselves to worthwhile endeavors.

PREPARATION

Gather Bibles, paper, pencils, blackboard and chalk, or newsprint and felt-tip markers.

Become familiar with the scripture passages included in this meeting. Study what each says about the life that a relationship with Christ gives us and how this can apply to boredom.

Study the Boredom Analysis Chart presented on the following page and draw it on the blackboard.

Prepare the room.

OPENING

Tell the group members you are going to name several activities and they are to express their opinion as to the amount of boredom each activity produces. When you say an item they consider boring, have them say "boring." If the activity is not boring, they should remain silent.

Here are some words you can use: algebra class, evening news, English class, astronomy, soap operas, Mr. Rogers, nursing home visitation, history class, football games, classical music concert, golf game, worship service, missionary slide show, family reunion, politics or documentary films.

THE "MEAT" OF THE MEETING

Based on the responses, choose five items that seemed to be the most boring. Create a Boredom Analysis Chart on a blackboard or newsprint similar to the one presented on the next page. Fill in each activity in the column on the left, and as a group fill in the other columns.

Split into five small groups and assign each group one of these scripture passages: John 6:63; 8:31-32; 10:10; Romans 12:2; or Philippians 4:8-9. Each group is to work together to ascertain what is being offered in its passage, what is being required according to the scripture and how that item can help overcome boredom. If you have a small gathering, you may want to divide into two groups and give each group more than one passage to study.

Distribute pencils and paper. Ask the youth to list across the top of the page four or five current interests such as sports, auto repair, home economics or computers. Beneath each item have them list the names of people with whom they share that activity. Give them time to evaluate their list and ask if they spend their time with a variety of people or with the same people. Ask if an exclusive sharing of time could exacerbate boredom.

Ask the youth to list across the top of the back of their paper several activities in which they are not yet involved but could be. Ask each person to create columns of names under each item of people who are now involved in that activity. Be sure to encourage the youth to include people who are of different ages than themselves. Ask if such interaction could relieve boredom.

As an optional exercise, you can have the group list on the blackboard or newsprint as many items as it can in which a person can spend a typical afternoon or evening. Use the following symbols to evaluate each item:

"$"	expensive
"¢"	cheap
"T"	requiring more than three hours of time
"S"	seasonal such as ice skating or swimming
"#"	requiring more than one person
"1"	can be done alone

RESPONSE (OR CLOSING)

Go around the circle and give each person an opportunity to share something he or she has learned.

Close in prayer asking God to challenge each person to become involved in something meaningful and purposeful.

Boredom Analysis Chart

Activity	Time of Day for Activity	Place Where Activity Occurs	Purpose of Activity	Cause of Boredom	Solution to Overcome Boredom
History Class	1:05 - 1:55 After lunch	Un-Air-Conditioned Classroom	Graduate Learn about others' mistakes	Environment Motivation	Improve Environment Search for Purpose

BREAKFAST BUFFET BIBLE STUDY

by Bruce Nichols

PURPOSE

To conduct study breakfasts as an alternative for teenagers who find it difficult to attend afternoon or evening youth ministry events.

PREPARATION

Prepare a four-month schedule for host families and youth Bible study leaders. Each host family should plan to provide a warm and open atmosphere and also to prepare the breakfasts. Breakfasts can be served buffet-style with youth gathered in one area of the house for talking, planning and fellowship. In planning menus, special dietary needs should be considered. Ask the youth to bring money to help defer the breakfast cost.

The youth assigned to lead the Bible study should be given ample time and guidance for preparation.

Publicize the breakfast through the church newsletter, bulletins, announcements, bulletin boards, newspapers and radio.

Everyone uses his or her Bible, notebook and pen.

For the study example given in the "Meat" of the Meeting, you'll need construction paper, magazines, glue and scissors for each participant.

OPENING

Greet each other and share the peace of Christ. Say a prayer and then eat the breakfast in a relaxed manner. Fellowship together, share joys and concerns, and talk about current issues, school and family. After breakfast, help clean up.

THE "MEAT" OF THE MEETING

Each study is different, here is one example:

Love, God and Me

Ask each of the participants to define love. Then hand out the construction paper, scissors, glue and magazines and ask the young people to make craft representations of their definitions.

Tell them to use their imaginations. One person might cut the word "Love" out of paper and glue on pictures from the magazines that remind him or her of love:

Another could cut out a heart and add other finishing touches:

Discuss the definitions and crafts and then have the youth read Solomon 1:1-4.

Ask, "What is human love like?" Allow time for each person to share.

Delve deeper by asking, "What is God's love like?"

RESPONSE (OR CLOSING)

Turn to 1 Corinthians 13:1-13 and have each member read a verse aloud. Talk about God's love in us and ask, "How do we pass on God's love to others?"

Discuss the differences and similarities between God's love and human love. Ask the participants manners in which God's love has grown and changed within them.

Turn again to 1 Corinthians 13:4-7 and have the youth choose one of the traits, research it, and then try to integrate it into their own lives.

Conclude with a circle prayer with the youth holding hands. Give thanks and praise for the love of God in our lives and also for the strength to live the traits listed in Corinthians.

If the breakfast takes place on a weekday morning, share rides to school.

HELPFUL RESOURCES

Sing a Song of Hope, Augsburg, 426 S. 5th St., Minneapolis, MN 55415.

GROUP Magazine, P.O. Box 481, Loveland, CO 80539.

BREAKFAST IN BED

by Cindy S. Hansen

PURPOSE

To provide a fun way to have fellowship with the group in a new environment.

PREPARATION

Gather paper plates and on the underside print different verses of the study. For example, if you were studying Psalm 121, write Psalm 121:1-2 on the bottom of one plate; Psalm 121:3-4 on the bottom of another plate, and so on. Various topics can be used for this breakfast-in-bed study time: Psalms, Proverbs, parables, Ten Commandments, fruits of the spirit, temptation of Jesus and stories of Old Testament characters.

Assign menu items to different people in the group. One person can bring eggs, others muffins, bacon, juice, coffee. Others can be assigned to bring flatware, napkins, cups and Bibles. Breakfast can be served potluck style.

A week before this activity, pick one youth or sponsor to surprise. Arrange the rendezvous with a member of the household so that person can open the door at the appointed hour.

Assign pre-meeting preparations to various group members.

OPENING

Breakfast in bed is a chipper way to start the day. Gather the group in the church parking lot to car pool with the breakfast items to the intended destination. Enter the bedroom of the "victim" and wake him or her with a loud chorus of: Good morning to you, good morning to you, good morning dear sleepy head—good morning to you. (Sung to the tune of "Happy Birthday.") Proceed to eat breakfast, then move into a Bible study using the following technique:

THE "MEAT" OF THE MEETING

One at a time, as the youth finish eating, have them turn the paper plate upside down and read the scripture, then open a Bible and read aloud the verse. The youth then answers the following:

1. What is the picture of man you see in this verse?
2. What is the picture of God?
3. What does this verse mean to you?

Allow time for discussion after each verse. When the next person is finished eating, he or she follows the same procedure.

For example: If the plate has Psalm 121:1-2 written on it, the youth would read: "I lift up my eyes to the hills. From whence does my help come? My help comes from the Lord, who made heaven and earth." The answer to question one might be, "Man lives in a troubled time and has many struggles." The answer to question two might be, "God is all powerful and he made everything." The answer to question three might be, "The Lord is my help—all I have to do is look for him." Continue until everyone has had a chance to answer the questions.

RESPONSE (OR CLOSING)

Close with a prayer thanking God for the food for our bodies as well as food for our thought made possible through the Bible study.

If surprise breakfasts don't work for your group . . . try meeting for a regularly scheduled snack hour (everyone brings a treat such as cookies, milk, chips or dip). Or arrange a weekly soup supper. (The guys bring cans of soup and the girls bring crackers and cheese.) Meet at the church kitchen or meeting room or in other members' homes. Rotate the meeting site each week and use the previously described Bible study technique.

WE ARE FAMILY

by Wesley Taylor

PURPOSE

To illustrate that just as the body is made of many members yet is one body, so the church is made of many members, yet is one in the body of Christ.

PREPARATION

Order the film **Water and Spirit**, Teleketics, 1229 S. Santee, Los Angeles, CA 90015. **The String** film from Mass Media Ministries, 2116 N. Charles, Baltimore, MD 21218 is optional.

You'll also need Christian music (see Resources for suggestions), a record player, film projector and screen.

Gather a water pitcher, glasses, ball of string and a cross 2- to 3-feet tall.

OPENING

Read aloud 1 Corinthians 12:12-27 then sing together or listen to "You've Got a Friend." Follow this with silent meditation and then pray:

Great God, who cares for us so much, we come to you to understand the meaning of the love of Jesus Christ for our lives. Help us to be careful and caring with each other. Help us to consider the other person as we consider our own needs. Forgive us when we have been too quick to put down and too irritable with a different opinion. Help us to celebrate the healing and forgiveness that nourishes our lives and empowers us to reach out with love to each other. May we care for one another as brothers and sisters bound together in a family. In Christ's name. Amen.

Introduce the subject of community by presenting this reading:

Community is more than contact; it is caring, compassion, concern, comforting, creating, celebrating, conversing, communion and service. Community is always becoming—never complete. Two or more share life together, risking to show pain, loneliness, fears, angers; receiving understanding, support, encouragement and relationship. Community involves risking error for another's sake, losing oneself for a great cause, responding to a need for enhancing the qualitative character of human life.

W. Stanley Smith Jr.

THE "MEAT" OF THE MEETING

Take time for quiet reflection and meditation and have the youth listen in silence for God and to think of concerns for each other.

Read aloud 1 Corinthians 13, then in small groups share the meaning of love by defining Christian love, Christian friendship and Christian community.

Read aloud the following adaptation from Ephesians 4:15-16:

Lovingly follow the truth, living love and honesty, and so become more like Christ who is the head of his body—the church. Under his love the whole body is fitted together perfectly and each part in its own special way helps the other parts, so the whole body is healthy, full of love and growing into completeness.

To demonstrate this, solemnly pour each member a glass of water and in unison sip the water.

In your own words explain that in the sharing of water, we are bound together, we recognize our commonality and dependence upon something other than ourselves.

Water is the holy symbol of baptism, the entrance into Christ's community and a representation of our new life.

RESPONSE (OR CLOSING)

View the film **Water and Spirit** and then discuss it.

Explain that when we gather together in Christian community, the risen Christ is with us. As the risen Christ is experienced between people, a beautiful thing happens—the gift of family and love.

Appropriate songs for this point are "Give Me Your Hand" by Robert Blue, **Hymnal for Young Christians**, and "By My Side" by **Godspell**.

If you have time, view the film **The String**.

Tie the string to the cross and pass the ball of string from person to person until all are connected to the cross. Read Ephesians 4:1-6.

After the youth have returned to their seats, tell this story.[1]

Sundar Singh and a companion were traveling through a pass high in the Himalaya Mountains. They came across a man collapsed in the snow. Singh wanted to stop and help the unfortunate man, but his companion refused, saying, "We shall lose our lives if we burden ourselves with him."

But Singh would not think of leaving the man to die in the cold and snow. As his companion bade him farewell, Singh lifted the poor traveler onto his back. With great exertion he bore the man onward, and gradually the heat from Singh's body began to warm the frozen man, who revived. Soon both were walking together. As they walked, they saw a body in the snow. It was Singh's former companion—frozen by the cold.

Have a quiet time together to think about the story, then sing, "Peace I Leave With You" in the **Hymnal for Young Christians**.

HELPFUL RESOURCES

"Let's Be Friends," **The Group Retreat Book**, by Arlo Reichter, et al., Group Books, P.O. Box 481, Loveland, CO 80539.

"You've Got a Friend," by Carole King or James Taylor.

"By My Side," **Godspell**.

Hymnal for Young Christians, FEL Publications, 1543 W. Olympic Blvd., Los Angeles, CA 90015.

---

[1] **Parables**, (Saratoga, Calif.: Saratoga Press, March 1983), Vol. 3, No. 1, p. 2.

PEW PEEVES

by Gary Richardson

PURPOSE

To take a humorous and positive look at those annoying, nerve-racking little things that happen in church.

PREPARATION

Gather enough paper, pens and pencils for the group; posterboard or chalkboard; and copies of the following samples from **Pew Peeves**, which is available from Group Books, P.O. Box 481, Loveland, CO 80539.

Soloists with a Julia Child voice.

When you're a few minutes late for church, hoping to slip into the back pew, and the usher parades you to the first pew.

OPENING

Allow everyone to read the **Pew Peeves** samples or purchase copies of the cartoon book which contains 80 pages of pew peeves.

Spend a few minutes listing "peeves" the young people have about anything relating to your church. Write those peeves on a chalkboard or posterboard—anywhere easily viewed by the young people.

Then have each person secretly choose a pew peeve and act it out. The rest of the group tries to guess the peeve.

At this point, take a few minutes to imagine what the perfect church would be like.

THE "MEAT" OF THE MEETING

Have your group read the following Bible passages that relate to the church: Psalm 100:3-4; 133:1; Matthew 18:20; John 10:14-15; Romans 12:4-5; 1 Corinthians 12:13; Galatians 3:27-28; Ephesians 2:19-21; 4:1-16; Colossians 1:18; 1 Peter 2:4-5.

Ask the group to respond to these statements and questions:

● All church members are Christians.

● A Christian should get his or her serious problems under control before he or she becomes involved in a church.

● Churches are made of people

trying to find God.

● By the New Testament definition, this youth group can be considered a church.

● A Christian can worship just as effectively alone as he or she can by being involved in a church.

● Why do many Christians have a lot of peeves? Is it okay to say bad things about the church? Why or why not?

● What are positive things you can say about the church?

RESPONSE (OR CLOSING)

Return to the list of pew peeves the group made and rank the group's top three peeves. Then list steps the group could take to deal with those peeves.

As a group, list things the youth group itself does that other people in the church might list as peeves. List steps the group could take to do away with those peeves.

Close with a prayer thanking God for the opportunity to worship as a congregation—peeves and all.

PEOPLE CONNECTION

by Dean Dammann

PURPOSE

To have participants experience togetherness and to understand how the body of Christ, the church, is held together.

PREPARATION

Make copies of the Checklist in the "Meat" of the Meeting or write the questions on a chalkboard.

Gather enough pencils, paper and Bibles for the group.

OPENING

Form groups of six to eight. The person with the biggest hands serves as group leader.

Take a few minutes to get acquainted if necessary. Have the group share favorite family times or activities.

Ask the youth to recall the most significant or meaningful spiritual experience that happened to them in the church fellowship. Instruct them to write a brief paragraph to identify the occasion—when, where and why it was meaningful. Each person in turn shares his or her paragraph, making additional explanation as necessary.

THE "MEAT" OF THE MEETING

Distribute and discuss the Checklist.

After everyone has shared, discuss any new learnings gained from the experience.

Each group's next activity is to

Checklist

Choose two items that best describe your feelings about the opening activities.

- I was surprised by what (name) shared.
- I feel closer to members of the group than I did at the beginning.
- I felt uncomfortable sharing my experience.
- I was surprised that (name)'s experience was like mine.
- I was excited about sharing my experience.
- Other

Share the two items you checked and explain why you chose those.

---

develop a "people machine," which is an action human sculpture. Each member becomes part of a machine that acts out an activity. Because it is a machine, each part functions as part of the whole. To replicate a crane, there would be wheels or caterpillar treads, an engine, controls, the crane part, the hook or bucket and the operator. As the machine is assembled, the youth should be sure to connect each part (person) and plan a specific action for each part.

Groups should plan their machines in secret so the other groups are not aware of their plans. They should practice "running" the machine as much as possible without revealing its identity.

Take time for each small group to demonstrate its machine for the total group. After each group performs, have the other groups decide what machine was modeled. Each group should try to reach consensus in its guess. Distribute paper so that the guesses can be written down and compared after all groups have demonstrated their machines.

As a total group share the guesses. Choose the machine in which all the parts best worked together.

Return to the small groups and read Ephesians 4:14-16. Discuss these verses as related to the concept of the body of Christ as a people machine. Each group should examine ways the people machines enhance or enlarge understanding of the youth's part in the body of Christ, the Christian church.

Verse 16 indicates "the whole body is held together by every joint with which it is provided." Read Ephesians 4:12—5:21 and have the youth identify the specific actions which might break their connection with the other parts (people) of the body or which build connections within the body (church). Have the participants make a list by noting verse numbers and key words on a sheet of paper. Compare the lists.

RESPONSE (OR CLOSING)

Have the youth choose one of the "connection" actions which needs attention in their lives. As a closing, pray a short prayer bringing this concern to the Lord. Then join hands and pray the Lord's Prayer together.

YOUR CHURCH

by James P. Reeves

PURPOSE

To present the history of your church and to tie that to present-day philosophies and learnings.

PREPARATION

Collect literature about the history of your church. Gather paper and pencils. Invite your pastor and also ask a church member who has had many years of membership.

Arrange for a pianist to play an older song from your church hymnal. Arrange for a guitarist to perform a contemporary Christian song.

OPENING

Open with everyone singing the classic church hymn. Present a brief church history relying on information about the denomination and your church.

THE "MEAT" OF THE MEETING

A church elder can discuss the church from the perspective of being present through many changes. Your pastor can explain the history of the denomination and its theological concepts.

If yours is an older denomination, present "ancient" church rules on dress and conduct. The pastor can talk about changes such as those in wedding ceremonies and vows.

Involve the youth in a discussion about future roles of your church. Discuss with the youth reasons for changes. Ask what changes they would like to see initiated or if there are any "old ways" they'd like to see renewed. Ask what the youth see as their specific roles in the future of the church.

RESPONSE (OR CLOSING)

Explain the opening hymn was representative of the early-day church and that now they are going to hear music that represents contemporary Christianity. Introduce the guitarist.

Open a short discussion time on the differences between the early-day music and the present-day music. Does the change in music reflect change in church tradition?

Distribute the pencils and paper and have the youth write one tradition and one recent change they like. Have them also write one tradition they would like to change and one new facet of Christianity that could require caution.

Have the guest speakers close with prayer thanking God for traditions as well as changes.

GOD AND COUNTRY: A CHRISTIAN VIEW

by Ed Rush

PURPOSE

To help youth view patriotism as Christians and to help youth recognize Christ as the ultimate authority.

PREPARATION

You will need construction paper and felt-tip markers in red, white and blue, an American and a Christian flag, coins from different countries or in different denominations, pencils, Bibles and songbooks.

Make copies of the Freedom Questionnaire and A Christian Patriot listed in the Response section.

Schedule a person to come to the meeting who was born and reared in America and a person who has become a citizen through naturalization. The youth will interview the guests on the subject of patriotism.

Gather slides or prints of Norman Rockwell's paintings of "The Four Freedoms." Check with your local library for copies.

OPENING

Sing patriotic songs concluding with "America."

Introduce the two speakers to the group. Let each one tell his or her story and then let the youth in- terview the speakers on their thoughts about America.

THE "MEAT" OF THE MEETING

At this point, show prints or slides of Norman Rockwell's paintings "The Four Freedoms." Have the group sing "This Is My Country" for freedom of speech, "America the Beautiful" for freedom from want, "God Bless America" for freedom from fear, and "God of Our Fathers" for freedom of worship.

Give each youth a coin and have each tell whose image is on his or her coin. Have a youth read Matthew 22:15-22. Let the group share its understanding of Christ's answer to the Pharisees. Discuss the significance of this passage to our present society, relating it specifically to taxes or government services. End the discussion by reading Isaiah 9:6-7.

RESPONSE (OR CLOSING)

Divide into three groups for the following:

The first group will use the red, white and blue markers and construction paper to make thank-you notes for the persons interviewed.

The second group will fill out the following Freedom Questionnaire:

CITIZENSHIP

Freedom Questionnaire

Freedom of speech means:
(check one)
____I can say what I want, no matter whom I hurt.
____No one cares what I say.
____I have the right to express my views, as long as I am willing to listen to the view of others.

Freedom from want means:
____I have the right to take what I want from any source available.
____I do not have to work, the government will take care of my needs.
____I have the right to work and earn the things I want and need.

Freedom from fear means:
____I never have to protect myself, that is why we have police.
____I have the right to protect myself, even if I break the law or hurt an innocent bystander in doing so.
____I have the right to seek protection from the authorities and to protect myself within the law, then depend on the law to uphold my rights.

Freedom of worship means:
____I have the right to force my religious beliefs on others.
____I have the right to practice my religion, regardless of the law.
____I have the right to worship in my own way, without government intervention or direction.

Members of the third group will rank the following statements:

A Christian Patriot
A Christian patriot is:
____A person who loves God and his or her country.
____One who has been converted, spiritually and politically.
____A person who zealously supports his or her Christian beliefs as well as his or her beliefs about his country.
____One who serves God through the church and serves his or her country through the means available.
____A person who sees his or her Christian principles and moral values as helpful to his or her country.

Keep in mind all the statements have some degree of truth. Have the youth share their responses with others in their group.

Re-form the large group and pledge allegiance to the American and Christian flags. Sing the national anthem and close the meeting with prayer.

HELPFUL RESOURCES
Patriotic Songs, Bowmar Educational Records, 622 Rodier Drive, Glendale, CA 91201.

Gather 'Round, by Walter Ehret, Boston Music, 116 Boyleston St., Boston, MA 02116.

GETTING TO KNOW YOU

by Patrick M. Mulcahy

PURPOSE

To help group members recognize other members' uniqueness and to appreciate this diversity.

PREPARATION

Obtain one large sheet of posterboard. Gather Bibles, crayons or felt-tip markers, 3 x 5 cards, paper and pencils for all.

If you have a small group, work through the following activities as a whole group. If your group is larger, divide into smaller teams of five or six in each, and have the participants work through different activities at the same time. (If you use this several-activities-at-one-time approach, enlist additional help to introduce and organize the activities.)

OPENING

On a table, place a sheet of blank posterboard and various colored crayons or markers. As group members arrive, have them trace their hands with the color that best represents how they are feeling and then write their first name in the middle of the hand outline. At the top of the posterboard write "Reach Out." Explain we can only get to know others by reaching out. Save the poster for future sessions as a reminder to the youth to "reach out."

Have everyone think of a self-descriptive word. The word's first letter must also be the first letter of the group member's first name. For example, John might think he is jolly, Bill might think he is best, Sarah might think she is super, and so on. Then, with the group sitting in a circle, one person says his or her name and then the descriptive word, the next person repeats the first person's information and then adds his or her own name and descriptive word, and so on. For example, John could begin by saying, "John, jolly." Bill would continue by saying, "John, jolly; Bill, best." Sarah would then say, "John, jolly; Bill, best; Sarah, super," and so on.

THE "MEAT" OF THE MEETING

Have the group read 1 Corinthians 12:14-27. Divide into small groups of threes or fours. Have half the groups study verses 14-19 and the other groups study verses 20-27. Instruct the youth to list passages that pertain to the youth group and to potential roles of individual members. Call the members together to report the groups' findings. Discuss how the youth group can be like the group described in the passage—especially in verses 25 and 26.

On 3 x 5 cards, group members should write their names and the following information:

● In the top left corner, an

animal that describes them.
- In the top right corner, a fruit or vegetable they would like to be.
- In the lower left corner, their fondest wish.
- In the lower right corner, a famous person—past or present—whom they would like to be for one week.

For example, a card could look like this:

koala bear   orange
Sharon
to be a   Martha
scuba   Washington
diver

Assign each group member a partner (or let youth choose their own) and have the youth discuss the information on the cards. Allow five to 10 minutes for each pair to get to know each other's likes, dislikes, dreams, and so on. Then ask each group member to design and draw a "gift" for his or her partner. Get the whole group together for the gift exchange. Encourage gift-givers to explain the gift choice.

RESPONSE (OR CLOSING)

Pass out paper and pencils or felt-tip markers. Ask each group member to draw a magazine advertisement that sells himself or herself. Youth members should consider:
- their finest features (talents and personality)
- traits that make them desirable (what they can do for others and society)
- what makes their product (them) unique.

Encourage the youth to draw pictures, design logos and write catchy verses. When they are finished, display the ads one at a time and see if group members can guess which person is advertised.

Close this session with a prayer of thankfulness for each individual in the group. Ask that the group, as the body of Christ, will be strong because of its diversity.

AIN'T GOT NO RESPECT

by Bill Pieper

PURPOSE

To help participants understand that respect comes from God and is to be shared by the children of God.

PREPARATION

Gather songbooks, Bibles, pencils and 3 x 5 cards.

Write out each of the following scripture verses on four 3 x 5 cards:

- Galatians 5:25; 6:2, 10
- Ephesians 5:21; 6:1-4
- Philippians 4:8-9
- Colossians 3:12-15

On two 3 x 5 cards write these outlines for role playing:

Role play 1: Four students are standing in the school hallway. Three are talking about something in common, such as a sports event. The fourth person is trying to be a part of the conversation, but the others only give him or her token recognition.

Role play 2: One person is idolizing another, fawning over his or her every word and action. The worshiped person is loving the attention.

Select young people to do the role plays and give them time before the meeting to think of their parts.

Make copies of the following study sheet:

Luke 18:9-14 Study Sheet

1. If I had been a Pharisee listening to Jesus tell this story, I would have . . .
   a. punched Jesus.
   b. got mad, but said nothing.
   c. been ashamed.
   d. been speechless.
   e. other (explain)
2. Looking at my life and thinking about this story of Jesus, I feel more like . . .
   a. Jesus.
   b. the bystanders.
   c. the Pharisee.
   d. the tax collector.
   e. not even in the story.
3. If I could compare the way I show respect for others (especially those who are not my friends) to a football game, I would be . . .
   a. in the locker room.
   b. sitting on the bench.
   c. in the thick of the game.
   d. behind in the game.
   e. sitting in the crowd.
   f. face down in the mud.
   g. totally exhausted.
   h. doing my best in the game.
4. If God were my coach and were talking to me about respect, he would . . .
   a. chew me up and spit me out.
   b. bench me.
   c. encourage me.
   d. kick me out of the game.
   e. understand me.
   f. send me back in to try again.

OPENING

Begin with songs, then divide into small groups.

Have each participant reflect on the following and share his or her thoughts:

- Recall a time when you felt respected.
- Recall a time when you felt you were invisible.
- Think of a time you genuinely respected someone. Did your behavior reflect this respect?

THE "MEAT" OF THE MEETING

Have the actors present their role plays. Explain the respect the group will be discussing will fall somewhere between the two extremes these role plays represent.

Ask the group members to share some of the respect-killing phrases they hear in school such as, "When God was passing out brains you must have been out of the room."

Ask the participants how they feel when they or good friends are treated this way. Have them share this in their groups.

Distribute the study sheets for Luke 18:9-14. Have the participants read the selection, complete the study sheet and share the responses.

After the discussion, explain respect begins with the right relationship with God. Remember who we are—first, we are sinners. Second, we are no better than anyone else in God's eyes. Third, we need forgiveness. God gives us the forgiveness and respect we need. We can learn from God's word how we should act.

Distribute the cards containing the Bible verses. Have each group read its passage and then share it with the others. What are the instructions God gives his people about how they should treat each other?

Read Galatians 6:7-8 and 1 Thessalonians 4:9-12. Ask what the verses say about our actions.

Have the young people write a positive statement as to how they will change their attitude toward respect and how they treat others.

Have them complete the statement, "If I could make a change in my life right now I would _____ _____ ."

Share these responses within the small groups.

RESPONSE (OR CLOSING)

Tie the discussion together by explaining: The lack of respect can hurt ourselves and others. Only when we realize we are sinners forgiven by God can we feel respect and that as forgiven sinners we need to use God's word as a guide for our relationships.

Have the participants write a one-sentence petition about respect or relationships on a 3 × 5 card and incorporate these thoughts into the closing prayer.

As a closing game have the group play Moving Pyramids. Each group of six forms a pyramid and in two minutes tries to move as far as it can. Give each pyramid several tries to see which can move the farthest.

HELPFUL RESOURCES

Praise the Lord, by Theodore Wuerffel, ed., Concordia, 3558 S. Jefferson Ave., St. Louis, MO 63118.

Songs for a New Creation, Augsburg, 426 S. Fifth St., Minneapolis, MN 55415.

INWARD JOURNEYS

by Tim Barnes

PURPOSE

To share ideas in a weekly "meet-your-peers" discussion format.

PREPARATION

List the topics that would be of interest to your group. For example: drugs, self-esteem, prayer, aging, marriage, war, dating, sex, cults, alcoholism, music and family roles.

Sign up host families. Make a roster of interested youth and note which ones will help drive others to the meeting sites.

Prepare the outline guide to give to the leaders of each meeting.

Outline Guide

Name of leaders: _____

Topic:_____

Songs: _____

Opening question:_____

Name three areas you would like to cover and questions for each:

1._____

Questions: _____

2._____

Questions: _____

3._____

Questions: _____

Materials such as tapes, filmstrips or handouts:_____
_____

Conclusion:_____

Prayer: _____

Write rules and guidelines, for example:
- What is said here stays here.
- Participate respectfully.
- Be dedicated and committed.
- Only one person talks at a time.
- Stay on the topic.
- Introduce new participants.
- End with prayer.

For each meeting you need to:
- Notify the youth of the meeting date and site.
- Prepare the topic outline or assign a youth to do so.
- Prepare music and refreshments.

OPENING

Open with up-beat songs and then a "mellow" one to quiet the group. You can substitute games instead of songs.

Introduce any new participants.

THE "MEAT" OF THE MEETING

Begin the meeting by giving an opening statement or questions pertaining to the weekly topic. Some examples are:
- Alcoholism: When is it acceptable to drink? What does the Bible say about drinking?
- Aging: What attitude does the Bible convey regarding aging? Who are respected elderly biblical characters? What is our attitude toward the elderly today?

● War: Why worry about war—it's all in the Lord's hands anyway. Do you agree or disagree with this? Why or why not?

Keep the meeting flowing by following the Outline Guide and having other questions in mind when discussion lags.

RESPONSE (OR CLOSING)

After discussion has reached a high point and the time is about over, the group tries to form a conclusion. For example: Although we are in God's hands and therefore should not worry about war, God expects us to deal responsibly with his world and help preserve peace.

End each meeting with a prayer and announce the next meeting time, site and leader.

COMMUNICATION

STICKS AND STONES . . .

by James P. Reeves

PURPOSE

To point out that we can be cruel not only physically but also verbally; to help youth understand what the Bible has to say about verbal cruelty; and to show how to be honest and open without being unkind.

PREPARATION

Gather Bibles, pencils, chalkboard and copies of the quiz in the "Meat" of the Meeting.

OPENING

Form groups of twos or threes. Ask the youth to finish this sentence, "Sticks and stones may break my bones, but words . . ." Ask them not to use the well-known ending "but words will never hurt me."

An alternative would be a "graffiti" board with the title on a chalkboard or large paper. Instruct the youth to take turns writing answers under the title.

Discuss the graffiti and responses, then tell the young people the purpose of the meeting. Invite them to share times when they have been verbally cruel to others. Have there been times they have been hurt by others? What are some early memories of name-calling?

THE "MEAT" OF THE MEETING

Have everybody split into groups of four. Pass out the quizzes.

Positive Effects of Our Words

No.	Proverbs	Questions
1.	12:25	An _____ word can help an anxious person.
2.	17:27-28	No matter how you look at it, restraint is _____.
3.	20:3	It is an _____ not to fight.
4.	12:22	A truthful person is a _____ to God.
5.	15:1	A soft _____ turns away wrath.
6.	28:23	Correction is much better than _____.
7.	10:20	A good man is _____ listening to.
8.	11:12	A good man holds his _____.
9.	15:23	It is wonderful to say the _____ thing.
10.	15:4	Gentle words cause _____.
11.	21:23	A person who guards his mouth keeps out of _____.
12.	21:15	A good man loves _____.
13.	16:24	Kind words are like _____.
14.	19:11	A wise man restrains _____.
15.	12:18	Words of the wise _____.

Negative Effects of Our Words

No.	Proverbs	Questions
1.	14:23	Talk brings _____.
2.	6:12	A _____ man is a liar.
3.	18:1	A _____ man quarrels.
4.	26:28	Lying and flattery _____ others.

5. 26:23   Pretty words may hide a _____ heart.
6. 18:6-7   The lips of a fool bring _____.
7. 12:19   Lies are soon _____.
8. 17:9 (25:24) _____ hurts friendships.
9. 18:2   A rebel wants to _____.
10. 11:13   A gossip spreads _____.
11. 29:5-6   Flattery is a _____.

Positive Answers

1. Encouraging 2. wise 3. honor 4. delight 5. answer 6. flattery 7. worth 8. tongue 9. right 10. life 11. trouble 12. justice 13. honey 14. anger 15. heal.

Negative Answers

1. Poverty 2. wicked 3. selfish 4. wounds 5. wicked 6. fights 7. exposed 8. nagging 9. yell 10. rumors 11. trap.

The puzzle questions have been designed from The Living Bible version. Allow the groups to work on their own to finish. If you want, you can create competition to see who can finish first, but do not do so unless each group has a Living Bible version.

RESPONSE (OR CLOSING)

Review the answers. Ask the youth what they learned and have them summarize their findings. How can we be honest and open without being cruel? What does the Bible have to say about verbal cruelty?

Close in prayer asking God to guide us in our daily lives and to help us live as he wants.

COMMUNICATION

THOSE 'HUGGABLE' HUGS

by Cindy S. Hansen

PURPOSE

To have youth think about types of hugs and the related feelings. To get the group to think of when it is appropriate to hug.

PREPARATION

Gather felt-tip markers, pencils and Bibles for everyone and two sheets of posterboard.

Make copies of the following question sheet for each member:

The Squeeze Quiz

1. Which hugs are you comfortable with? Why?
2. Which hugs are you uncomfortable with? Why?
3. What good feelings are gained from hugs?
4. What bad feelings are registered because of hugs?
5. How do you decide which hugs are appropriate?
6. How do you decide which hugs are inappropriate?
7. Why do some people feel comfortable hugging and others not?
8. Is it easy for you to hug friends? moms? dads? brothers? sisters? other relatives? Why? Why not?

OPENING

Begin this meeting with a rousing game of Hug Tag. One person is "it" and tries to tag someone else—by hugging. You are "safe" only when you are hugging some- one else. Only two to a hug and you can't hug the same person two times in a row. You can hug for three seconds then you must hug someone else.[1] Try some variations with this game—have all players move in slow motion, hop on one foot or run backward.

THE "MEAT" OF THE MEETING

Gather the group in a circle and introduce the topic of hugs by saying that "touch is not only nice, it's needed. Scientific research supports the theory that stimulation by touch is absolutely necessary for our physical as well as emotional well-being."[2] How many agree? disagree? Why? Explain that this meeting examines our feelings about touch, different kinds of hugs, and when it is and is not appropriate to hug.

Begin a pantomime time. Ask for two volunteers to stand in the middle of the circle. The leader says one type of hug—the two in the middle must use their imaginations and pantomime the hug. Examples:

- Grandmother hug
- Cheek-to-cheek hug
- Bear hug
- One-arm hug
- Stuck-record hug
- Neck hug
- Waist hug
- Quick squeeze
- Stiff hug

Ask the group to think of other types of hugs. Volunteers are changed after each hug is pantomimed. Write the names of the hugs on a chalkboard or posterboard for later reference. Discuss the types of hugs just demonstrated. Have the youth experienced these kinds of hugs? Distribute and have the youth answer the Squeeze Quiz.

Divide the group in half and have each group discuss the quiz.

Read 1 Corinthians 16:20. What is a holy kiss? Do you have a similar greeting at church? Passing of the peace? Morning greeters at the door? What do you do if you are in church and want to greet someone with a hug and the person is not comfortable with it? What do you do if you are uncomfortable with "huggable" greetings at church?

Read Matthew 8:3,15; 9:29; 20:34. Does Jesus use touch in his ministry? How? How do people feel from his touch? How do you think Jesus would feel about each of the hugs that were demonstrated in the pantomime time?

RESPONSE (OR CLOSING)

After the discussion, hand each group a piece of posterboard and a marker. Tell each group it is now full of "hug experts." Instruct them to make a list of hugging guidelines. Keeping in mind the earlier discussion of types of hugs, feel-

ings of hugs and Bible verses. What are some guidelines? Which hugs are unbearable? Which are okay? Example:

1. Never smother a person with a hug if it makes him or her feel uncomfortable.

2. One-arm hugs and quick squeezes are acceptable for making people feel welcome at a church service or youth meeting.

At the bottom of the posterboard, have each group write its philosophy of hugs or touches. Example: "As a result of this discussion and Bible study, we decide that friendly hugs are okay and should be easily administered. Keeping in mind Romans 16:16: 'Greet one another with a holy kiss,' we will, 'Greet one another with a holy hug.' "

Gather in groups of threes. Each person in the trio shares a concern or a thanksgiving. Pray silently together and end with an Oreo Cookie hug. (One person stands in the center of the other two and gets squeezed.) Allow each person in the trio to be the center of the cookie hug. End the session with one big group hug.

[1]Lee Sparks, ed., **Try This One . . . Too** (Loveland, Colo.: Group Books, 1982), p. 29.

[2]Kathleen Keating, **The Hug Therapy Book** (Minneapolis, Minn.: CompCare Publications, 1983), p. 1.

THE ULTIMATE MIXER

by Karen Ceckowski

PURPOSE

To show the importance of each member and to find out something new and different about each participant.

PREPARATION

Supplies to gather (one for each participant): plastic cups, lunch sacks and napkins. Also, one electric blender, felt-tip marker, three cutting knives, a can opener, three pitchers, four bowls and a hair dryer.

Food items needed (all amounts based on a group of 10): three apples, three oranges, six bananas, a large can of frozen strawberries, three cans of fruit juice nectar, two cans of frozen fruit juice concentrate, a large can of pineapple juice (or one whole pineapple).

Also have on hand a Bible and 3 x 5 cards.

Label the lunch bags in consecutive number. Label each 3 x 5 card with a corresponding lunch bag number.

Assign food preparation to each member of the group by writing tasks on the separate 3 x 5 cards. The object is to get all fruit peeled and cut, juices mixed, frozen berries defrosted and all items in a bowl.

The cards can be prepared in the following manner:
● Card number one: Peel and cut one apple, one orange and one banana. Put in the bowl.
● Card number two: Peel and cut one orange and two bananas. Put in the bowl.
● Card number three: Mix three cans of fruit nectar.
● Card number four: Defrost two cans of frozen strawberries.

Place the numbered cards in the same-numbered sack. Randomly fill the bags with food items and utensils. Do not match the 3 x 5 cards with the proper food items. The object of this mixer is to make the members depend upon one another to finish assigned tasks. Be creative in your preparations.

● If the 3 x 5 card says to peel two apples, put a hair dryer and banana in the sack.
● Freeze the bananas and oranges the night before to make peeling a chilling experience.
● Use exotic fruits such as mangoes or kiwi.
● Assign a youth to collect all fruit peelings and make a centerpiece.

Prepare a work area. Youth can work at tables or on plastic bags on the floor.

OPENING

Introduce the Ultimate Mixer and explain that it will require following the basic instructions in 30 minutes. Before distributing the sacks, outline the rules:
● Each of you will be given a

paper sack. Don't look inside until the mixer begins.

- Inside the bag is a 3 × 5 card with instructions. Follow these carefully.

- In each bag are items that may or may not help you to complete the task. Other people may have the items you need. If you need to ask for an item, it's all right to do so, but you must tell the person something about yourself he or she does not already know.

- Are there any questions? If not . . .

- Begin.

THE "MEAT" OF THE MEETING

Call time after 30 minutes. Ask each youth to bring his or her items to one of the tables. Get the blender and cups. Take portions of the different fruits and juices and fill the blender. As you do this, explain that each person needed others to perform the tasks and as a group you need them to perform this final step—to work together. The Ultimate Mixer is now to take place. Turn on the blender and mix all ingredients.

RESPONSE (OR CLOSING)

Pour portions of the drink for each youth. Sit together as the youth enjoy the drink. Ask them to talk about facts they learned about other group members.

Close by having the youth read aloud Romans 12:4-5 and Hebrews 10:25. Discuss how the verses show the importance of others in our lives.

WHEN YOUR GROUP STOPS TALKING

by Patrick M. Mulcahy

PURPOSE

To ease the problem of non-communication (private conversations, daydreams, dead silence, tension) by getting group members to interact.

PREPARATION

Make one Group Evaluation sheet for each person (leaders included):

Group Evaluation

1. Why did you join this group?
2. What did you expect the group to be like when you joined?
3. Is that what you found? If not, was it better or worse? Why?
4. What did you expect from the group's leaders?
5. Is that what you found? If not, were they better or worse than you had expected? Why?
6. What did you expect from the group's members?
7. Is that what you found? If not, were they better or worse? Why?
8. My overall rating for this group is:

   A___ B___ C___ D___ F___

   Explain the grade you gave:
9. What I don't like about this group:
10. What I do like about this group:
11. What I can do to make this group better:

Gather paper, pencils and Bibles for everyone and one copy of the book, **Fuzzies: A Folk Fable**.

Fuzzies: A Folk Fable explains that the touch of "warm fuzzies" makes people happy. The story is an example of sharing, peace and simple happiness. The fable is essential to this session. This book is available from bookstores and Argus Books, Allen, TX 75002.

You also can make your own warm fuzzies for this session. Design the pompons or puff balls by wrapping a long piece of yarn around a 3-inch width of cardboard. Remove the yarn from the cardboard and tie it in the middle. Then use scissors to clip the loops. Trim it to a ball shape. As a final touch, you can add eyes.

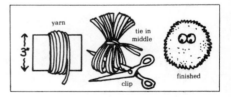

On a sheet of paper sketch a simple design:

OPENING

Distribute paper and pencils. Give the sheet with the design to one of the youth.

Have that person describe the design using only words—no gesticulating or body clues. The rest of the group tries to sketch what the person described. Compare the drawings to the original and stress the difference in interpretations. Note that it's difficult to understand everything heard, since people interpret the same message differently.

THE "MEAT" OF THE MEETING

Pass out the Group Evaluation forms and ask the youth to answer honestly. Allow 10 minutes for completion.

Discuss the Group Evaluations asking everyone, including leaders, to share responses.

God has a lot to say about how his people should relate to one another. Divide into groups of three or four and ask each group to read the following passages and list three to five ideas for relating better to one another.

The Bible passages are: Matthew 22:37-39; Luke 6:27-38; John 13:34-35; Romans 12:1-13; 1 Corinthians 12:12-27; Ephesians 4:1-7; 1 John 2:7-11; 4:7-12.

Then bring the entire group together and compare ideas.

Have everyone share ideas to improve the group. Be willing to establish new rules and be open to discussion. Get a group decision regarding new policies.

RESPONSE (OR CLOSING)

Read the story **Fuzzies**. Explain a "warm fuzzy" is another word for "hug." Have everyone give each other a warm fuzzy and pass out the fuzzies you made earlier.

End with a prayer for togetherness, happiness and better communication. Also add prayers for concerns mentioned during the session.

IT'S LOVE, IT'S LOVE

by Patrick M. Mulcahy

PURPOSE

To help the youth examine boy-friends and girlfriends in view of religious beliefs and family values.

PREPARATION

In advance gather Bibles and pencils or felt-tip markers for each youth. Prepare the What I Can Offer and What I Look For worksheets in the "Meat" of the Meeting. Prepare refreshments.

This meeting can be done well with a small or large group. If you have a large group, split them into small groups of six to eight. Assign group leaders to facilitate discussion and explain activities.

Ask three of the group leaders to present the skit in the Opening section. The three should understand the message they are to convey, but should not be over prepared, as this skit is best when improvised.

OPENING

Present the following skit:

Setting: Your family and you are seated around the dinner table. Your parents are giving you numerous reasons you should break up with your steady date. You've heard them before: Your steady date doesn't dress well, gets poor grades, causes you to get poor grades, supposedly is using drugs, or is not of the same religion.

You are telling your parents why they are wrong and why you still should be allowed to date this individual. You add they are old-fashioned, you're old enough to make your own decisions and your date doesn't have to please them as long as you're happy.

Opening line: Parent says, "About this kid you're seeing, we think you should break it up."

Closing line: Parent shouts, "Fine. We can make it so you won't see this no-good for at least six months. You're grounded!"

In groups, discuss:
- Who was wrong?
- What, if anything, could have been done to make both the parents and the teenager happy?
- If you were the teenager, what would you have done or said?
- If you were the parents, what would you have done or said?

Each group should start thinking about a skit for the Closing and choose three different youth to act the roles. This skit, however, will present the opposite viewpoint—a positive discussion between parents and teenager.

THE "MEAT" OF THE MEETING

Read 1 Corinthians 13:1-13. What does Paul say about love and dating? What should both partners be to each other? How should they treat each other?

Distribute the following What I Can Offer worksheets and give each person a few minutes to complete it.

What I Can Offer

Rate yourself from 1 (poorest) to 5 (best) on each of the following characteristics:

____Physical appearance
____Figure/physique
____Personality
____Intelligence
____Popularity
____Charm or charisma
____Clothing

Which of these are truly important to me?

What is my best feature?

What do I need to work on most?

Discuss the answers to the last two questions. Each person can pass on these if he or she is uncomfortable answering in front of others.

Distribute the What I Look For worksheets and give each person a few minutes to finish.

Ask the youth to discuss their selections and choice of ratings. Each group then should tell the large group the three main qualities its members look for in a date.

Return to the small groups and serve the refreshments. Use the refreshment break for the groups to work on the closing skits outlined in the Opening section.

RESPONSE (OR CLOSING)

Have each group present its skit.

What I Look For

What do you look for in a steady date? Check the qualities you most desire, but you can't have everything, so each quality costs you points. You only have 20 points, so choose carefully. You determine the amount of points each quality is worth.

____Is okay-looking
____Is good-looking
____Is a knockout!
____Has a good figure/physique
____Has a sense of humor
____Is extremely intelligent
____Is a good conversationalist
____Is popular
____Is athletic
____Is a good dresser
____Is well-liked by your friends
____His/her friends like you
____Your parents like him/her
____His/her parents like you
____Is honest
____Is not over aggressive
____Is considerate and polite
____Is wealthy
____Is genuinely caring
____Is of your religion

Close by praying the youth will choose partners they can genuinely love and who will help them draw closer to God and their parents.

HELPFUL RESOURCES

Sex, Love or Infatuation: How Can I Really Know?, by Ray E. Short, Augsburg, 425 S. Fifth St., Minneapolis, MN 55415.

DEARLY BELOVED . . .

by Denise Turner

PURPOSE

To make dating and marriage a threesome, with the Lord the third entity.

PREPARATION

Collect pencils and paper. Make copies of the Dearly Beloved . . . handout in the "Meat" of the Meeting section.

Invite a recently married couple to talk about married life and the adjustments they had to make. Encourage them to discuss expectations versus realizations, the elements of a happy Christian marriage, and what they wish they had known when they were dating. Ask them to concentrate on their dating experiences and the first year of marriage.

OPENING

Have the couple talk for five to 10 minutes. Then let the group ask questions.

THE "MEAT" OF THE MEETING

Divide into groups of five to seven. Ask each group to list six important characteristics to look for in a spouse and how those compare to what the young people look for in a date.

Regroup to share the ideas.

Distribute and discuss the following handout:

Dearly Beloved . . .
- Do you think being a traditional wife and mother is a fulfilling role for today's woman?
- Do you approve of house-husbands?
- Do you think it's better to be married or single?
- Do you think the women's movement has done more harm or good for society?
- Do you think a husband should be dominant in the home?

Ask for volunteers to do these role plays:

A wife is having difficulty telling her husband about an expensive outfit she recently purchased. One day, however, the husband opens the mail and reads the bill.

Two people dated steadily during high school. At the end of their senior year, the young man entered the military. Now he is home on leave and the girl must tell him she is dating someone else.

A husband and wife each have important business banquets on the same night. Each spouse forgot to tell the other. They have to decide which one they are going to attend.

Discuss the role plays together.

110

RESPONSE (OR CLOSING)

Divide into two groups—male and female. Ask each group to list three or more questions it wants to ask the other group. Put the questions into stacks and instruct the opposing group to take turns answering.

As a large group, discuss the meeting. Ask the youth how Christ can be kept as the center of dating and marital relationships. Join hands and pray for God's presence and guidance in relationships.

DEATH AND DYING

by Frank Zolvinski

PURPOSE

To examine the stages of death and dying, to relate to someone who has recently lost a loved one through death and to try to establish a Christian response to death.

PREPARATION

Make copies of the handouts: Things to Know (in the "Meat" of the Meeting) and On Death (in the Closing).

Contact a speaker who is knowledgeable on the subject of death. Possible contacts are a local hospital, hospice, ministerial alliance or psychologists. Also, you can contact your chamber of commerce for groups specifically to aid those experiencing death, such as Sudden Infant Death Syndrome (SIDS).

Gather pencils and paper for the entire group.

OPENING

Give pencils and paper to the youth and ask them to write any questions they have on death and dying.

THE "MEAT" OF THE MEETING

Introduce the speaker and encourage the youth to write questions or comments concerning the presentation.

After the speaker is finished, lead a question and answer period.

Distribute and discuss the following handout:[1]

Things to Know
Five Stages of Dying

A person might not go through all these stages. These steps might not be experienced in any order or sequence.
- Denial
- Anger
- Bargaining
- Depression
- Acceptance

What to Say to a Dying Person
- Is there anything you would like to talk about?
- Is there anything I can do for you?
- I've been praying for you.
- I'll baby-sit your children.
- I'll bring you something to eat.
- I'll drive you to the doctor.
- I'll keep you company so your spouse can go somewhere.

What to Say or Do at a Funeral
- Ask if there's anything you can do for the family.
- Listen to the family members and respond.
- A hug or touch can say more than words.
- Talk briefly about the deceased.
- Console the family.
- Experts think it is questionable to say, "It was God's will."

• Don't forget the family after the burial. Keep in touch, particularly several weeks after the death and during holidays or anniversaries.

RESPONSE (OR CLOSING)

Read the On Death prayer handout, with half the youth taking side one and the others side two.

Ask the youth if they agree or disagree with the statements in this handout. Which ones? Do they know anyone who recently has lost a loved one? How can the youth use this lesson to comfort the bereaved?

Read John 11:1-44 for a concluding prayer and thank God for his power over death and his promise of eternal life.

[1]Elisabeth Kubler-Ross, **On Death and Dying** (New York: MacMillan, 1970).

On Death
by Marie Gertrude Mlodzik

Side 1: I believe in death. I believe death is a part of life, a part of every life.

Side 2: I believe that we were born to die. . . to die that we may live more fully. Born to die a little each day to selfishness, to pretense, to sin.

Side 1: I believe that every time we pass from one stage of life to another, something in us dies: The innocence and spontaneity of childhood dies to the daring of youth, to the reasoning of maturity.

Side 2: I believe that death is the way of nature in a flower that fades, a leaf that falls, a raindrop that evaporates, a breeze that passes by.

Side 1: I believe that I taste death in moments of loneliness, of unlove, sorrow, and disappointment, when I am afraid, lose courage and give up, see my broken dreams, and every time I say goodbye.

Side 2: I believe that I am dying before my time when I live in bitterness, hatred and isolation.

Side 1: I believe that I create my own death by the way I live.

Side 2: I believe that life and death are one: that in the one same moment I can say that I am living and I am dying.

All: I believe that Jesus walked toward his death out of love and that he invites me to do the same.

Amen. So may it be.

DEATH IS NOT A DEAD END

by Cindy S. Hansen

PURPOSE

To discuss the fears of death that most have and to rejoice in the hope shared as Christians in the life to come.

PREPARATION

Gather Bibles, candles, pens and paper.

Turn off the lights in the meeting room and light several candles. (There should be just enough light to see for the writing exercise.) Play several appropriate record albums to set a somber mood.

OPENING

The youth receive a pencil and paper as they enter into the dimly lit meeting room. Introduce the topic of death by saying, "Although we are Christians, many of us still fear death and its unknown quality. Think of these feelings now: the negative, dark, scary feelings of death. Jot them down. They can be words or phrases." Allow a few minutes of silence. Announce that each individual in the group is going to write a Cinquain poem about feelings of death. This form of poetry originated in France and the name refers to the French word for the number five. Explain there are five lines in the poem. The first line is one noun. The second line is two adjectives or a phrase to describe the noun, and the third is three action words or a phrase about the title, the fourth line is four words to describe a feeling or feelings about the title. The fifth line is to rename the title in one word. Example:

DEATH
FINAL BREATH
LAST OF LIFE
LONELY, UNKNOWN,
  FRIGHTENING, DESPAIR
DARKNESS

The youth can use the feelings they wrote as they entered the room. Keep the lights dim as the poems are written. Invite individuals to share their poems with the large group. What are some of these negative feelings of death? Why do we have them? Were the poems similar in any ways? What is the most common, fearful feeling of death?

THE "MEAT" OF THE MEETING

Turn on the lights and break into small groups of five to six. Have each group read Psalm 23:4 and brainstorm for a way to pantomime its version of the valley of the shadow of death. What feelings come from this verse? Hope? Lighter feelings? Why? Take turns performing the skits.

Have the small groups read other verses on death: Isaiah 25:8; Hosea 13:14; Matthew 16:18;

1 Corinthians 15:54,55; 2 Timothy 1:7,10; 1 Peter 5:7.

What does the Bible have to say about death? Do we need to fear death as Christians? What is the hope that Jesus offers?

Keeping these thoughts of hope and salvation in mind—how does each person now feel about death? Better? How could you make sure your survivors would feel this hope and salvation after your death? If you could send a message, what would you tell people after your death? How could you assure them not to worry?

Distribute more paper and allow 10 minutes for each small group to plan a joyous funeral. How would you like people to feel at your funeral? Happy for you? How could you ensure they would feel that way? What would you include in the funeral service? Flowers? What kinds? Music? What kind? Would you want decorations? Would you want people to donate money to a charity, instead? What would you want the pastor to say? Share with the large group. How are these joyous funerals different from funerals you have attended?

RESPONSE (OR CLOSING)

Stop for a few minutes and think of the happy and hopeful feelings of death. Think of the happy feelings you wanted to share with guests at your joyous funeral. Jot them onto paper. Have everyone do a second Cinquain poem, this time with the happy, light feelings of death. Example:

DEATH
PEACEFUL REST
ONWARD TO HEAVEN
HOPEFUL, JOYOUS, WARM,
CONTENT
LIFE

Share the poems with the large group. Notice the difference between the two sets of poems. What are the reasons for the hope replacing the fear? Close with a prayer of comfort for those who mourn that they may know the peace that is in store.

HELPFUL RESOURCES

When Bad Things Happen to Good People, by Harold Kushner, Avon Books, 959 8th Ave., New York, NY 10019.

THE DECISIONS GAME

by Patrick M. Mulcahy

PURPOSE

To help the youth make decisions on the basis of their religious beliefs as Christians.

PREPARATION

You will need a Bible, paper and pencil for each person.

OPENING

Begin with the Indoor Scavenger Hunt game. Form teams of four to six. Ask for the following items, and the first person to find the item wins a point for his or her team. All items must come from pockets or purses.

Items can include: a picture of someone's mother, a purple comb, a pen with green ink, a 1971 penny, a school identification card from the previous year, or a Social Security card.

THE "MEAT" OF THE MEETING

Read Matthew 6:24-34 and discuss:
- What is the main message?
- How does it apply today?
- Do we worry too much about our next meal, clothing and other necessities? Why or why not?
- Do you think God will provide these things for us if we turn to him? Why or why not? How can we be sure?
- What should worry us? Elaborate.

Distribute paper and pencils. Have the youth tear the paper into five slips. Tell them you've taken over the world and will provide them with only the basic necessities of clothing, food and shelter. They are to write on the slips of paper five other things they want to keep. Everything else will be taken away. Next say you've changed your mind and will only allow them to keep four items. Have the youth tell which ones they would relinquish and then tear up that paper. Now repeat the process saying they can only keep three items. Continue until they have only one left. Say you would never ask them to give up the most important things in their lives, but you'd like to hear what it was anyway. Discuss what they kept and their reasonings.

RESPONSE (OR CLOSING)

Read the following letter that could be published in an advice column:

Help!

I don't know what to do.

I am a junior in high school and just got a job at a department store. I earn about $60 a week and can't decide what to do with the money.

It's not that I don't have anything to spend my money on—I just can't decide what to spend it on. I have to save for college because my parents

116

can't help me, I could use a car to get around and I'd like some spending money for records, clothing and stuff like that.

The other day I saw a magazine advertisement with a starving child from one of the Third World nations. It talked about how I could give so much of my money to help the kid. Then I got to thinking about how many people could use money— people that are a lot worse off than I am.

What should I do?

Jim

Have each person write what he or she would tell Jim to do. Have each youth read his or her response and discuss these.

Close with a prayer that the Spirit will help us make decisions based on storing treasures in heaven.

DO YOU EVER WONDER?

by Dean Dammann

PURPOSE

To have participants identify troubling questions about the meaning and purpose of life, and to find hope and meaning from this Bible study.

PREPARATION

In advance arrange for rental of the film **Do You Ever Wonder?** The film is available from religious film libraries or from Johnson Nyquist Productions, 23854 Via Fabricante D1, Mission Viejo, CA 92691.

Make copies of the I Wonder Bible study in the Opening section. Or the questions can be written on a chalkboard.

Gather Bibles, pencils, 3 × 5 cards and newsprint or chalkboard. You also will need a screen and projector.

OPENING

Distribute paper and pencils. Have the group complete the following sentences:

I Wonder

● I wonder most about myself when . . .

● The things I wonder about most are . . .

● When I wonder about the future, I . . .

● Many people I know wonder about . . .

● My parents generally wonder about . . .

Tell the youth to keep their replies for a discussion after the film.

Explain: "We are going to see a film titled **Do You Ever Wonder?,** which is developed around four songs on the theme of 'Who am I?' After viewing the film we will share our sentences." Begin the film.

THE "MEAT" OF THE MEETING

Form groups of three or four. Discuss the film. Have each youth complete the following sentence: The scene in the film that really spoke to me was . . .

After each youth has responded, share the sentences completed in the opening activity.

Instruct each small group to decide on a common concern regarding the meaning of life, and then relate this to the entire group.

List these ideas on newsprint or chalkboard. Explain: "The fact that we have questions and concerns about (insert an issue mentioned by the group) the meaning and purpose for our lives isn't unique to our time. Paul speaks about this in his note to the Corinthians. He wrote, 'For since, in the wisdom of God, the world did not know God through wisdom.' (1 Corinthians 1:21). Read 1 Corinthians 1:18—2:16 and look for answers to the question, 'How are we to find meaning and purpose in our lives?' "

List these responses on newsprint.

RESPONSE (OR CLOSING)

Distribute the 3 × 5 cards. Ask the youth to write a short prayer beginning with the words, "Lord, help me . . ." They need not write their names on the cards.

Collect all 3 × 5 cards and use the thoughts as a closing prayer.

FAMOUS BIBLICAL DOUBTERS

by Glen Miles

PURPOSE

To enable youth to compare their own doubts and fears to those experienced by biblical people and to encourage young people to express their faith despite occasional fears and doubts.

PREPARATION

Gather posterboard, multi-colored construction paper, pencils, pens, 3 x 5 cards and Bibles.

Print on posterboard:

Famous Biblical Doubters
1. Exodus 4:1: Moses, "Sorry, God, wrong number."
2. Exodus 16:3: Israelites, "Mannaburgers, again?"
3. Jonah 1:1-3: Jonah, "Not me, God, I hate them!"
4. Luke 1:12-20: Zechariah, "Me? A father? No way!"

Prepare and make copies of the Doubters Worksheet in the "Meat" of the Meeting.

Post the posterboard in the meeting room.

OPENING

Distribute the construction paper and ask the youth to tear the paper into a symbol that in some way represents what it means to know God. Ask the participants to share their symbols and what they represent. Example: A question mark could represent uncertainty of who God really is or clouds could indicate heaven.

THE "MEAT" OF THE MEETING

Ask for a volunteer to read Matthew 28:11-15. Share with your group a brief explanation of who the chief priests were and what they did. List potential reasons for their doubts: These Jewish religious leaders were afraid of losing their power or were looking for a different type of Messiah. Ask the youth to think of other reasons.

Refer to the Famous Biblical Doubters poster. Divide into four small groups and distribute the Doubters Worksheet. Ask each group to answer the questions according to scripture passage. Group one reads Exodus 3:1-11; 4:1; group two reads Exodus 16:1-3; group three reads Jonah 1:1-3; 4:1-11; and group four reads Luke 1:5-20.

Doubters Worksheet
1. What are the characteristics of the famous biblical person's doubt?
2. What do the doubters have in common with the chief priests?
3 What were some of the causes of the doubts of the biblical people?
4. What are some of the causes of your doubts?

Have each group choose a spokesperson to report its findings to the entire group.

Explain to the youth that all the doubters they read about went on to great things. Jonah wasn't that happy about it and the Israelites weren't perfect, but they were successful in spite of their doubts.

Distribute 3 x 5 cards and pencils. Ask the youth to write their own doubts and fears about Christianity. After a few minutes ask for volunteers to share.

Ask the youth to compare and contrast their doubts with those of the people just studied. Ask if it helps to know the doubts of these people. Why or why not? Have you ever doubted your ability to do something and then discovered you were good at it?

RESPONSE (OR CLOSING)

Ask a volunteer to read Matthew 28:16-20. Following the reading, ask the youth to turn over their 3 x 5 cards and finish this sentence, "Despite my doubt, I can go into the world and spread the gospel by . . ." Allow time for each person to finish and ask for volunteers to share their answers.

Close in prayer asking for strength to believe.

DREAMS . . . GOD'S FORGOTTEN LANGUAGE

by Paul M. Thompson

PURPOSE

To explore dreams, to learn more about oneself and to study situations in the Bible in which dreams are mentioned.

PREPARATION

Gather Bibles, pencils, paper, straight pins, construction paper and make copies of the Dream Question sheet and Dream Discovery Process.

Cut name tags from the construction paper in shapes related to night, sleep and dreams—such as stars, moons, pillows, beds and owls.

Note: This meeting length is 90 minutes, depending upon the discussion allowed.

OPENING

Have the young people fill in their names on their tags and write a word or phrase to complete the following statements:

● As a child I used to daydream about . . .

● A commonly occurring dream for me is . . .

● I remember my dreams — always, usually, sometimes, seldom or never (choose one).

● A song or book that mentions a dream is . . .

● A dream come true for me would be . . .

● A favorite dream of mine is . . .

● Dreams that scare me are . . .

When everyone has completed this activity, divide into smaller groups according to the shape of the name tags. Have each person discuss three statements from his or her name tag. Have the youth pin on their tags.

THE "MEAT" OF THE MEETING

Gather the young people and explain they will be studying dreams, both their own and some of those mentioned in the Bible. Continue by saying: "We don't pay much attention to dreams today. In fact, we ignore dreams to the point that some of us don't believe we dream. Scientists have proved that everyone dreams, but some of us no longer remember our dreams. Even if we remember them, we dismiss dreams as being silly or unimportant and forget them before the day has ended. It hasn't always been this way. Dreams are an important part of other cultures. In biblical times dreams were seen as a way that God communicated with people. Jacob, Joseph, Nebuchadnezzar, Gideon, Daniel, Job, Solomon, Jesus' father, and the wise men all had important dreams.

"Our dreams still can be a way that God tells us something about ourselves. God created us and all that we are, including our dreams. If we believe that God's creation is good, then it makes little sense to ignore parts of it because we don't understand. Dreams can be a way that enables us to learn more about ourselves. Dreams include the deepest rumblings of our subconscious, working on things we all face. Let's take some time and pay attention to our dreams."

Assign each group one or more of the following biblical passages:

● Jacob's ladder, Genesis 28:10-20.

● Joseph with the Pharoah, Genesis 41:1-32.

● Solomon asks for wisdom, 1 Kings 3:3-14.

● Daniel interprets Nebuchadnezzar's dream, Daniel 2:1-45.

● The wise men and Joseph are warned about Herod, Matthew 2:12-23.

Have each small group complete a Dream Question Sheet and then share with the whole group.

Dream Question Sheet

Who is dreaming?

Who interprets the dream?

What does the dream tell about the situation?

What does the dream say about the dreamer?

What does the dream tell us about God?

Is the dream psychic (foretelling the future) or personal (telling about the person who is dreaming)? Note: Today most dreams are personal and psychic dreams occur rarely.

What is God saying to the dreamer?

What is God saying to us in the story of the dream?

How does the dream change the persons involved?

RESPONSE (OR CLOSING)

Have the young people find a partner to work on their individual dreams. The pairs take turns leading each other through the Dream Discovery Process.

Dream Discovery Process

Have the person relax, close his or her eyes, uncross arms and legs and take several deep breaths.

When ready, have the person tell you the dream in the present active tense, for example, "I see an old house," not, "The dream was about a house . . . "

Have the person become the significant person or object in the dream and describe feelings such as "I am the house. I'm old, broken-down and empty."

At the conclusion of the dream, ask the person if he or she would like to change the ending. If yes, ask the person to use his or her imagination and describe the new ending. For example, "I'm inviting my friends over and we're fixing the house. One is painting, another is bringing flowers."

Tell the person to open his or her eyes when ready.

Afterward, talk about the experience with your partner. It is sometimes fun for pairs to share their experience with the whole group.

Note: At no time does one partner "interpret" another's dream. The exercise is designed for the experience rather than analysis.

Gather in a large circle and encourage each person to complete these sentences:

• God has helped me through a nightmarish time in my life by . . .

• God has made a dream come true by . . .

When finished, have everyone join hands in a circle. Close with each person offering a prayer. Suggest a prayer of help during times of nightmares or a prayer of thanks for dreams come true.

DEALING WITH OUR EMOTIONS

by Ben Sharpton

PURPOSE

To identify some of the different emotions young people experience, to reassure the participants that others have similar feelings and to lead them to identify positive steps to manage such emotions.

PREPARATION

Collect 3 x 5 cards, pencils, blackboard and chalk or newsprint and felt-tip markers, and Bibles.

Become familiar with the passages of scripture in the "Meat" of the Meeting. Think through the thoughts and feelings that Jesus might have felt during each situation.

If you have an assortment of slides of your group, show them at the beginning of the session. It can be effective to show pictures of the faces of different members of your group as you play a song about emotions, such as "Feelings," or "You've Got a Friend."

OPENING

Begin with songs or skits. Welcome newcomers and include announcements about upcoming events.

Ask the group members to name as many emotions as they can that young people face. As these are mentioned, have someone list them on the 3 x 5 cards. Examples are: sadness, frustration, depres-

sion, craziness, enthusiasm, joy, anger, anxiety, shyness or fear.

Place the cards in the middle of the circle. One at a time volunteers pick the top card, read the emotion and tell how they usually react when they feel that emotion. If they prefer not to respond to that emotion, they can place their card on the bottom of the stack. Always give people a chance to pass.

If the participants decide to respond, they choose the next person who will pick a card. Explain that a person who has already participated in this activity cannot pick a card twice. After everyone has had a chance to participate or all the emotions have been mentioned, move to the next activity.

THE "MEAT" OF THE MEETING

Refer to the feelings you have just studied. Ask the group to identify the five most prevalent emotions and list them in a column on the left side of a blackboard or newsprint. Next to each emotion, list some of the most common causes for that emotion. Finally, list possible behaviors for each emotion. Continue to work with each feeling until you have completely filled the chart. (Consult the Emotion Chart in the Closing section for the format.) During this activity you will be working with the left half of the chart. Don't reveal the right half until you reach the Response section of this meeting.

Explain that Jesus faced many situations which would have brought about certain feelings. Ask volunteers to read the following verses: Mark 3:1-6; 4:35-41; 10:13-16; 11:12-14; 14:32-42; John 10:22; 11:28-37.

Ask the group members to share what they believe Jesus may have felt and how he reacted in each situation. Pinpoint an emotion for the passage.

RESPONSE (OR CLOSING)

Return to the Emotions Chart and ask a volunteer to read Galatians 5:22-23. Quickly list each of the "fruits of the spirit" on the blackboard or newsprint.

Review the first emotion the group listed, the possible causes

and the typical behaviors such emotions evoke. Ask the young people to choose one of the "fruits of the spirit" that they would rather feel than the negative mood they are now reviewing. For example, when feeling depressed, they would probably rather feel joyous. Create the column "Desired Emotion" and list those feelings in the first box.

Explain that often the youth may have to do something to feel a certain emotion. If they wish to feel happy, it often helps to do something that has made them happy in the past. Ask the youth to suggest activities that might bring about the desired emotion they just listed. After everyone understands the process, move to the next listed emotion. Work through all five to find things that can be done to change one's emotions.

Emotion Chart

Emotion	Possible Causes	Behaviors	Desired Emotion	Activities to Cause Desired Emotion

When all five emotions have been covered, explain that prayer for help and guidance is also important in working through feelings. Also point out that some emotions are so intense they may require special help from a competent counselor. Encourage the young people to seek help during such times. Allow for discussion.

Close with sentence prayers from every participant asking God for help and support in handling emotions. Be sure to thank him for emotions and for the help he provides.

HELPFUL RESOURCES
Songs and Creations, P.O. Box 7, San Anselmo, CA 94960.

Try This One, Group Books, P.O. 481, Loveland, CO 80539.

Fun 'n Games, Youth Specialties, 1224 Greenfield Drive, El Cajon, CA 92021.

LOVE THY NEIGHBOR

by Arlo R. Reichter

PURPOSE

To help young people gain an understanding and appreciation for persons from other racial or ethnic groups by hosting a meeting and potluck.

PREPARATION

Gather Bibles, hymnals, paper, pencils, newsprint, felt-tip markers and masking tape.

Meet in advance with leaders from a church of another ethnic or racial group. Plan with them a pot-luck dinner in which participants bring foods representative of their culture.

Both church leaders should inform participants to bring a food dish and also family pictures or other items representative of individual racial or ethnic roots.

Prepare the meeting area with room for discussion, display of the cultural items and an area for storing and serving food items.

OPENING

As the participants arrive, have them display their pictures and memorabilia.

Allow participants from both groups to choose songs of their culture, with all joining.

State the purpose of the meeting and invite the participants to enjoy sharing during the meeting. If more than one language group is present, have translators at the meeting. Encourage the use of all languages so everyone has the experience of hearing a different tongue.

Have the participants pair with someone from the other ethnic group. Direct the pairs to share their names and then show each other the family pictures and other display items. After about 10 minutes of conversation, have each pair join with another pair and then each share one thing they learned about the other's racial or ethnic group.

Within the foursomes, have the two from the same church list three things they think are important for the others to understand about their racial or ethnic group. Ask them to write these on paper. Then the two from the other church do the same. Have the foursomes share their items with the entire group and then write these on newsprint and post for all to view.

THE "MEAT" OF THE MEETING

The church leaders share three important things others should understand about their racial or ethnic group. These can be drawn from the items the youth have listed or be in addition. The leaders can also use this time to explain religious differences and similarities. Limit each adult to 15 minutes.

Encourage all youth to ask additional questions concerning racial or ethnic relationships and social conditions.

Ask each group to write on newsprint one thing it learned in the meeting and to suggest a concrete idea that can be done to bring future interaction between the two church youth groups. Ideas include: joint work projects, visit the other church worship service, view and discuss a film, or meet for another party or potluck.

RESPONSE (OR CLOSING)

For the closing worship, have the participants form a large circle of chairs. Begin the worship by affirming the sharing of the participants and the learning which came from the event. Invite the participants to thank God for the sharing and for new friends and new understandings. Read Galatians 3:23-29.

Ask each person to think through the meeting and then complete the statement, "Tonight I thank God for . . . " After each response, have the group repeat,

"We thank God for you." Some responses are: new friends, a chance to share with people of different backgrounds, and leaders who help take risks to reach out.

Invite the youth to join hands. As the adults read each line of the following prayer, the youth repeat it:

We thank God for difference.
We thank God for each other.
We thank God for new friends.
Help us to be one in Christ.
Help us to be witnesses of faith.
Help us to be like Jesus.
Bless us, O Lord.
Strengthen us, O Lord.
Amen.

Enjoy the potluck and fellowship.

HELPFUL RESOURCES

Intercultural resources and materials are available through many denominational groups. Contact your library or chamber of commerce for ideas. If you are unable to arrange the intercultural meeting, use audio-visual aids from denominational groups.

YOUTH GROUP ON TRIAL

by Matthew E. Hartsell

PURPOSE

To aid the group in evaluation of its positive and negative conduct and to find solutions as needed.

PREPARATION

You will need paper, pencils, posterboard, felt-tip marker and chairs.

Write a "J" on six to 12 pieces of paper and have blank papers for the rest of the group. These are to be drawn at the beginning of the meeting to determine a jury. The number of your jury depends on the size of the group.

Prepare five to 10 charges against the group. The charges should make the youth think about the group as well as their own personal lives. Make the charges practical to your situation. Some should be obviously false, others irrefutably true, still others questionable. Examples: This group does not sing loudly enough. This group is accused of taking money from the collection plate. This group is interested in the study of Jesus. This group is accused of being unfriendly to visitors.

Ask an adult to be the judge. Have her try to dress the part and wear a black robe such as a graduation gown.

Tell the judge she is to explain the courtroom procedure, keep order, dismiss the jury and recall it for the verdict.

Ask another adult to be the prosecuting attorney. He is to dress in a three-piece suit and tie. He will read the charges and try to present supporting facts. He should present testimony that is irrefutable and also evidence that is foolish. Examples: Because the church funds are running low, it is conjectured the youth have been stealing from the collection plate. Or, it is thought that the youth group is not singing loudly enough—if it were, the singing would be loud enough to raise the dead.

Appoint a youth to be the bailiff. The bailiff starts the trial by saying, "Court is now in session." (Pause). "All rise," (as the judge and prosecuting attorney enter), "the honorable (judge's name) will be presiding."

Print posters that read "Youth Group on Trial" and include the time, date and room of the trial. Place the posters about the church.

In the front of the meeting room put a small table and chair for the judge. Nearby put six to 12 seats in two rows for the jury.

OPENING

Have the youth draw the papers for the jury; have the bailiff call those forward who drew "J's" and seat the jury.

Remind the other youth they are in court and to act accordingly, maintaining a respectful mood.

The bailiff calls in the judge and prosecuting attorney.

THE "MEAT" OF THE MEETING

The judge introduces the prosecuting attorney, and also explains to the youth they are to act as their own defense. The attorney reads the charges, one at a time. After each charge is read and facts are presented, the youth are permitted to defend themselves. The prosecuting attorney may ask the youth to clarify their statements, and he may add statements as well. Try to get as many youth involved as time permits.

The judge calls time after 30 minutes.

The jury then is given the written charges that were discussed and a piece of paper and a pencil for notes. They are sent to a private room to discuss whether the group is guilty or not on each charge. After 10 minutes, they return to the courtroom and explain their verdict based on the facts received.

RESPONSE (OR CLOSING)

Informally discuss the charges and possible solutions to the problems and shortcomings of the group. Write down the solutions on a posterboard and post those for all youth as a reminder. Place the most emphasis on praising the group members for their positive points.

Remind the youth we are on trial for Jesus every day. As a group and individually, we need to keep a clear record for Jesus. Read 1 John 2:6 and explain briefly that Jesus is not only our judge, but also our example to follow in the "courtroom of life." Remind them to try to walk in the same way in which Jesus walked.

Tell the youth that even though we daily are on trial for Christ, we are not saved by works. Jesus loves us and forgives us our shortcomings.

Have two or three youth close in prayer asking for God's wisdom, partiality and truth.

YEARLY EVALUATION

by Frank Zolvinski

PURPOSE

To sponsor an end-of-year evaluation for senior high group members to get their feedback regarding activities.

PREPARATION

Gather pencils and make copies of the Evaluation in the "Meat" of the Meeting. Make the evaluation relevant to your group by listing classes, speakers, retreats and activities that your group has done. Structure the forms so there is plenty of room for the youth to write answers.

Make refreshments for the end of the meeting.

OPENING

Explain to the youth their input will be used to evaluate the past year's program and their suggestions will be utilized in planning the upcoming year's activities.

THE "MEAT" OF THE MEETING

Distribute the Evaluation forms and pencils.

Evaluation

Instructions: Please help us evaluate this past year's program. Your suggestions will help us in planning next year's activities. Above all, be honest and fair in your remarks. All suggestions and comments are welcome.

Use the following scale: 1-poor, 2-fair, 3-good, 4-very good, 5-excellent, NA-does not apply.

1. Classes and Content
(List classes, films, guest speakers and programs.)

2. Activities
(List sports, plays, parties and special events for holidays.)

3. Prayers and Experiences
(List variety, meditation, spontaneity, reflective readings, formal prayer, music and poems.)

4. Retreat
(Include time, place, length, size of group, facilities, food, talks, presentations, staff, pastor, discussions, services and activities.)

5. Staff
(Rate interest in students, friendliness, maturity, enthusiasm, sincerity, fairness, leadership, ability to answer questions and ability to listen.)

6. In Conclusion
I would rate this past year:
I would come again next year:
I would encourage a friend to attend:
I would like to help plan next year's activities:
I would be interested in meeting this summer:
I would be interested in joining other activities our church offers:

7. My words of wisdom for next year's group are:

RESPONSE (OR CLOSING)

Honor the students with special refreshments. Allow them to socialize one last time as a group. Point out other activities they can do such as young adult classes and Bible studies. If they are planning to attend college, invite them to visit while home on college vacations.

Close with a prayer asking for God's guidance in their futures.

WHAT IS IT
TO BE A CHRISTIAN?

by James P. Reeves

PURPOSE

To tailor a meeting to youth who have not yet accepted Christ, and to help them accept Jesus as their personal Savior.

PREPARATION

Prepare copies of What Is Salvation to Me? (in the "Meat" of the Meeting), and My Salvation (in the Closing).

OPENING

To introduce Christianity, explain that the youth are going to play a game about love. Briefly explain the Christian concept of love, then play the Love Room.[1]

Love Room

You'll need two separate rooms.

Begin by explaining, that everyone at times has trouble showing love. Occasionally cliques and groups of friends hurt others by rejection. This group exercise may help.

Send four or five people to each room. Keep the rest of the group in another room.

One by one, the leader sends a person into the first room for a few minutes. The people in the room have been told ahead of time to ignore the newcomer who has been instructed to introduce himself or herself and to try to join the group.

After the newcomer has been in

that room a short time, the leader takes him or her to the next room. Again, the participant introduces himself or herself, but the people in that room enthusiastically greet the newcomer, smile and hug him or her. The participant stays in that room to greet the others in the same way.

After everyone has experienced the "cold room" and the "love room," have a discussion on how each person felt in the rooms. Relate the experiences to everyday life.

THE "MEAT" OF THE MEETING

Ask the youth to explain: What does it mean to be a Christian? How do you become a Christian? What process did you go through?

Divide into three groups and have each of the groups answer one of the sections of the handout:

What Is Salvation to Me?

What do the following scriptures say about salvation?

Group one:
  Isaiah 59:1-2
  Romans 3:10
  Romans 6:23
  Romans 3:23

Group two:
  Isaiah 53:5-6
  Matthew 26:28
  John 3:16; 10:10
  Romans 5:8

134

1 John 5:11-12
2 Corinthians 5:21
1 Timothy 1:15; 2:5
1 Peter 2:24; 3:18
Group three:
  Mark 1:15; 8:35
  John 1:12
  Romans 5:1-2
  Ephesians 2:8-9
  1 John 1:9
  Revelations 3:20

In simple terms, summarize your scriptures and share with the entire group.

RESPONSE (OR CLOSING)

Prepare an evaluation designed for your group. Following is an example:

---

[1]Thom Schultz, ed., **More . . . Try This One**, (Group Books: Loveland, Colo. 1980), p. 42.

My Salvation

Tonight was the first time I ever heard the message of how to receive Jesus Christ. I feel:

Because I now know the message, I want to receive Jesus as my savior:

Are you a Christian now? How do you know? Can you pinpoint a specific time you accepted Jesus? Or, have you always felt the Lord's presence?

If you are not now involved in a Bible study, would you be interested in joining one?

I am not a Christian, but I want more information:

Pray: Lord Jesus, please come into my life and be my Savior and Lord. Please forgive my sins and give me the gift of eternal life.

WHEN I FAIL

by Ben Sharpton

PURPOSE

To have the young people recall past experiences of failure. To evaluate the experiences in relationship to our success-oriented society and to suggest scriptural guidelines for coping with failure.

PREPARATION

Become familiar with the handout used in the first part of the lesson. Prepare your own definition of success. Read the scripture verses and become familiar with their implications regarding failure.

Study the material in the Response section and prepare your presentation.

For each member make copies of How Do You Spell Success?

How Do You Spell Success?

Fill in each blank with a word that begins with the letter preceding it. Use words that describe a feeling which accompanies success and met goals.

G_____
O_____
A_____
L_____
S_____

Rank the following successes by placing a 1 before that situation that you face most often, and an 8 before the situation that you face the least. Continue with the other items until you have ranked all.

____school
____family
____friends
____athletics/hobby
____job

____God
____personal experiences
____other (explain)

Place a check (✔) by any of the following reactions that describe how you respond to unmet goals.

____throw a temper tantrum
____bottle it up inside
____hit something
____sulk or pout
____resolve to try harder
____talk it out
____get depressed
____ignore it
____other (explain)

Now, go over the last two exercises and circle the "failures" that you think most of your friends face (that is, the most common failures). Also, circle the most common reactions to failure.

Gather Bibles, pencils, chalk or felt-tip markers, paper, copies of the handout, and blackboard or newsprint.

OPENING

Distribute pencils and copies of How Do You Spell Success? Give everyone five minutes to finish, then split into groups of five or six and allow the youth to share answers. Encourage the groups to respond positively, as there are no right answers.

THE "MEAT" OF THE MEETING

Explain your definition of success. Include the concept of failure as not reaching goals and expectations. Explain that failure is inevitable; we all fail in some areas of our life but what matters most is how we respond.

Distribute pencils and paper. Have each group list three goals of life, such as happiness, success, wealth, friendship or prestige. After a few minutes have the groups copy the goals on the blackboard or newsprint.

Assign one goal to each group and have it list the steps for achieving the goal and also list the consequences of failure. Allow five minutes.

Assign each group one of the following scripture passages: Romans 8:1; 8:28 and 1 John 2:1. Ask each group to find the goal in the passage and to list consequences of failure. Ask the young people the difference between the scriptural goals and those of our success-oriented society. Compare the consequences of failure between the two.

Write the following on the blackboard or on newsprint:

F eelings
A nalyze the situation
I ndividuals involved
L ook for alternatives

Explain that when we fail, we should briefly study feelings. Are we overreacting? letting failure depress us? passing the buck? We must be careful not to dwell on the feelings because it could keep us from moving ahead.

Objectively analyze the situation. Look at the events that led to the failure. How much control could we have over such events? How much responsibility do we actually have for the failure?

Look at the others involved in the failure. What did each person contribute to the solution? We should ask how our relationships with others contributed to the situation. Which individuals should we could go to for help?

The final step is to study alternatives. Ask what we could have done differently, then evaluate options for future situations. What warning signs can we look for in preventing a reoccurrence? A good practice is to list three actions that we can take. Date the actions on a calendar and follow through.

RESPONSE (OR CLOSING)

Include daily prayer for forgiveness (if necessary), guidance and insight, and we will be moving toward becoming the new creatures God intended.

As a final activity, create a "recipe for handling failure." List all the ingredients and instructions on the blackboard. For example, "Stir in three cups of confession to a heaping pot of prayer. Add a dash of optimism, bake for some time in a warm atmosphere of love and acceptance."

Or read the following case study and ask the group to prepare specific suggestions:

Bob was having a tough time. It began when he tried out for basketball. He was too short and just didn't make the team. He was crushed. He had really wanted to make the team and had practiced several hours every day, but he was cut on the last day of tryouts. His girlfriend was a cheerleader, and shortly after that broke up with Bob to date the team center.

He did keep his job at the hardware store and let that occupy most of his free time and thoughts. The manager had given Bob the responsibility of locking up every night. Just last week Bob left the store and forgot to lock the front door. Someone walked in during the night and stole several hundred dollars worth of merchandise.

To top it all, Bob received a "D" on his report card which was issued today.

He has come to you with his story. What do you say? How can you comfort Bob?

WHAT IS FAITH?

by Ben Sharpton

PURPOSE

To lead young people to define faith and to explore ways in which they can utilize that faith.

PREPARATION

Study the handout printed in the "Meat" of the Meeting and the suggested scriptures used in this session.

Prepare your own definition of faith and think of personal examples of faith for you to share.

Gather Bibles, pencils, chalk or felt-tip markers, 3 x 5 cards, flashlight, blank paper, copies of the handout and blackboard or newsprint.

OPENING

If you want, begin with games or songs (see Resources).

Distribute the 3 x 5 cards and pencils. Ask everyone to complete the sentence, "Faith is . . ." No one should sign their cards. Collect the cards and read the answers.

Read the following quotes and ask the group members if they agree or disagree:

● "Faith is an intellectual leap of trust"—O. Dean Martin.

● "Without faith it is impossible to please God"—Paul (Hebrews 11:6).

● "Faith is simply the way to tap the spiritual power that is available to us"—Steve Clark.

● "Faith—a personal answer to the question, 'Where do I place my ultimate trust?' "—Stephen Jones.

● "There is nothing now known that was not initially a matter of faith"—W.T. Purkiser.

● "Faith consists in the recognition that it is God who makes the grain grow, and in loving and glorifying him in thanksgiving"—Paul Tournier.

● "Faith makes it possible for us to count on and cooperate with what God is doing"—Steve Clark.

● "Doubt is the growing edge of faith"—O. Dean Martin.

● "Faith consists in thanking God for our deliverance and in attaching ourselves to him"—Paul Tournier.

● "Revelation demands response. Faith is the name we give this response when it is unfavorable"—W.T. Purkiser.

● "Expectant faith often means we have to do something before we see God act"—Steve Clark.

● "Faith is the beginning of all knowledge and wisdom"—Jennifer Wright.

● "The difference between faith and presumption lies in the fact that real faith is rationally defensible. Belief is not irrational prejudice. It is the mind reaching out into the yet unexplored"—W.T. Purkiser.

● "I believe in the sun, even when it is not shining. I believe in love, even when I feel it not. I believe in God, even when he is silent"—Unknown.

THE "MEAT" OF THE MEETING

Distribute the Faith handout. Give each person enough time to do the exercise.

Have the group members share their answers. Then ask them to share experiences in which they have known people who have had great faith and who have been used by God through this faith. Tie this in with times people have stepped out on faith, trusting God.

Faith

"Now faith is being sure of what we hope for and certain of what we do not see."
Hebrews 11:1 (New International Version)

"Now faith is the assurance of things hoped for, the conviction of things not seen."
Hebrews 11:1 (New American Standard Version)

"Now faith is the substance of things hoped for, the evidence of things not seen."
Hebrews 11:1 (King James Version)

"What is faith? It is the confident assurance that something we want is going to happen. It is the certainty that what we hope for is waiting for us, even though we cannot see it up ahead."
Hebrews 11:1 (Living Bible)

Circle the translation that appeals most to you.

Underline any words you don't understand.

What is meant by the "substance" (assurance) of things hoped for, and "evidence" (conviction) of things not seen?

SUBSTANCE:_____
_____
_____

CONVICTION:_____
_____
_____

Here are two definitions of faith. With which do you agree?

● Faith is taking all intellectual and rational arguments for a subject (which aren't enough for proof in themselves), followed by a firm belief in that subject based on these evidences and substances.

● Our faith, and the faith of our forefathers, is the proof that what we believe is true. Faith is our evidence.

Now, fill in this chart:

	Who acted on faith?	What did they do?	What was God's response?
Hebrews 11:7 and Genesis 6:13-22			
Hebrews 11:8-10 and Genesis 12:1-4			
Hebrews 11:11 and Genesis 17:19			
Hebrews 11:17 and Genesis 22:1-10			
Hebrews 11:23 and Exodus 2:2			
Hebrews 11:29 and Exodus 14:22-29			

Define faith: I believe that faith is:

RESPONSE (OR CLOSING)

Pass a flashlight around the group and ask how it is similar to faith. Some possible responses include:

● A light is made to shine and not be hidden. So also our faith ought to be evident and not disguised (Mark 4:21).

● We have the power to turn the light on or off just as we have the ability to aid God's power or inhibit it through lack of faith (Mark 5:5-6).

Read 1 Corinthians 16:13 as a closing prayer.

HELPFUL RESOURCES

Songs, Songs and Creations, P.O. Box 7, San Anselmo, CA 94960.

Try This One, Group Books, P.O. Box 481, Loveland, CO 80539.

Fun 'n Games, Youth Specialties, 1224 Greenfield Drive, El Cajon, CA 92021.

FAITH

BRANCHES OF THE VINE

by Mark Mustful

PURPOSE

To allow parents and their teen-agers the opportunity to tell of their love of Christ and each other.

PREPARATION

Put one long string of Christmas tree lights on the floor of the meeting room. This will serve as the "vine" for the Close of the meeting. Collect sheets of 9 × 12 construction paper, 3 × 5 cards (two per person), scissors, glue, rulers and pencils.

Set a date for the meeting. Contact a few people to arrange, serve and clean up a potluck dinner.

Send invitations to families with teenagers and express the purpose of the meeting. Attach an R.S.V.P.

Announce the meeting in the church newsletter and bulletin.

Arrange for one youth and one parent to give a brief testimony about the way in which their faith has given them a greater love for their children or parents. These two will share their experiences during the Opening of the meeting.

OPENING

Begin with a brief introduction, dinner prayer and the meal.

After everyone has eaten, begin the devotional. Explain how we often neglect to express our feelings of endearment to each other as parents and children and that we sometimes avoid such expressions.

Read John 15:1-17 which says that we are branches of the vine, Jesus. We are commanded to love each other. Explain how, through this scripture, we will begin to create a visual vine and branches that will help us to see the truth in this passage as it affects our lives.

Introduce the parent and teen-ager and have them give their brief testimonies. Encourage them to tie John 15:1-17 to their message.

THE "MEAT" OF THE MEETING

Clear the tables and start the activity. Everyone receives scissors, glue, a ruler, two 3 × 5 cards, construction paper and a pencil. The participants are to cut off a 1 × 9 inch strip from the top of their construction paper which will be used to form the "branch." Fold the remaining paper in half. Take the sheet and cut out a teardrop-shaped leaf so there will be two identical leaves. Glue the 1 × 9 inch strips end-to-end. The leaves are glued to the branch leaving space on the inside end of the branch to connect it to the vine. As this dries, the participants write on the note cards events in which they felt a special love for their parent or child because of their relationship to Christ. These cards are to be glued to the center of the leaves. See the example:

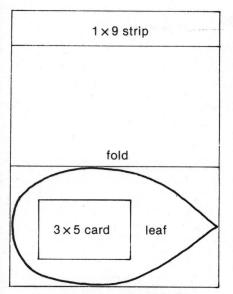

1 × 9 strip

fold

3 × 5 card   leaf

9 × 12 construction paper

RESPONSE (OR CLOSING)

Gather around the string of lighted Christmas tree lights. Each family brings its branch and lays it on the floor so that the inside of the branch connects to the string of lights. This forms a vine with branches. Turn off the other lights in the area and express how this display is an example of Christ's relationship to our families. He is the vine and we are the branches—rooted in his love.

Ask the participants to create a prayer that thanks God for this relationship. Invite people to share their thoughts, one at a time, in a circle prayer.

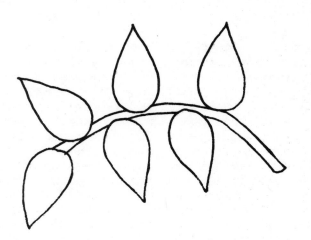

FAMILY TIES

by Rickey Short

PURPOSE

To enable teenagers to understand parental concerns, to show means of improving family relationships and to help youth contemplate their roles within the home.

PREPARATION

Gather paper, pencils, felt-tip markers and several Bibles.

For each participant prepare copies of the handouts What Bugs Parents and Me in My Family, both on the next page.

Note: The Me in My Family information can be presented orally rather than in writing.

OPENING

Distribute felt-tip markers and one or two sheets of paper to each participant. Ask the youth to draw their family in a situation such as at the dinner table, in the car or on a picnic. They are to use colors that tell something about the members of their family.

When the youth have completed their drawings, have them explain who the people are, the colors used and the scene depicted. For example, "My mother is always cheerful, so I used yellow to represent her."

To facilitate the discussion, the leader can begin by explaining his or her drawing.

This activity quickly introduces each person's family to the group and reveals who has brothers, sisters or grandparents at home. Single-parent situations often are related in the drawings. It also helps the teenagers express predominant feelings about family members.

THE "MEAT" OF THE MEETING

Distribute pencils and the What Bugs Parents worksheets and allow time for completion.

Discuss the answers with the youth and show them that parents have emotions and feelings, too.

Tally the answers to find the most common ones and discuss possible reasons for the concerns.

Distribute the Me in My Family worksheets and have the youth answer all questions.

Discuss answers and compliment the youth who best applied themselves to the questions.

RESPONSE (OR CLOSING)

Select two or three of the following scriptures and ask different youth to read aloud: Galatians 6:9-10; Ephesians 4:29; 6:1-3; Colossians 3:13; 3:23-24; James 1:19. Ask ways in which the scriptures relate to parent-teenager relationships.

Ask the young people to make a quick statement about what they have learned that will help them understand their parents better and one thing they are going to do

What Bugs Parents

1. Circle the item that you think has placed the most stress on your parents within the past year:
   a. moving
   b. money
   c. death in the family
   d. divorce
   e. major illness
   f. depression
   g. me
   h. other

Explain your answer.

What did you do to help during the stressful time?

2. Parents worry their teenager will (select five):
   a. take drugs
   b. get in a fight
   c. get expelled from school
   d. have to get married
   e. fail a class
   f. skip school
   g. get married too early
   h. not get married
   i. drink alcohol
   j. smoke cigarettes or marijuana
   k. have an abortion
   l. never get a job
   m. join a gang
   n. not go to college
   o. move out or run away
   p. wreck the car
   q. not be popular
   r. turn into a religious or cultist fanatic
   s. other (explain)

Me in My Family

● My family's greatest strength is . . .

● My parents dream I will . . .

● The best way to improve communication between parents and teenagers is . . .

● The most important lesson I learned from my parents is . . .

● My family most enjoys . . .

● My family needs to do more of . . .

● If my parents told me to "grow up" they would mean . . .

● I can help my parents by . . .

● My parents are usually right about . . .

● My parents are usually wrong about . . .

● I wish my parents would . . .

● On a scale of one to 10 (one is poor, 10 is excellent), my family is . . .

immediately to improve family life.

Form a circle and let each give his or her interpretation of, "Honor your father and your mother, that your days may be long in the land which your Lord your God gives you."

Close with a circle prayer and ask for love and respect for parents.

HELPFUL RESOURCES

"Family of God," **Songs**, compiled by Yohann Anderson, Songs and Creations, P.O. Box 7, San Anselmo, CA 94960.

An Adolescent in Your Home, Public Documents Distribution Center, Department 19, Pueblo, CO 81009. Stock number 017-091-0020-2.

GETTING ALONG WITH BROTHERS AND SISTERS

by Dave Pearce

PURPOSE

To examine sibling relationships and to encourage introspection and improvement.

PREPARATION

Gather Bibles, songbooks (see Resources), paper, pencils, milk, saucers, balls of yarn, blackboard or newsprint.

Collect pictures of cats, kittens, brothers and sisters. Intersperse the pictures about the meeting room.

Make copies of the Sibling Situations handout in the Response section.

Publicize the meeting and encourage the youth to attend in cat costumes such as the Cat in the Hat, Garfield or Top Cat.

OPENING

Open with games such as:

String Ball Nose Push: Line up the teams and have members use their noses to unroll huge balls of yarn or string around a goal.

Milk Lapping: Have several students lick up small bowls of milk. Watch for slurpers.

Back Scratching: Have everyone get in a circle and claw everyone else's back gently then switch directions.

Cat Costume Awards: Give a special award for best costume called The Cat's Meow.

Introduce the theme by explaining that kittens often battle with one another. They want the most of mother's milk, and the runt may get left out. They battle—sometimes playfully—sometimes in earnest. This is much like the real family siblings battling for parental attention, and injustices sometimes occur. In the interplay, children learn about life and love.

THE "MEAT" OF THE MEETING

Divide into small groups and hand out copies of the Sibling sheet for discussion.

Have each group share the most powerful insight from its discussion.

If you have time, have each group role play brother and sister situations. Discuss the role plays and ways the situations might have been resolved.

RESPONSE (OR CLOSING)

Write traits such as these on the blackboard or newsprint in two columns.

Negative	Positive
jealousy	love
pride	acceptance
injustice	servanthood
territoriality	sharing

Encourage the students to relinquish negative traits while adding positiveness. Ask, "What are some

Sibling Situations

Cain and Abel (Genesis 4:1-16)
● How can disobeying our parents or God get us into problems with brothers and sisters?
● How does jealousy manifest itself in your family? What does it cost?
● How can you avoid jealousy and overcome it?

Jacob and Esau (Genesis 25:19-34; 27:1-40)
● How does manipulation harm families?
● How can we trust God and be less selfish in our brother and sister relationships?

Jesus' brothers and sisters

(Luke 8:20)
● Who are his brothers and sisters?
● How can we let him be close to us?
● How can being close to Christ affect our relationship with our real siblings?

The prodigal's brother (Luke 15:11-32).
● How are we to feel about siblings who mistreat our parents?
● How can you know the difference between loving and serving your brothers and sisters and letting them abuse and mistreat you?

of the ways we can express positive traits in our relationships with brothers and sisters?"

Close with prayer asking that the participants find God's love and utilize it in their relationships with brothers, sisters and parents.

HELPFUL RESOURCES
Young Life Songbook, Young Life National Services, P.O. 520, Colorado Springs, CO 80901.

PARENTS ARE PEOPLE, TOO

by Lawrence Bauer

PURPOSE

To allow the youth to discover lines in family communication, to assist in clarifying attitudes on family lifestyles and to show methods of defusing conflict.

PREPARATION

Gather Bibles, newsprint, crayons and chairs. (Songbooks are optional.)

Number sheets of paper from one to 10 and tape them to the wall.

Note: This meeting takes one to two hours to complete, depending on the amount of discussion time.

OPENING

Open with songs and use music between sections of the meeting to assist in transitions.

Have the youth choose partners by finding people who have the same number of letters in their names.

THE "MEAT" OF THE MEETING

Announce, "Half of you will be A's and the other half B's—decide quickly. All A's raise their hands. You are the parents. B's are the teenagers. The situation is the teenagers refuse to clean their rooms and this has caused the parents to be irritated. B's cover your ears. Parents, you are beside yourselves. Your child's room is a pigsty—old sandwiches, tons of garbage—and you're sure something is alive under the trash. You have talked until you are exasperated.

All A's cover your ears. You are good people, B's, with one exception. It's your room. You feel that your parents don't have to enter this area, so they shouldn't be concerned.

"Parents stand on chairs with the teenagers facing you. Parents have 45 seconds to express their displeasure. Teenagers must stand and take it. Reverse places and teenagers have 45 seconds and parents can say nothing.

"Finally, A's and B's sit facing each other. The parent has 45 seconds to express displeasure and the youth has 45 seconds to respond."

The group leader asks the entire gathering:

- Parents, how did you feel in each situation?
- Teenagers, how did you feel?
- Was it more difficult to argue sitting down?
- If so, what does that tell us?
- When you argue, do you ever say anything you regret?
- Relate the last time you were in a similar situation and if you could have reacted better.

THE "MEAT" OF THE MEETING

Discuss briefly how emotion controls rational thought. Speak on the importance of controlling emotions to allow for clearer communication.

Break into groups of four to six and give each crayons and newsprint. Have the group members draw their kitchen table, and explain in the "old days" the table was where family discussions took place. As they draw, explain colors can mean different things such as red is anger, blue is happiness or serenity, green is hope and black represents heavy anger. Have them draw each family member at the table. Say, "Remember who talks with whom and draw lines to represent discussion such as thunderbolts if argumentative, broken lines if talk is sporadic, crooked lines or straight, etc.

Upon completion members share their drawings and explain the meaning of the colors and lines.

Gather as a large group and ask what the young people discovered doing this activity. Can they utilize what they've learned? How?

Tell the young people you are going to read a series of statements and after each one they should go to the number on the wall indicating their opinion. One means they totally agree with the statement, 10 means they totally disagree. If the youth have no opinion, they stand in the middle of the room. Then allow two people from the "agree" side to question people on the disagree side of each issue.

They are allowed to change positions if their opinions change.

The leader reads these statements one at a time and coordinates the activity:

● Parents overdiscipline teenagers by making too many rules.

● Teenagers are irresponsible. They want the privileges of adulthood but not the responsibility.

● The family is no longer the main social unit.

● Family desires must be superior to individual desires.

● Christian families have fewer problems communicating than non-Christian families.

Gather and ask what surprised the youth the most about the response. How would their parents have responded to each statement? If time permits, replay the game with the youth representing their parents' attitudes.

RESPONSE (OR CLOSING)

Read Ephesians 4:1-16 and give a short message on the body of Christ and family and how the units are interwoven. Say that we are to "speak the truth in love and grow in every way into him who is the head, into Christ."

Close with a prayer thanking God for families, asking him for guidance in communicating and working through family conflicts.

HELPFUL RESOURCES

Sing With Young Life, Young Life, P.O. Box 520, Colorado Springs, CO 80901.

THE PARENT-YOUTH GAME

by Gary Moran

PURPOSE

To relax and enjoy the fellowship of youth and parents.

PREPARATION

Gather a Bible for the closing devotion, blackboard or newsprint to use as scoreboard, a lectern, tables and chairs.

Set the two tables at the front of the room with four chairs behind each with a lectern in the middle. Place a blackboard nearby.

Assign a youth to read 1 Peter 5:1-7 and a parent to read 1 Timothy 4:12, and have them prepare a closing devotional based on the two scripture passages.

Select four parents and their children to play the game that is explained in the Opening.

Bring gifts to award to the winning team.

OPENING

Begin with a prayer of thanks for this fun opportunity to gather as families. Ask God to bless everyone at the meeting.

Explain the rules of the game. The youth will leave the room while their parents answer four questions. The youth enter and try to guess their parents' answers. Next, the parents leave and the young people answer four questions. Their parents enter and try to guess their children's answers.

The object of this contest, based on the **Newlywed Game** television show, is to see which youth-parent team can answer the most questions. Announce that there will be prizes for the winning team.

THE ''MEAT'' OF THE MEETING

The four young people leave the room and their parents answer the following questions:

- My child's favorite singing group is . . .
- My child would be most likely to admire:
  1. Superman
  2. a muscle builder
  3. a scientist
- The funniest thing I've ever seen my child do is . . .
- My child thinks of his or her parents as:
  1. a clean-up crew
  2. spies
  3. award-winners

The youth return and try to answer as their parents answered.

Next, the parents leave and the youth answer the following:

- If my family's life was a television show, it would be most like . . .
- My dad would most like to be:
  1. a newsman
  2. a sports hero
  3. a movie star

- My mom would rather:
  1. knit something useful
  2. spend a night on the town
  3. go on an African safari
- If I compared my life with that of my parents when they were my age, theirs would seem:
  1. embarrassingly tame
  2. about the same as mine
  3. unmentionably wild

The parents then return and try to answer as their children answered.

Award the winning team with prizes.

RESPONSE (OR CLOSING)

The parent and teenager chosen during the Preparation will read the scripture passages and give their devotional.

For a closing prayer, try an open-ended sentence such as: "Dear Lord, thank you for parents because . . ., thank you for young people because . . .."

LIVING IN SINGLE-PARENT HOMES

by Denise Turner

PURPOSE

To share feelings about single-parent homes, to provide support to those in such homes and to help the young people understand God is always with them.

PREPARATION

Gather Bibles, paper, pencils, blackboard and chalk.

OPENING

Ask: What causes divorce?

Direct the young people to brainstorm and call out quick answers. Jot the ideas on the blackboard. If they need help, ask what they think about changing attitudes toward marriage, altered roles for women, or mistakes the church is making in the area of family and marriage.

THE "MEAT" OF THE MEETING

Divide into groups of five or six. Direct each group to spend about 10 minutes listing at least 10 questions a young person whose parents are newly divorced might want to ask God. Tell them to word the questions as if God were going to drop by earth for a news conference and answer them.

Ask the groups to exchange lists and then answer the questions as they think God might answer them. Spend another 10 minutes on this, and then ask the groups to share the questions and answers.

Talk for a few minutes about the special problems that arise in a home where a parent is widowed.

Talk about the stages of grief—denial, emptiness, anger and freedom—and ways these feelings apply to people touched by both death and divorce.

Ask for volunteers to participate in the following role plays. Allow discussion after each one. What would you do differently? What would you do the same?

● Several youth are trying to comfort a friend's parent who has just lost his spouse.

● A youth feels he or she is being asked to choose between parents. The youth decides to talk with a minister or counselor.

● A young person is angry with his or her parents because they have divorced. He or she is getting poor grades in school and hanging with the wrong crowd. A friend decides to have a talk with the youth.

● A teenager is living with a single parent. The parent decides to begin dating again, and the youth is angry, hurt and confused. They talk about it.

RESPONSE (OR CLOSING)

Ask: How can you help a friend who is trying to cope with living in a single-parent home?

Encourage those who are not in that situation to think of ways they have seen young people help each other. Encourage the others to talk about ways their friends have helped them. Jot ideas on the blackboard.

Read Romans 8:28-39. Explain God can use everything that happens to bring about something that is good. Talk about God being present in all situations.

Ask the youth to share one thing about their homes for which they thank God. Lead the group in a prayer of thanks for these things.

HELPFUL RESOURCES

Check with your library for books on the grief process and coping with divorce.

WHO'S AFRAID OF . . .

by Lawrence Bauer

PURPOSE

To help adolescents understand that fear is normal and to encourage them to overcome fear by trusting in the Lord.

PREPARATION

Collect Bibles, 3 x 5 cards, pencils, blackboard or newsprint. Songbooks are optional.

OPENING

Open with several rousing songs. Music can be used between sections of the meeting to assist in transitions.

Play a game to get everyone relaxed and ready for the meeting. Have a Pantomime Time! Divide the youth into groups of threes or fours. Instruct each group to act out a really strange action such as chewing a piece of gum. Each person must be included in the action—so one could be the stick of gum, one could be the wrapper and another could be the mouth. Other pantomime ideas are: flying a kite, a bowl of ice cream on a hot day, an automobile dashboard (with all the gauges), a typewriter, and a brush involved in house painting.[1]

THE "MEAT" OF THE MEETING

Distribute the cards and pencils and have the young people gather in a large group. Relate a time when your worries or fears caused an overreaction and feeling of foolishness. Try to give a humorous example.

Ask the participants to raise their hands if they are afraid of the dark, snakes, the boogeyman or something in the closet.

Tally the answers on the blackboard and explain briefly that adults also have fears. Give examples such as rejection, loneliness, death or poverty.

Have the youth write something that scares them now and ways the group can help. Invite them to share their feelings.

Ask the participants to write of a time when they were afraid of something and they later realized their fears were unfounded.

Ask someone to read aloud Luke 9:10-17. Let the youth talk about worry. What are some reasons that we worry? Is worry ever necessary? How does this scripture reading help us? What are other ways God comforts us and takes care of us?

RESPONSE (OR CLOSING)

Close with the song "He's Got the Whole World in His Hands." Add a prayer of thanksgiving for God's presence in fearful, worrisome times.

---

[1]Adapted from Lee Sparks, ed., **Try This One . . . Too** (Loveland, Colo.: Group Books, 1982), p. 9.

THE PRODIGAL DAUGHTER

by Walter Mees, Jr.

PURPOSE

For young people to realize the connection between actions and consequences and to help them see more than one side of an issue through debate.

PREPARATION

Gather pencils, paper and song-books.

Ask someone to be prepared to close the meeting with prayer.

Prepare and duplicate the following information:

THE PRODIGAL DAUGHTER

Lorrie just celebrated her 18th birthday. She is not married, has a 6-month-old son, and has been supported by her boyfriend Fred who is not the father of her baby. A week ago Fred left her saying he was in love with someone else.

Lorrie did not tell the father of her baby about the pregnancy. She has lost contact with him and cannot remember his last name.

Lorrie's parents, Chuck and Barbara, live in the city and are respected members of a local church. Chuck teaches high school and Barbara is a nurse. They had high expectations for Lorrie, but she never did as well in school as they thought she should. In fact, a year ago Lorrie quit school and left home after an argument with her parents about a boyfriend and her poor school performance. Lorrie's brother is in graduate school, and

her sister is in high school.

She has telephoned her parents twice in the past year—when her baby was born and at Christmas. Her parents have not called her.

In two weeks the rent will be due on Lorrie's apartment, and she has a three-day supply of food.

What should Lorrie do or not do? Read each suggested action and write down your reason.

1. Return to parents' home.
2. Move in with girlfriend in the same situation.
3. Apply for Aid for Families with Dependent Children (AFDC), which provides cash, food stamps and medical aid.
4. Investigate school or job training programs.
5. Move in with a 29-year-old man she met last night at a party.

OPENING

This meeting can be opened with several songs from your group's favorite songbook or with the following game.

Divide the group into small circles of six to eight youth. Ask the young people to give their name and a color that best describes how they are feeling. Each person must precede his or her name by remembering all the other names and colors, for example, "This is John and he's blue and that's Mary and she's pink."

When everyone is done, have the

participants explain why they picked their color.

THE "MEAT" OF THE MEETING

Distribute pencils and papers with the story of Lorrie plus suggested actions. Give the young people a certain amount of time to read the story and write down reasons for each action. Ten to 15 minutes should be adequate.

When everyone has finished writing, separate into discussion clusters of five. Number the members of each cluster. One's will give their reasons for choosing or not choosing answer one from the story of Lorrie. Two's will give their reasons for choosing or not choosing answer two, etc., until all five have shared. Allow five minutes for the small group to discuss the reasons, seeking a consensus. Don't wait for the youth to reach a final conclusion; stop them in mid-debate. Renumber the members and have them repeat the sharing process until they have debated all five alternatives.

Reassemble the group and ask a member of each cluster to report on her or his impression of the best action for Lorrie.

RESPONSE (OR CLOSING)

Ask if anyone can think of advice Jesus gave about such a situation. Responses might include the parable of the prodigal son (Luke 15:11-32) and the story of the woman caught in adultery (John 8:1-11).

Discussion may lead to action number one as Lorrie's best choice. However, that choice would depend upon her parents' ability to respond as the prodigal son's father or like Jesus, and not every parent can do that. Even though some parents are unable or unwilling to forgive, the church should be able to do so. Questions to consider are: How could the group be Jesus to Lorrie, if she were a member? How could each person be Jesus to Lorrie? Don't forget the baby. How could the group help them both?

Close with prayer and enjoy the refreshments.

HELPFUL RESOURCES

Study governmental aid programs such as AFDC. Contact your local social service office for more information or brochures.

Research job training and school programs for unwed mothers by calling a nearby employment or job training service.

Study **Bread for the World**. Write: 4600 N. Kilpatrick Ave., Chicago, IL 60630.

THE FORGIVENESS GIFT

by Steve Allen

PURPOSE

To emphasize God's gift of forgiveness and to enable youth to learn to practice this forgiveness.

PREPARATION

Collect Bibles, dictionary, paper, pencils, metal wastebasket, matches, 3 x 5 cards, overhead projector, screen, cassette player, chalk and chalkboard (or newsprint and felt-tip markers).

Select music to play as the youth arrive. One suggestion is "Forgiven" on the album **A Song in the Night** by Silverwind, recorded by Sparrow records.

For each participant prepare copies of the Forgiveness handouts in the "Meat" section and the Match the Person With the Sin handout in the Response section.

Place a piece of posterboard in the meeting room with the word "prison" written on it. This is for the role play.

Set up the projector and screen and cue the cassette player with the "Forgiven" song.

OPENING

As the participants enter, distribute pencils and 3 x 5 cards. Have the members write a personal sin or problem. Instruct the youth to put the card in their shoes.

Begin an active game such as volleyball or a relay race. After the activity, have the youth discuss the feelings of the sin that trouble them.

Divide the youth into three groups for the forgiveness study. Distribute the handouts and have each group follow the directions.

THE "MEAT" OF THE MEETING

Refer to Matthew 18:23-35. Choose 11 youth and have one read the passage while the others act it out. Discuss the role play and ask the youth to explain how they would have felt if the part they played would have really happened.

Discuss ways we are to forgive others and the positive results that come when we do. List the following on the newsprint or chalkboard:

● Forgiving others communicates God's character and plan.[1] Explain that failure to forgive others goes against God's plan.

● Forgiving others lets people know forgiveness is really possible. Emphasize that people must believe in God's forgiveness and respond to this belief by forgiving others.

● Forgiveness gives the forgiver peace of mind. Have the youth read Colossians 3:13,15.

● Forgiving the person who has sinned against us shows we have received God's forgiveness of our

157

Forgiveness

Group 1

1. List as many sins you can think of that God will forgive.

2. Read Matthew 12:31. What does this verse mean?

3. What does each of the following statements mean to you?

● One of God's specialties is forgiving!

● God does not lock us into past sin.

● God frees us from past sin to take us to a future of usefulness.

Group 2

1. Use the dictionary to define forgiveness.

2. Put in your own words what it means to forgive.

3. Read 2 Corinthians 5:18. As Christians we are to be in the ministry of reconciliation.

4. Use the dictionary to define reconciliation.

Group 3

1. Read Ephesians 4:32. What does this verse mean?

2. Is forgiving others an option or a mandate for a Christian?

3. Read and discuss Matthew 6:14-15.

4. Read Matthew 18:21-22. How many times should we forgive?

---

sin against him. Explain if we really believe and accept God's forgiveness, we will offer it to others. Read Matthew 18:33-35 and discuss it.

● Why is it hard to forgive others? Let the youth respond. Refer to the Forgiveness handout and ask the youth to discuss how many times they should forgive. From these responses discuss Matthew 18:22, that Jesus continued to forgive and that no one should keep score of the times forgiveness is made. Refer to 1 Corinthians 13:5 and explain this is the only way to forgive—with love.

Have the youth read and discuss Matthew 7:2 and James 2:13. Have one youth read Ephesians 4:31—5:2. Discuss how we are to have the ministry of reconciliation.

Write "Forgiveness—What About Home?" on the transparency and show it with an overhead pro-jector. Refer to Luke 15:11-31 and talk about the conflict in the home and forgiveness.

On the transparency, outline the following points on forgiveness within a family:

● Awareness of the conflict (awareness that you have sinned).

● Recognition (acknowledgment of your contribution to the conflict).

● Confrontation (action must be taken after your acknowledgment). Read 2 Timothy 2:22-24. What is its message? Why is it difficult to admit mistakes?

● Seek for oneness of heart (although this does not mean you have to always agree).

● Reaffirm your love for each other. Read 2 Corinthians 2:8.

RESPONSE (OR CLOSING)

Distribute and have the youth complete the following worksheet:

Match the Person With the Sin

1. Moses	a. Persecuted Christians
2. Lot	b. Had temper tantrums and sexual affairs
3. Samson	c. Peeping Tom, adulterer and schemer of murder
4. Paul	d. Ruthless tax collector
5. David	e. Slept with his daughters
6. Jacob	f. Deserted his wife
7. Abraham	g. Murderer
8. Matthew	h. Cheated his brother, lied to his father

Answers: 1 (g), 2 (e), 3 (b), 4 (a), 5 (c), 6 (h), 7 (f), 8 (d).

Discuss the worksheet with the group and point out that God works wonders with sinners. Although we sin—God forgives us and leads our lives if we ask him to do so.

While the song "Forgiven" is playing, ask the youth to bow their heads and consider its message.

After the song, ask the youth to take the 3×5 cards which they put in their shoes at the start of the meeting and place the cards in the metal wastebasket. Carefully burn the cards.

Pray that the sins may be overcome just as the flames consumed the cards.

HELPFUL RESOURCES

Davis Dictionary of the Bible, by Richard Baker, Baker, P.O. Box 6287, Grand Rapids, MI 49506.

[1]Knofel Station, **Check Your Morality** (Cincinnati, Ohio: Standard Publishing, n.d.), pp. 131-132.

DUST IN THE WIND

by Lawrence Bauer

PURPOSE

To better understand God's ability to forgive, to help youth learn to forgive others and to show how to "let go" of a sin.

PREPARATION

Gather Bibles, 3 × 5 cards, pencils, blackboard or newsprint, a large bowl or metal wastebasket, matches and several copies of the prepared Forgiveness handout in the "Meat" of the Meeting section.

OPENING

Have participants group by birth months. Groups should have four to six members. Choose group leaders by whoever had the most for breakfast.

Have the youth identify themselves. If they don't know each other, they can give their names and explain why they are at the meeting. Ask if they have a picture of themselves in their wallets and, if so, to pass the picture around. Then ask how many words they can use to describe themselves — male/female, teenager, daughter/son, student, job.

The leaders then organize the groups to perform short skits on forgiveness. Ideas might be mimes or enactments of events in the Bible based on forgiveness. Or use the topics: Forgiveness is . . . Forgiveness is not . . .

THE "MEAT" OF THE MEETING

Have the participants regroup and give one person in each group a copy of the Forgiveness handout. This person will serve as the discussion leader.

Forgiveness

- Have someone in your group read the story of Hosea and Gomer in the book of Hosea.
- Talk about Hosea forgiving Gomer.
- Could you do that?
- Do you sometimes feel like Gomer? Why or why not?
- What does forgiving have to do with Christian friendship?
- Can you think of other examples of forgiveness in the Bible?
- Is forgiving others hard to do? Why or why not?
- Is self-forgiveness difficult? Why or why not?

RESPONSE (OR CLOSING)

Reassemble in one group and give everyone a 3 × 5 card. Each person is to list one sin that is separating him or her from God. Assure the young people no one else will see what they have written.

Explain that God's forgiveness is

160

even stronger than Hosea's for Gomer, and that God's cleansing power is our greatest gift.

The leader is to take his or her card, put it into the bowl and burn it. While it is burning, each person should silently walk foward, put his or her card in the fire and say,

"My sin is forgiven."

After all have done this and have had time to meditate, sing "Pass It On." Close with the Lord's Prayer.

HELPFUL RESOURCES
Sing With Young Life, Young Life, P.O. Box 520, Colorado Springs, CO 80901.

THE GIFT OF FRIENDSHIP

by Gary Moran

PURPOSE

To explore aspects of Christian friendships and to strengthen relationships within the youth fellowship. To sponsor an event and invite other youth.

PREPARATION

Prepare the Attractive Qualities and Quality Questions handouts in the "Meat" of the Meeting.

Gather a record player, 30 pieces of string for each person, pencils, paper, chalkboard and chalk.

Find a song that has a message concerning friendships or relationships and prepare a brief devotional based on the song. Some suggestions are: "You've Got a Friend," by James Taylor; "You Needed Me," by Anne Murray; "Bridge Over Troubled Water," by Simon and Garfunkle; or "Thank You for Being My Friend," by Andrew Gold.

OPENING

Play I Have Never . . . Give each participant 30 pieces of string. One person begins by saying, "I have never . . . (something he or she has never done)." Everyone who has done what the speaker has never done gives the speaker a string. If no one in the circle has done it, the speaker gives each player a piece of string.

The winner is the player with the most pieces of string.[1]

THE "MEAT" OF THE MEETING

Have the youth sit in a circle and give paper and pencils to each.

Instruct the youth to title the paper "Pleasing Traits." Tell the young people to look around the circle and jot down some of the pleasing qualities and personality traits of the other members. No names should be listed—just descriptive words such as punctual, sense of humor, friendly or reliable. Have the youth study their own lists to see how many of the traits could be applied to themselves.

Ask: How can you improve your less pleasing traits? Have you told your friends in the group any of the things that you like about them? Why not? Remind the youth it's the traits in many people they don't like, not the people. The information on the papers should remain confidential.

Distribute the Attractive Qualities list:

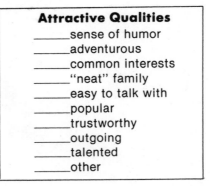

Attractive Qualities
_____sense of humor
_____adventurous
_____common interests
_____"neat" family
_____easy to talk with
_____popular
_____trustworthy
_____outgoing
_____talented
_____other

Ask the youth to rank these characteristics in order of importance in regard to how they choose friends. Divide into groups of six and discuss the sheets.

Distribute the Quality Questions handout to the groups and have them discuss it:

Quality Questions

● Why do you come to this group?

● What are some of the good things about our group?

● How is this group different from a group of friends at school?

● Which school friends could you invite to come to our group activities?

● What kinds of activities would you like our group to sponsor for our church, other churches and other friends? (Such as lock-ins, speakers or field trips.)

Share some of the insights from the small groups with the large group. On a chalkboard, write the activities suggested from the last question on the sheet. What events would be fun to sponsor as a youth group? Who could help with the planning? Who would we invite?

RESPONSE (OR CLOSING)

Choose one of the activities from the list and form a special event committee to organize it. Be sure to include publicity (posters, flyers), set-up, program and refreshments.

Form a circle and listen quietly to the song about friendship and share a few brief remarks about its message.

Close with individual prayers thanking God for friends.

---

[1]Lee Sparks, ed., **Try This One . . . Too** (Loveland, Colo.: Group Books, 1982), p.26.

YOU'VE GOT A FRIEND

by Margaret Tyree

PURPOSE

To help youth identify basic characteristics of a friend, to decide the kind of friends they are, to categorize friendships, and to examine scriptures that refer to Christlike qualities that youth can model in their relationships.

PREPARATION

Gather a record player, newsprint, paper, pencils, felt-tip markers or crayons, tape, a hat and Bibles.

Prepare copies of the Friendship Survey in the "Meat" of the Meeting.

Select several Christian songs or other recordings that pertain to friendship such as "You've Got a Friend" by Carole King.

Gather pictures of people doing activities together as friends such as biking, eating or chatting. Place the pictures about the meeting room.

Arrange the chairs in a circle and place a Bible, songbook, pencil, paper and marker on each one. Put the hat in the middle of the circle for the opening game.

OPENING

Sing a familiar Christian song that pertains to friendship. Then play Secret Friends.[1]

Begin this game by explaining Paul wrote in 1 Thessalonians 3:12, ". . . abound in love to one an-

other." Tell the youth this is a too often forgotten Christian concept.

Read aloud and discuss Matthew 22:39; John 13:35; 15:12; and 1 Thessalonians 3:12 to explore the vital role of loving one another as a part of Christian growth.

Have the youth write their names on slips of paper and put them into the hat. Each member then draws a name from the hat.

Tell the youth that during the upcoming week they are to:

• Write to the person whose name you drew. Tell them their traits you admire and why they would make a good friend. Include in this letter your favorite scripture verse or one that has been helpful.

• Pray daily for the person whose name you drew.

Next, divide into small groups. Distribute the markers and newsprint to each group and tell the youth to write traits of a friend. Encourage them to draw pictures to aid in their descriptions. If they have trouble thinking of several traits, call attention to the friendship pictures that are about the room. As they are making their lists, play the recording that addresses friendship.

Tape each group's newsprint list to the wall.

THE "MEAT" OF THE MEETING

Discuss the characteristics that

were most often listed. Are all the traits desirable? Can any of the traits be undesirable? Do good friends have to possess all these traits? Do you possess these traits?

To further explore these characteristics, distribute the Friendship Survey and have the youth answer the questions.[2]

Friendship Survey

1. How many friends do you have?

2. Do you have friends of both sexes?

3. Do you have friends who are five years younger than you are?

4. Do you have friends who are five years older than you are?

5. What's the craziest thing you've done with friends?

6. Who would consider you a friend?

7. What qualities do you have that make you a friend to others? List three.

8. What qualities does your best friend have?

9. Are your parents your friends? Why or why not?

10. Do you have any really close friends?

11. Do you have more or fewer friends than you had a year ago?

12. Are you a good friend? Explain.

Assign each small group one of these scriptures: Proverbs 17:17; 18:24; Galatians 6:1-10; Ephesians 4:31-32; Colossians 3:12-15. Discuss the ways these scriptures relate to friendship.

Re-form one large group and share the small group insights.

Ask if these characteristics are realistic to today's world.

Read and discuss John 15:13. What does it mean to lay down your life for a friend? Ask the youth to name people who were legendary friends, such as Anne Sullivan and Helen Keller. (Friends who gave their lives to each other in a special way.)

RESPONSE (OR CLOSING)

Draw a line down the center of a large piece of newsprint. Ask the youth to name characteristics of Christ and list these in one column. Then ask specific examples the youth can employ in their daily relationships and list these traits on the right side.

Ask the youth to name the best characteristic a friend can have. Discuss the answers.

Sing a few songs that deal with the subject of friendship such as "Pass It On" or "They'll Know We Are Christians by Our Love."

Remind the youth of the names they drew earlier. Encourage them to be Christlike and to think of other things they can do for their friends.

Form a circle and ask the youth to put their arms around one another for a time of prayer and thankfulness for friendship.

HELPFUL RESOURCES

Bible commentaries, read scriptures on friendship and friends.

The Interpreter's Dictionary of the Bible, Abingdon, 201 8th Ave. S., Nashville, TN 37202.

[1]Thom Schultz, ed., **More Try This One**, (Loveland, Colo.: Group Books, 1980), pp. 58-59.

[2]Dr. Arlo Reichter, et al., **The Group Retreat Book** (Loveland, Colo.: Group Books, 1983), p. 155.

CELEBRATING YOUR GIFTS

by Patrick M. Mulcahy

PURPOSE

To have each youth look at the failures and successes of his or her life, with emphasis on successes and the knowledge that he or she is a talented individual chosen by God for a part of his plan.

PREPARATION

You will need a Bible, paper and pencil for each person. Gather a few rolls of toilet paper.

OPENING

Open with the game All You Need. Have the group sit in a circle and pass the rolls of toilet paper. Tell the youth they are to take as much as they think they'll need for the duration of the meeting. Explain there is no toilet paper in the bathrooms (because you just took it) and they should take some "just in case." After the participants have taken a supply, explain they now need to share one thing about themselves with the group for each piece of toilet paper they have in their possession.

THE "MEAT" OF THE MEETING

Read 1 Corinthians 12:12-31. Discuss the fact that all people have talents and gifts and God intends them to use the gifts for his plan. It doesn't matter what the gifts are, all are important.

Distribute paper and pencils.

Each person is to write the three greatest successes and three worst failures of the past year. Allow a few minutes for this. The leader should do this, too. Discuss and openly share the participants' answers. Emphasize that failures are only temporary setbacks. We pick up and go on utilizing our talents and successes.

On the other side of the paper, have the youth list all their talents. They should consider: sports, music, scholastic ability, community service, public speaking, acting, dancing, sewing, cooking, crafts, painting, sketching, sculpting, writing, organizing, leadership and anything else.

Each person should share and discuss his or her list. Stress that all the talents are great and are gifts from God and should be used for the best possible goal.

RESPONSE (OR CLOSING)

Divide into groups of six to eight. Ask each team to quickly write and prepare a funny skit—in the style of a television commercial. The skit should emphasize the bad things commercials say about people to get them to buy products. The commercials should be geared to people who need help with body odor, bad breath, ugly teeth, slippery dentures, sinus trouble, athlete's foot, iron-poor blood, dandruff, acne, age spots or whatever. The youth then explain how their product can help.

The commercials should be 30 seconds to one minute. Afterward, talk about the silliness of many commercials. Emphasize that to make money, the commercials de- grade people and make a major case of small problems. Commercials such as these often can create feelings of insecurity.

Thank God that he doesn't think of us as commercials often portray people.

WHO IS GOD?

by James P. Reeves

PURPOSE

To emphasize the importance of studying about God.

PREPARATION

Prepare copies of the Let's Imagine handout in the Opening section. Each person will need paper and pencils.

Have an overhead projector or chalkboard, chairs and a blindfold.

Arrange the chairs in the meeting room.

OPENING

This creative project is useful to get young people interested in studying about God.

Divide into small groups of four to five. Describe the following situations and give each group 20 minutes to finish its task.

Let's Imagine

Situation: Let's imagine you and your crew are on a spacecraft traveling through space charting the galaxy. You happen to meet another spacecraft during your flight through the stars. The meeting is friendly and positive. Modern technology has provided you with a device that allows you to speak to your new space friends in their language and they in yours. During your conversation they explain to you their search for a new God and they pose the question, "Who or what is God to you?"

Your task for the next 20 minutes is to explain God to these creatures and friends. Remember, they know nothing of earth and its history, so avoid using Bible jargon and phrases common to earth people.

● How do you explain God's name or names?

● Can you see God?

● How does God communicate and how do earthlings communicate with God? (Remember that our word "prayer" means nothing to these creatures, so how do you explain prayer?)

● Do you fear God?

● How do you worship this God?

THE "MEAT" OF THE MEETING

Reunite the group and have the young people share the concepts of God.

How similar or different is this God with the God we know in the Bible? Did you have to stretch your thoughts any to use non-biblical words or phrases?

On the basis of your work, why do you think it might be important to study about God?

Explain to the youth that it has been said, "There is something exceedingly improving to the mind in a contemplation of divinity."

Continue to explain we improve ourselves as we think about who God is and what he is like. We can also explore the recesses of our minds through contemplation of God.

Ask and discuss means to improve oneself, self-image or attitude in life, by getting to know God better.

Present this illustration on the importance of studying about God: Blindfold a volunteer and walk him or her about the room. Explain that to disregard a study of God would be like going blindfolded through life, tantamount to being without direction. Life is a waste without this knowledge, because God made this world and to know how to function in it requires a knowledge of the one who made it.

On the blackboard or overhead write these five steps to get to know God:

To Know God
• God has spoken to us through his word, the Bible, which gives us his plan of salvation.

• God is Lord of all creation. He made all we see and rules over all. We are his creation and should worship and adore him.

• God is our Savior. He rescued us from our guilt and sin by sending his son to die for us on the cross.

• God is one in three persons. God the Father purposed the redemption of the world. God the Son secured it at the cross. The Spirit helps to apply this truth to our lives.

• Our walk in God's spirit means responding to God's revelation in trust and obedience. We should worship him, pray to him, serve others for him, and follow his desires for us to do his will. We must live our lives as God reveals it from his word.

RESPONSE (OR CLOSING)
Ask the youth to bow their heads, close their eyes and think about these two questions:

How well do I know God?

How well would I like to know God?

After a brief pause, ask the youth to think of ways in which they can better get to know God.

After an appropriate amount of time, say, "Let's pray about that desire right now, you pray quietly and I will pray aloud."

HELPFUL RESOURCES
Off the Shelf and Into Yourself, by Terry Hall, Victor Books, P.O. Box 1825, Wheaton, IL 60187.

Knowing God, by J.I. Packer, InterVarsity Press, P.O. Box F, Downers Grove, IL 60615.

Break-Through, by Jay Keeler, Zondervan/Campus Life Book, 1420 Robinson Road, Grand Rapids, MI 49506.

God's Book for God's People, by John R.W. Stott, InterVarsity Press, P.O. Box F, Downers Grove, IL 60515.

GOD'S ATTRIBUTES

by James P. Reeves

PURPOSE

To allow youth to increase their knowledge of God by studying specific attributes and to get to know themselves better in the process.

PREPARATION

Gather newsprint, blackboard, hymnal, paper, pencils, colored pencils, crayons, felt-tip markers, glue, tape and several copies of the shield drawing in the "Meat" of the Meeting.

OPENING

Introduce the concept of God's attributes by saying that we can learn to accept ourselves and to accept all that happens to us when we get to know God.

Read the following paragraph to the youth:

"There is tremendous relief in knowing that his love to me is utterly realistic, based at every point on prior knowledge of the worst about me, so that no discovery now can disillusion him about me, in the way I am so often disillusioned about myself, and quench his determination to bless me. There is, certainly, great cause for humility in the thought that he sees all the twisted things about me my fellowmen do not see ... and that he sees more corruption in me than that which I see in myself ... He wants me as his friend, and desires to be my friend, and has given his son to die for me in order to realize this purpose."[1]

Ask: Which attributes of God were mentioned in this paragraph? (List these on the blackboard.) Ask if the youth agree or disagree with the opinion of God stated in this paragraph.

THE "MEAT" OF THE MEETING

Explain you will be looking at the amazing and wonderful attributes of God that touch us every day. These attributes are God's power, presence, knowledge, loving concern and proven authority.

Divide into five groups and assign each group one of the following topics.

Each group should complete the project in 30 to 40 minutes.

● **All-powerful creator.** Read Psalms 19:1-6; 29:3-9; 65:9-13. Write a front page story for the Jerusalem Journal. Write more than one story if time allows. Have at least two "photographers" draw pictures on this topic.

● **God is everywhere at once.** Read Psalm 139:7-12. Either do a pantomime to present a message on this topic or write an advertisement brochure to celebrate the fact that God is omnipotent.

● **The "I-know-it-all" God.** Read Psalm 139:1-6. Create a book cover for your Bible that reflects this message.

● **The God of loving concern.** Read Psalms 8:3-9; 86:11-13. Fill in and decorate the coat of arms for

170

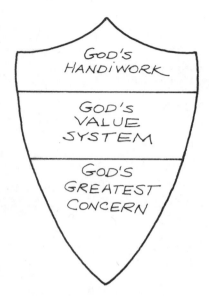

God's Handiwork

God's Value System

God's Greatest Concern

God. (Distribute art supplies.)

● **God's power demonstrated.** Read 1 Corinthians 15. Develop a choral reading to emphasize the idea of God's power of death. (Use responsive readings from the church hymnal as a guideline for designing your choral reading.)

RESPONSE (OR CLOSING)

Regroup and share your results. Praise the groups for their efforts.

Distribute paper and pencils to the youth and have them write their responses to the following: God is all knowing, all powerful, all seeing and all loving. Because of this, I need to contemplate_____ _____. Apply this at home and at school.

How should this statement alter what you feel about yourself and others? What should you do in your life to exemplify this?

Close with a prayer asking God to open your heart, mind and eyes to that which God wants you to comprehend.

HELPFUL RESOURCES

It Is Finished, February 1982, GROUP Magazine, P.O. Box 481, Loveland, CO 80539.

---

[1]J.I. Packer, **Knowing God** (Downer's Grove, Ill.: InterVarsity Press, n.d.), p. 37.

IN SEARCH OF GOD'S WILL

by Karl Blaser

PURPOSE

To help young people find and accept God's will for their lives and to help them see how God revealed his will to the people of the Bible.

PREPARATION

Gather seven balls (such as basketballs, volleyballs and footballs), seven towels, two rectangular tables, blankets or sheets large enough to cover the tables, a watch with a second hand (or a stopwatch), Bibles, pens, paper and posterboard.

On the posterboard, write out these verses: Psalm 119:58; Proverbs 3:5-6; Matthew 6:25-27; 7:7-8; Romans 8:28; and Ephesians 5:17.

Make copies of the Eight Steps to Discover God's Will, as listed in the Closing section.

Select three or four Bible characters and write scripts telling how God called them to his will. Refer to the sample dialogue and questions in the "Meat" of the Meeting section.

Each dialogue should be about five or seven minutes in length. Characters to consider for the skits include the disciples, Abraham, Sarah, Mary, Jonah, Moses, Elijah, Samuel, Isaiah, Joshua or David.

Enlist adults to play the roles and go over the lines with them.

Help the actors prepare their costumes and props. Items can include robes, fake beards, sandals, makeup and props such as staffs and a slingshot.

Set up the opening crowdbreaker. Put the two tables end-to-end with just enough space between for a person's head. Drape the sheets across the tables and put the seven objects on the table. Use the towels to cover the items.

Post the scriptures you wrote on the posterboard.

OPENING

Open with prayer asking the Lord to use the meeting to help you learn more about his will in your lives.

Ask five volunteers to leave the room. After they have left, enlist another volunteer (such as a pastor or sponsor) to come to the tables. Have this person put his or her head between the two tables, place a towel over his or her head and arrange the sheets so that the appearance is given that there are eight objects on the table, rather than the seven. Tell this person to yell or make a face when the towel is raised.

Explain to the group that the five volunteers will be returned to the room individually and will be told they are participating in a timed contest to see how quickly they can identify the eight objects on the table. Encourage the group to get excited and cheer. This will make the contestants push harder and add fun when the towel is lifted to reveal the head.

As each contestant returns to the room, explain that on the word "go" he or she is to race alongside the table grabbing the towels and shouting the name of the object he or she uncovers.

After all the contestants have participated, ask the group how this contest and God's will for their lives are similar. After a brief discussion, explain that even before they were born God had a will and plan for their lives and that, although his will might not seem clear now, in time God will reveal it. In the same manner the contestants did not know the identity of the objects on the table until they lifted the towels.

THE "MEAT" OF THE MEETING

Read the scriptures on the posters and ask the young people to give you one word per verse that summarizes their interpretation of the scripture.

Explain that according to these verses, God does have a will for their lives and has known it from the beginning of time. They are to seek his will yet are not to worry about his design because "in everything God works for good with those who love him, who are called according to his purpose" (Romans 8:28).

Say, "Now that we have discussed this, let's look at some Bible characters. We'll see how they were called by God, how the Lord showed them his will and the way it affected them."

Before you bring each actor into

the room, tell the youth where to turn in their Bibles. For example, "Turn with me to Exodus 3 where we will learn about how God showed his will to Moses."

At this point the biblical character, in this case Moses, enters. A sample dialogue is:

Moses: Hi, leader. Hi, everyone. What a place for a time warp.

Leader: Moses, what are you doing here?

Moses: Well, actually, I thought I'd come to talk about God and how he called me into his ministry.

Moses can now tell the story in his own words, read directly from the scriptures, or make this into a question and answer period.

Sample questions can be: How did God's will for your life become known to you? What was God's task for you? Did you question the will of God? If so, how did God deal with you? Did God help you with your task?

After the character has told his or her story and answered any questions from the group, introduce the scripture for the next character and in this manner continue with each skit. More than three skits are likely to become repetitive.

RESPONSE (OR CLOSING)

Ask the young people what they learned from the skits. Lessons from Moses can include:
● God uses everyone despite handicaps.
● God prepares us throughout life.
● God controls the future.

After this discussion, ask, "Does God still call us in the same way he called these Bible characters? If not, how does he call us?"

Hand out the Eight Steps to Discover God's Will. Ask the youth to work through it. If you have time, discuss the answers.

Read Proverbs 3:5-6 and pray for the wisdom to recognize and accept God's will.

Eight Steps to Discover God's Will

1. Use your intelligence.
   - Most people have the ability to analyze and choose between right and wrong.
   - God is pleased when we use our ability to think.
   - Response: What do I think is God's will for me?
2. Face yourself realistically.
   - Take a good look at yourself. Be objective, but don't be afraid to strive for a goal.
   - There are things you can and cannot do. Don't be overwhelmed by what you can't do, rather focus on the gifts you have.
   - Response: What can I do to learn God's will?
3. Read your Bible.
   - The will of God will not go against scripture.
   - God's will has more meaning with study. "Thy word is a lamp to my feet and a light to my path" (Psalm 119:105).
   - Response: What is one thing I can do to better understand the Bible?
4. Commit yourself to God.
   - Re-evaluate your ambitions and goals. Don't hesitate to reach for the stars.
   - Develop a strong will and character by seeking God's guidance instead of your own and by seeking advice from spiritual leaders.
   - Give your problems to God. "Cast all your anxieties on him, for he cares about you" (1 Peter 5:7).
   - Response: What is one thing I can do to draw closer to God?
5. Pray for guidance.
   - Spend time thinking and meditating.
   - Response: What is one area of my life that most needs guidance from God?
6. Study the circumstances.
   - God operates his will within life situations.
   - Learn from your mistakes.
   - Rest in God's love for you (Romans 8:28).
   - Response: What kinds of circumstances in my life have revealed God's will?
7. Wait patiently on the Lord (Habakkuk 2:3).
   - Response: How difficult is it for me to be patient?
8. Be flexible about your decisions. God may want you to do one thing for a little while and change later (Acts 8).
   - Response: In any given situation, do I see only one option or many options?

TEMPTATIONS

by Paul Copeland

PURPOSE

To help young people understand that temptation provides wrong answers to pressing questions.

PREPARATION

Gather a bucket or small trash can, magazines, newspapers, 3 × 5 cards, Bibles, pencils or felt-tip markers, paper, chalkboard or overhead projector.

OPENING

Begin by playing the Scripture Mixer![1]

Scripture Mixer

Distribute slips of paper with vital parts of well-known Bible scriptures on them. Let everyone roam about introducing himself or herself to one another and read their piece of scripture. If he or she finds someone with the corresponding scripture, stay together until the scripture is completed.

For example, the person with a slip reading, "Even though I walk through the valley of the shadow of death" must find the person with, "I fear no evil, for you are with me," and the other people with the rest of the 23rd Psalm.

THE "MEAT" OF THE MEETING

Discuss:

Are there degrees of sin such as white lies and big lies?

Are some sins unforgivable? See Matthew 12:31-32.

What are turning points in the Bible caused by sin?

Read Romans 3:23. Does this mean we can sin repeatedly?

From memory, name the Ten Commandments. Now refer to Exodus 20:3-17. Silently think of any commandments you recently have broken.

What commandment did Jesus give us? Read John 13:34.

RESPONSE (OR CLOSING)

Lead a discussion about pollution of our natural environment. Guide the group in its discussion to discover that there also can be "sin pollution in a Christian life."

Place a trash can in the center of the room. Distribute magazines, newspapers and 3 × 5 cards. Ask the group members to cut out or write the word or phrase of something that contributes to "sin pollution" in their lives. The list can include items such as lying, bad habits, greed, jealousy, evil companions or going to questionable places. Place each of these in the trash can.

Ask each youth to select a card or cut-out from the trash can and write on the back ways to eliminate the "sin pollution." Let the youth share their responses.

On chalkboard or overhead write:

175

Two ways to deal with sin pollution
Your Way
God's Way

Share 2 Timothy 2:22. Encourage the group members to realize that one way to deal with sin pollution is to have several friends who really love Christ! Discuss the impor-tance of living a Christian life.

Select 10 youth to read the Ten Commandments.

Close with the Lord's Prayer.

---

[1]Thom Schultz, ed., **The Best of Try This One**, (Loveland, Colo.: Group Books, 1981), p. 22.

THE STRAYING AND THE STRAIGHT

by Dean Dammann

PURPOSE

To help the good news of God's great love be made more real for all participants. To have participants relate God's love to their times of straying. To have participants repent of self-righteousness and reaffirm their dependence on Jesus Christ.

PREPARATION

Make copies of the Bible and Study questions in the "Meat" of the Meeting or write the questions on a chalkboard for all to read.

Gather paper, pencils and Bibles for the group.

OPENING

Form groups of six to eight. The person with the darkest hair leads the group.

Take a few minutes to get acquainted. Have the youth share a good thing that happened during the past week.

THE "MEAT" OF THE MEETING

Distribute paper, pencils and the handout:

Study Questions

Television and newspapers frequently carry stories of lost children. When these incidents occur, a massive search usually is started until the child is found. To explore how it feels to be lost or to have lost something, do one of the following:

A. Recall a time in your life when you were lost. Write a brief report about the experience, including your feelings.

B. Recall a time when you lost something that was important to you. Write a few notes about the experience. Identify your emotions.

The youth share their reports; those who answered "A" begin. Before those sharing "B" begin, talk about the common elements in the stories. The groups should make a list of the feelings experienced. The "B" experiences should then be shared. Find the common elements in the stories and make a list of the feelings experienced.

Luke 15 has three stories about being lost—the lost sheep, the lost coin and the lost son. The latter story is often referred to as the story of the prodigal son. Refer to the first two stories in verses 1-10. In groups discuss possible reasons Jesus told the stories.

Bible Questions

To dig deeper into the theme of this Bible study quickly read Luke 15:11-32. Note the attitudes and feelings you think were exhibited by. . .

- the lost son.
- the father about the lost son.
- the elder son.
- the father about the elder son.

If you were to put yourself into the story of the lost son, where would you fit? On the continuum below indicate where you think you are right now:

"Strayed" 9 8 7 6 5 4 3 2 1 "Straight"
(lost son)   (elder son)

The youth should share self-ratings and reasonings. (If your meeting area allows, replicate the continuum on the floor and then have each member of the group take a place physically to demonstrate his or her location. While standing, have each share why he or she chose the particular location.)

Explain: From the stories of Luke 15, it is clear that God celebrates when people are no longer lost. The stories also give insights as to the response he expects from "sons." See verses 7 and 10. God expects us to . . .

As people try to fit the role of being "respectable," they can lose sight of what God expects. Make a list of how Christians today fall into the traps of being straight, respectable and pious as did the Pharisees and teachers of the law in Luke 15:2. Example: criticizing those who don't attend church or Bible classes.

Individually identify where you have strayed or flaunted your piety. Silently confess and pray for God's forgiveness.

RESPONSE (OR CLOSING)

Sing a song to celebrate God's forgiving love or share a sentence prayer beginning with the words, "I thank and praise God for . . ."

GOOD OL' GUILTY ME

by Joani Lillevold

PURPOSE

To explore feelings of guilt and to celebrate the forgiveness we have in Christ.

PREPARATION

Collect Bibles, pencils, paper, a watch, and prepare two signs: one printed "Agree" and the other "Disagree."

Place the "Agree" and "Disagree" signs at opposite ends of the room to represent a continuum.

OPENING

Introduce the study topic by using this information:

Guilt. It's one of those haunting feelings that creeps into your life and before you know it, grabs control. It's a vicious monster you seemingly can't avoid.

As much as that squeamish feeling prevails, you might be surprised to learn how sparingly the Bible refers to guilt. Even though the Old Testament refers to guilt more than 100 times, the New Testament only uses the word "guilty" six times and the word "guilt" twice (both times in John 9:41).

Regardless of biblical reference, guilt remains a struggle to those who try to live a Christian life. Apart from Christ, we're hopelessly trapped by sin. When we look honestly at who we are, we fall short of the ability to supply the cleansing, freeing power needed. Only in connection with Christ can we hope for joy and forgiveness.

Guilt can be embarrassing, uncomfortable and difficult to talk about; however, I want you to share as you feel—don't share if you don't want to.

To get in touch with personal perspectives, let's begin with this agree/disagree exercise. (Explain the "Agree" and "Disagree" signs at opposite ends of the room represent ends of a continuum.) As I read the questions, stand somewhere along the imaginary line that best describes how you feel about the following statements:

● Most people feel guilty about things that really shouldn't bother them.

● People should feel guilty; it makes them change their ways.

● If someone hurts you, saying it's "okay" is the same as saying, "I forgive you."

● You can usually tell when a person is guilty.

● God uses guilt to make us better people.

● The more guilt you feel, the worse you are.

● If you don't feel guilty about something, you probably are not guilty.

● Guilt is easy to dismiss.

THE "MEAT" OF THE MEETING

If your group is large, form

179

groups of six to eight for the discussion activities. Gather in a circle. Tell everyone to silently read Romans 3:19-20. Then ask one volunteer to read those verses aloud. Ask each person, beginning with the person who woke up the earliest that day, to complete this sentence, "I know when I've sinned, because . . ."

Ask participants to close their eyes. Say: "We're going to use the next three minutes to do something that we usually don't take the time to do. I would like you to get in touch with what's inside of you—your thoughts, your feelings, who you are. (Read Romans 3:19-20 once more.) Pause now and reflect on times or a specific time you've felt really guilty about something. I'll be keeping track of the time, so you don't need to worry; I'll let you know when it is time for you to open your eyes."

After three minutes say, "With your eyes still closed, let me read someone else's feelings about guilt." (Read Psalm 51:1-12.)

Have people open their eyes. Encourage each person to share these thoughts with the group:

When I feel guilty, I . . .

When I heard the words of the Psalm, I felt . . .

Guilt devastates. If we stopped here, life would be empty and hollow. But we don't stop here. As Christians, our guilt doesn't need to control us. A life-giving focus doesn't center on ourselves alone —but on our connection with Christ. By his resurrection, we are freed from the mess of guilt.

Together read Romans 3:21-24. Note the shift in action. God is the Actor, the Doer, the One who puts people right. Have each person find a partner. Distribute pencils and paper to each pair. Instruct each pair to read Romans 3:21-24 and write two questions about the verses. To get the youth started, you can suggest questions:

One thing we don't understand is _____

When we read _____, we wonder why _____

What does it mean when it says _____

When partners have written two questions, they should exchange the queries with another pair. Have each couple write answers to the questions they've received. After sufficient time, gather the entire group. Have each pair read the questions and their answers. Encourage further discussion and questions. Ask: What did you learn about the passage? Are there issues that need more study? How can you make these words come alive in your life?

God puts us right with him through his son, Jesus. That's a gift! We experience that special gift of forgiveness and a new life through each other.

Read this statement to your group, "It is about as easy to absolve yourself of your own guilt as it is to sit in your own lap" (Frederick Buechner). Discuss that idea. For fun, have each person try to sit in his or her own lap.

God places people in our lives for the privilege of living what is meant to forgive and be forgiven. End your time together with a celebration of forgiveness and freedom from guilt.

Have your group members form two lines that face each other; have the youth face the partner they had from the previous activities. Ask each person to think of a guilt struggle that he or she is facing. Encourage partners to share those feelings. If they feel uncomfortable, remind them that no one is forced to share.

RESPONSE (OR CLOSING)

Now lead the young people into a quiet time between themselves and God. They can remain facing their partners. Have the youth silently read 1 John 1:9. Encourage the youth to pray to God and confess their guilty feelings and ask him for cleansing and freeing. Remind them to thank God for his promise of forgiveness. Allow three to five minutes for this prayer time.

Ask partners to express the forgiveness and love we have in Christ by saying to each other, "God loves you; you are forgiven!"

Forgiveness is cause for celebration. Have everyone stand in two lines. One by one, each person walks between the lines. As each person walks through, have others extend a sign of love and assurance of forgiveness such as hugs, handshakes, pats on the back and words of care.

After everyone has gone through the line, join hands in a circle for a giant hug of celebration.

RESPECT FOR THE DISABLED

by Sandra Wilmoth

PURPOSE

To consider practical manners and respect for the disabled.

PREPARATION

Invite a disabled person to speak about day-to-day matters and what the able-bodied can do to make life easier.

In advance have group members write questions such as: How can people help the disabled? Is our church handicap-accessible? What stores in our area need to make more concessions to the disabled?

Contact your library and other resource centers for printed material that can be copied and distributed. Prepare copies of Tips for Aiding the Blind in the "Meat" of the Meeting section.

Note: Other speakers can include a teacher from a local school who works with the disabled, a social service worker, or city official who has knowledge of policy and procedure for working with disabled employees.

OPENING

Introduce the guest speaker. The speaker can talk about physical barriers and other problems that make day-to-day existence more difficult for the disabled.

THE "MEAT" OF THE MEETING

Have the speaker answer the previously written questions. Encourage discussion and more questions.

Distribute literature you may have obtained and copies of:

Tips for Aiding the Blind

There are things a sighted person can do to aid the blind. The following pointers are designed for day-to-day situations you might encounter:

● Talk to the blind person. Don't think that because a person is blind, he or she also is deaf.

● Don't take the blind person's arm, let him or her take yours so that you, the sighted person, are leading, not pushing. To take a blind person's arm and push him or her along can be hazardous, especially when approaching stairs.

● As for the door, lead the blind person through. If the door opens in, tell the blind person on which side the door opens so he or she can put out a hand and you can continue walking through together.

If the door opens out, stay in front of the blind person, pull the door open, and tell the blind person the door is on the left or right. But if the blind person has a guide dog, it might not be necessary for the sighted person to help.

● To help a blind person enter a car, lead him or her to the car and put his or her hand on the doorhandle. Allow the blind person to open the door. This helps the person get his or her bearing.

● To go up or down stairs, don't try to count the steps.

The logical thing is to say, "Here are

stairs." Specify whether they go up or down.

As you, the sighted person, continue leading, your arm goes up and the blind person knows you're still going up stairs. Once your arm levels off, the blind person knows there are no more steps.

When descending steps, start down first, don't insist the blind person step down at the same time.

● To get on an escalator: When no one is waiting to get on, put the person's hand on the rail. He or she can then use his or her feet to find a step. Once the person is on, get on behind him or her.

● When you approach a table, take the person's hand and place it on the back of the chair and let him or her figure out where to sit.

● When seated for dinner, don't give commentary unless there's something strange about the place setting—if the dinner napkin is in the water glass. You don't need to say, "The fork's on the left, the knife and spoon are on the right and the plate's in the center."

● When the food is served, the sighted person can look at it like a clock, and say, "The meat is at 12 o'clock, the beans at 3, the roll at 6 and the salad at 9."

If the blind person asks, cut his or her meat, but wait for the blind person to tell you what he or she needs. Don't grab the plate and start cutting as if he or she were a 3-year-old.

● Behavior around guide dogs is important: Don't pet the dog!

● Try not to criticize the dog. The dog is not a machine. Dogs have personalities; like people, they also have idiosyncrasies.

● If you're walking with a blind person and the dog takes off in the wrong direction, which means your blind friend also is going the wrong way, don't call the dog. There may be a reason the dog is going the wrong direction. If not, call to the person, not the dog.

RESPONSE (OR CLOSING)

Introduce an activity to let the youth actually experience blindness during the next week. Each person picks a partner and one will be blindfolded while the other is his or her companion. Then switch the roles. Go to a shopping mall, out to eat, walk in the park—experience what an everyday activity would be like without sight. Record feelings and discuss them at the next meeting.

Ask the guest speaker to close with prayer.

HEAVEN IS . . .

by Cindy S. Hansen

PURPOSE

To provide a time for youth to voice thoughts about heaven, to imagine what heaven is like, and to discuss scripture references about heaven.

PREPARATION

Gather a Bible, paper, pencils, crayons, tape, a record player and a white piece of posterboard.

Obtain the song "Dear Father" by Neil Diamond on the **Jonathon Livingston Seagull** album, or other types of "heavenly" music.

Cut the piece of posterboard in the shape of a cloud and at the top print "Heaven is . . ."

Write the words to the song "Heaven Is a Wonderful Place" on a chalkboard (optional). This can be found in the songbook: **Kids Praise**, Marantha Music, Word, 4800 W. Waco Dr., Waco, TX 76703.

Mix a batch of sugar cookie dough and refrigerate it for the optional activity in the Response section. You also will need an oven, frosting and decorating candies.

OPENING

Hand out paper, pencils and crayons and instruct the youth to draw a picture of heaven. Tell them to incorporate the letters of the word "heaven" in their drawings. For example, if they think heaven is full of angels, an H could be the body of an angel; E, the wings; A,

the head; V, the legs; E, the feet; and N, the songbook. At the bottom of the page have the youth finish the sentence, "Heaven is . . ."

. . . a place with angels singing praises to God.

Save these pictures until the Response section.

THE "MEAT" OF THE MEETING

Play "Dear Father" or other samples of "heavenly" music and instruct the young people to mingle. Periodically stop the music. At each musical rest, the youth choose a partner and answer the following questions as the leader asks them:

● What is one word that describes your feelings of heaven?

● It has been said that earth is the real heaven or the real hell. Do you agree or disagree? Why or why not?

- What types of activities will we do in heaven?
- What does it take to get into heaven?
- Do you think St. Peter will meet us at the pearly gates? If not, how will we know we are in heaven when we get there?

Next, instruct the young people to find a partner with the same color of eyes. The partners answer the following questions as the leader asks them. Allow a few minutes for each question.

- Mark 12:25 says, "For when they rise from the dead, they neither marry nor are given in marriage, but are like angels in heaven." What are angels in heaven like?
- Will we meet our family in heaven and have the same relationships?
- Isaiah 66:1 says, "Thus says the Lord, 'Heaven is my throne and the earth is my footstool; what is the house which you would build for me, and what is the place of my rest?' " Compare earth to a footstool. Why is it that way?
- Compare heaven to a throne. Why is it that way?
- How does thinking about heaven make you feel about problems on earth?

RESPONSE (OR CLOSING)

Gather in a large group. One at a time, have the participants share their pictures of heaven from the Opening and the answers to "Heaven is . . ."

Ask the youth if their thoughts of heaven remained the same or changed since the beginning of the meeting. Discuss the differences and similarities of the participants' definitions of heaven.

On the back of their pictures of heaven, have the youth write a prayer of thanks for God's presence on earth as well as in heaven. Share these in a closing circle prayer. Have the young people tape their pictures to the posterboard labeled "Heaven is . . ." and sing the song "Heaven Is a Wonderful Place."

If time permits, participate in a variation of Cookie Decorators.[1] Each person is given a small amount of cookie dough that was prepared before the meeting. Ask the youth to make one or two cookies that represent something discussed in the meeting (angels, thrones, clouds, pearly gates). Bake the cookies in an oven (10-15 minutes) and add frosting and decorating candies.

Display the finished cookies and ask the youth to explain the design. After sharing the ideas, share the cookies.

---

[1]Thom Schultz, ed., **More . . . Try This One** (Loveland, Colo.: Group Books, 1980), pp. 40-41.

HEAVEN

THE PEACE OF CHRIST

by Maryellen Reidy

PURPOSE

To share the peace and joy of Christ in an interdenominational gathering of high school youth.

PREPARATION

Leaders from churches within the community plan topics or themes they would like to present at the weekly gatherings. A schedule is prepared as to when each participating church will host the youth. Plan to begin a new theme every six weeks.

Each hosting church prepares by planning a presentation, devotional, prayer time, songs, games and refreshments.

Materials for each meeting include Bibles, hymnals, musical accompaniment, audio-visual aids, games and literature.

OPENING

Begin with songs and then move to a game that will relax the youth and make them feel comfortable.

For example: Give each person a name tag as he or she enters the hosting church. On the back of each tag print one of the following: hair dryer, lawn mower, sports car, locomotive, alarm clock or typewriter.

When the young people are gathered in one large room, instruct them to begin making the noise of the item that is written on their name tags. All typewriters gather, all sports cars, lawn mowers, and so forth. No other noises are allowed.

Instruct the small group participants to get acquainted. Then each group thinks of a way its item could be useful to get members to attend the interdenominational meeting. The hair dryer group might say, "We're the hair dryers and we're instrumental in grooming people's hair so they look their best and want to come." Let imaginations work freely when thinking of the usefulness of lawn mowers or locomotives.

THE "MEAT" OF THE MEETING

Have a church leader give a presentation that's based on the scriptures and that relates to the overall theme for each week.

Examples of themes include:
- A study of Acts
- The lives of the disciples before and after Christ's death and resurrection
- Comparison of the Gospels
- Old Testament giants of the faith
- The Israelites' journey to the promised land
- Job and his "friends"
- Witnessing
- Cults
- Drugs
- Dating
- College

- Careers
- Lent and other church seasons

RESPONSE (OR CLOSING)

Conclude each meeting with a prayer of thanksgiving for the time to gather as God's children.

The host church serves refreshments. Remind the group of the date and location of the next meeting.

GROWING OLDER

by Linda Webster

PURPOSE

To acquaint young people with some of the joys and concerns of the elderly and to help them consider the aging process in their own lives.

PREPARATION

Find the poem **Rabbi ben Ezra** (Grow Old Along With Me . . .), by Robert Browning, available in many poetry books; the Beatles' recording, "When I'm 64" in the **Sgt. Peppers Lonely Hearts Club Band** album (and copies of its words); gather a record player; paper and pencils.

Invite an older person to share with the group and be a part of the whole meeting.

Note: This meeting can lead to further studies on death and dying, specific joys and concerns of aging (such as Social Security or retirement), and service projects for the elderly.

OPENING

Welcome and introduce your guest to the group. Have each person share his or her name and describe an "ideal age." What makes that age special?

Have someone read **Rabbi ben Ezra**. Discuss the poem using questions such as: What do you think the poem is saying? Do you really think the best is yet to be? How is the "first of life" related to the "last of life"?

THE "MEAT" OF THE MEETING

Pass out paper and pencils and have each member list 20 things he or she loves to do. After the youth have had time to do this, code each item on the list as follows:

$ = costs money.
1 = can be done alone.
E = involves the use of special equipment.
65 = will be able to do when 65.

As a group, discuss the lists in terms of the possibility of limited finances, widowhood, never married, health or physical ability. Help participants think about the activities they enjoy and are engaged in now. Is there long-term potential for enjoyment and participation?

Listen to "When I'm 64." Have copies of the words available. Determine what year it will be when most of the participants reach the age of 64. Discuss what they think the world will be like then and how they see themselves as a part of it.

Invite your guest to share his or her feelings regarding aging. Make this an informal time and allow opportunities for discussion and questions.

RESPONSE (OR CLOSING)

Invite the participants to share

one thing they hope to accomplish in their lives—make this a personal goal rather than career goal. Little comment needs to be made about these except to acknowledge and appreciate them.

Share some of the apostle Paul's thoughts as he wrote to his "son in the faith" Timothy (2 Timothy 4:6-8). It is thought that Paul wrote these words with the knowledge that his life and ministry on earth were soon to be completed. Notice as the passage is read what Paul feels he has accomplished.

How do you think Paul felt growing older? Do you think Timothy listened to what Paul said? Have you had special relationships such as Timothy and Paul's? Who is an older person you respect and admire today?

Read Jesus' promise, "And lo, I am with you always, to the close of the age" (Matthew 28:20). Allow a few moments for the youth to discuss this promise and the feelings it brings. How do they feel about their concerns of aging after hearing this verse?

Ask the guest to close with prayer thanking God for the joy of growing older with his presence.

AN INTERGENERATIONAL EVENT

by Arlo R. Reichter

PURPOSE

To build relationships between youth and senior adults in the church; to help the elderly understand youth; and to help young people articulate their perspectives, feelings and faith.

PREPARATION

Select hymns and a scripture reading for the opening. Invite senior adults who are willing to share their past experiences.

Prepare a list of appropriate questions for sharing. The youth and elders can prepare the questions in advance. (Sample questions are in the "Meat" of the Meeting.) Arrange a comfortable meeting room.

Invite senior adults to bring early-day family pictures and ask the youth to bring current pictures of family and friends. Prepare a place to display the pictures. Post the photographs as the participants arrive.

You can ask all participants to bring a special food item that reflects their heritage.

Note: If one senior adult for each youth is not able to attend, adapt by having two or three young people for each senior adult. If no senior adults are available from your church, do this activity with a local nursing home or senior citizen recreation center.

OPENING

Open the meeting with a welcoming statement, singing, praying and reading of scripture verse.

Ask the participants to pair with someone from the other age group.

Have the pairs introduce themselves and tell how long they have been active in the church. Have them share their first memory of a church—when, where and what kind of experience they had. Ask each person to introduce his or her "new" friend to the rest of the group.

Have the pairs tell each other about the pictures they brought explaining when, where and why it was taken.

THE "MEAT" OF THE MEETING

Have the pairs discuss the previously prepared questions. Keep the process moving by giving the questions one at a time.

Examples of questions are:
● What problems did the senior adults face when they were young?
● What problems do youth have today?
● What influences other than parents did the senior adults have when they were growing up?
● What influences do today's youngsters have other than parents?
● Compare church involvement of the elders when they were grow-

ing up to the participation of to-day's youth.

● How did the senior adults express their faith (confirmation, baptism, testimonies, devotionals) when they were young?

● How do today's youth express their faith?

● How did each become a person of faith?

● Other subjects can be: family life, social issues, biblical applications to life and education.

Call the group together and ask each person to share something he or she has learned. As each person shares, have the entire group repeat, "That's great!"

RESPONSE (OR CLOSING)

Close with a devotional that encourages their relationships. An appropriate text would be 1 Corinthians 13.

You may want to:

● Serve the potluck dishes or refreshments.

● Have the participants exchange names and addresses.

● Suggest the participants sit with their "new" friends in Sunday worship with an explanation to the congregation of the meeting that has taken place.

● Keep the pictures on display for several weeks.

JEALOUSY

by Cindy S. Hansen

PURPOSE

To become aware of jealousy, to understand everyone experiences it and to find ways to deal with this emotion.

PREPARATION

Prepare a question sheet on the topic of jealousy and make copies for everyone:

Jealousy

1. Most people my age react to jealousy by:
2. I'd get jealous if . . .
3. Can we make someone jealous? If so, why would we want to?
4. What are other feelings related to jealousy?
5. What makes jealousy so dangerous?
6. How does jealousy lead to other emotions?
7. Do people ever have good reasons to be jealous? If so, when?
8. Is jealousy between members of the same sex as strong? Why or why not?[1]

Gather Bibles, paper, crayons and pencils for everyone.

Get a paper bag and fill it with pieces of paper. Write on each piece either one noun (time, boy, castle, etc.), one verb (guzzled, typed, ran, etc.), one adjective (beautiful, ugly, magnificent, etc.), or one adverb (quickly, slowly, grudgingly, etc.). Include enough words so that everyone will have one.

OPENING

Tell the group members they are going to be storytellers and they are going to tell a story about jealousy. Begin passing the bag. The first person draws a slip of paper and must make up a sentence to begin the story using that word. For example, if the first word chosen was "boy" the person could begin with, "Once upon a time there was a boy named Jim." Then the bag is passed to a second person. If the word is "ugly" the next line could be, "Jim was a nice boy, but he was afraid that people thought he was ugly." The storytelling continues, staying with the theme of jealousy. The last person in the circle ends the story with a moral (using a word from the sack). Example: If the word is "time," "The moral of the story is: Jealousy is a waste of time . . . try to get away from it." A variation of this game can be done with actors. Choose people to act out the story as it progresses through the narration.

THE "MEAT" OF THE MEETING

Webster's dictionary describes jealousy as, "Resentfully

suspicious of a rival or a rival's influence. Resentfully envious."[2] Ask for other definitions of jealousy. What does jealousy feel like?

Distribute the jealousy question sheets. Allow time for everyone to finish. Gather them in groups of threes or fours. Share answers to the questions.

Have the small groups read Proverbs 6:34; 14:30; 27:4; Solomon 8:6; 1 Corinthians 3:13; 13:4; James 3:16. What does each verse have to say about jealousy? Does each verse have a personal message? How do these verses help "cure" jealousy?

Read Philippians 4:7-8. Does this offer any other ideas to end jealousy? What are some of the ways each person deals with this emotion?

RESPONSE (OR CLOSING)

Using some of the suggestions, have each small group design a jealousy cure. Distribute paper and crayons or markers. Describe the ingredients of the cure. How many times a day do you have to use this cure? For how long? What is its name? What are other direc-

tions that are necessary to have a complete cure? Share with the large group. Example:

Ingredients: 70 times 7 good thoughts.

Dosage: Three times a day for as long as needed or when symptoms of jealousy occur. Additional help for complete cure: Gargle with good thoughts and follow by reading Philippians 4:7-8.

Close with a circle prayer. Each person says a need or a thanksgiving. Everyone in the group then prays aloud for the person on his or her right. End the prayer by thanking God for his help during the difficult emotions of life.

HELPFUL RESOURCES

Feelings, by Willard Gaylin, M.D., Ballantine Books, 10 E. 53 St., New York, NY 10022.

---

[1]"Sexual Jealousy Is Worldwide," GROUP Magazine (March/April 1984):A11-A12.

[2]Webster's New World Dictionary, 2nd ed. (New York: Simon and Schuster, 1980).

THE ADVENT OF CHRIST

by Bill Pieper

PURPOSE

To prepare for the Advent of Christ by involving young people in thought-provoking study and meaningful activities.

PREPARATION

Gather paper, pencils, Christmas carol songsheets or albums (see Helpful Resources), and a record player.

Have youth bring Bibles from home.

Make copies of the Prepare Ye the Way of the Lord study sheets:

Read the following, "You have just received a telephone call in which Jesus Christ has informed you that tomorrow night he will be at your home for dinner and you are to prepare the feast."

Have the students list five to 10 things they would have to do to prepare for this visit. Allow a few minutes to discuss these lists within the small groups.

THE "MEAT" OF THE MEETING

Have the group silently read

Prepare Ye the Way of the Lord

1. Read Luke 3:1-18. Why is it necessary to prepare for the Advent or the coming of Christ?
   a. John says, "Prepare the way of the Lord."
   b. We have to get into the spirit of Christmas.
   c. We are threatened with an unquenchable fire.
   d. It is expected.
   e. Jesus is coming.
2. Rate yourself on a scale of one to 10 as to where you are in your preparation for Advent. (One is totally prepared and 10 is absolutely unready.)

3. Share with your group why you do or do not feel prepared.

4. The Christmas season is almost here. Complete this statement: In preparation for the Advent, I will . . .

5. Share your preparation item with your group.

OPENING

As the participants arrive, play Christmas carols (tapes or recordings). To open the meeting, sing carols. Then divide into small groups.

Luke 3:1-18 and make one of the following pencil marks by appropriate verses:

! = makes you feel good or excited.

? = you do not understand.

194

✔ = worth remembering.

Have members in the small groups share their verse notations. Invite youth to share their interpretations of those verses that others did not understand.

Hand out the Prepare Ye the Way of the Lord study sheets. Share the thoughts about what it means to prepare for the coming of Christ.

RESPONSE (OR CLOSING)

Gather in a large group and think of Advent activities to do together. Ideas include: Bake Christmas cookies for shut-ins; carol for shut-ins, hospitals and nursing homes; make decorations for the church; or raise funds to contribute to hunger organizations.

Close by singing carols such as "O Come, O Come, Emmanuel."

HELPFUL RESOURCES

Carols of Christmas, Augsburg, 426 S. Fifth St., Minneapolis, MN 55415.

HAVE YOU SEEN JESUS?

by Lee Sparks

PURPOSE

To help young people sort their thoughts and feelings toward Jesus, to encourage a positive response from them toward Jesus.

PREPARATION

Obtain one songbook with "Have You Seen Jesus My Lord?" and a few other upbeat songs. A good resource is **Songs**, Songs and Creations, P.O. Box 7, San Anselmo, CA 94960.

Collect a good variety of pictures of Jesus. Check with your church or other neighboring churches for these pictures and post them in the meeting room.

Gather a blackboard or a large newsprint pad, felt-tip markers, paper, pencils, Bibles, old white dress shirts (one for each person and a few extras in men's large size), and newspapers or other protective material to put under the shirts during the opening activity.

Obtain one copy of **Try This One . . . Too**, available from Group Books, P.O. Box 481, Loveland, CO 80539. This book is full of ideas for youth groups.

Make refreshments. Prepare the Jesus Is . . . worksheet described in the Response section of the meeting design.

Note: The white shirts can be found in closets, uniform supply services, second-hand stores, garage sales, flea markets, etc. Or have each youth bring an old white shirt from home.

OPENING

Begin this meeting with a few rousing songs and gradually move into more mellow tunes. End with "Have You Seen Jesus My Lord?"

Pass out the white shirts and do the White Shirt Party described in detail on page 50 of **Try This One . . . Too**. This creative activity helps youth better get to know each other and themselves.

Spread a few newspapers over the floor. Give each person a felt-tip marker and a shirt. Have the youth write 20 things about themselves on their shirts (such as birthday, favorite color or favorite Bible verses). When everyone is finished, have them wear the shirts for the rest of the meeting.

THE "MEAT" OF THE MEETING

Pass out paper and pencils. Ask the youth to write 10 words used by their friends, adults, famous people and others to describe Jesus. Ask volunteers to read their lists. Write these words on the newsprint pad (or blackboard). Discuss: What words were used most? least? Do you agree with all the words?

After you've made the big list, have the young people stand next to the piece of artwork that best depicts how they understand Jesus. Have volunteers give reasons they stood next to each particular picture. Ask why Jesus is seen in different ways by different artists.

Break into smaller groups (about five persons per group). Take turns reading these passages: Mark 2:5-12; 14:61-64; John 8:51-58; 10:30-39; 14:6-14. Have one person in every small group write the theme of each passage. What does Jesus say about himself? Share these with the whole group.

If you have time, repeat this process with Bible passages in which others describe Jesus: Matthew 16:15-17; John 5:18; 11:25-28; 1 Peter 2:22-24.

RESPONSE (OR CLOSING)

Pass out the prepared Jesus Is . . . worksheets. The sheet lists clarifying statements (add your own if you want):

Jesus Is . . .

____a close friend

____someone people my age are embarrassed to talk about

____someone to turn to when I hurt

____someone who cares for the poor

____someone who died for me

____someone who cares for people, no matter what

____a judge

____a person who gives new life

____a loving father

____a punisher

____other (explain)

Ask the youth to rank these statements. (Mention that all the statements have some degree of truth.) "1" is most important; "10" is least important. Have the youth compare their sheets with people around them and explain why they ranked the statements as they did.

Ask each person to pick one word or phrase that *best* describes his or her belief right now about Jesus. Encourage honesty. For example, tell the group that it is okay to have some doubts about Jesus. Encourage persons to feel free to write something like, "You're someone special and I want to know you better, Jesus."

After everyone has chosen the word or phrase, ask the people to write it with a felt-tip marker on a shirt in the center of the room. This shirt will be Jesus' white shirt. After this, have the people write the same word or phrase on their own white shirt (see the Opening section of this meeting design).

Close with singing "Have You Seen Jesus My Lord?" and a group prayer. Enjoy the refreshments.

CHRISTIAN JOY

by Mark Reed

PURPOSE

To lead youth to a practical understanding of Christian joy and to assist them in securing and maintaining that joy in their lives.

PREPARATION

Collect felt-tip markers, three sheets of posterboard, chalkboard, chalk, pencils, paper, three 3 x 5 cards for each person, tape and Bibles.

If you use the laugh tape or giggle record in the Opening you will need to purchase one or make your own. Make one by recording four or five people in a small room. One person starts chuckling, then giggling, another joins, then another, until everyone is roaring with laughter.

Bring a tape player or record player to the meeting.

Write one of the following incomplete sentences at the top of each posterboard:

There is joy in . . .
If it feels good . . .
Happiness is . . .

Post the signs about the meeting room.

Ask a youth to lead several choruses about joy such as: "The Joy of the Lord Is My Strength," "Rejoice in the Lord Always," "There Is Joy in Serving Jesus," and "I've Got the Joy, Joy, Joy, Joy."

Arrange chairs in a circle with the chalkboard in front.

Copy the Joy in Jesus discussion guide in the "Meat" of the Meeting section. Make one copy for every four or five youth.

OPENING

As the youth arrive, distribute markers and ask them to complete the posterboard sentences with a word or phrase (in graffiti fashion).

After everyone has written ideas, ask the song leader to begin the choruses.

As an option, play the game Poor, Poor Puppy. One person selects someone in the circle and tries to make that person laugh or smile. The person may only touch or pat the other person on the head and say, "Poor, poor, puppy." If the person cannot break the subject's solemn look after saying this three times, the player must move to someone else. No other words may be spoken but gestures and facial expressions are unbounded. Play passes to the person unable to keep a straight face.

Another "laughable" activity is to play a laugh tape or giggle record. Start the tape without introduction—soon everyone will be laughing.

THE "MEAT" OF THE MEETING

Divide into small discussion groups with a sponsor or leader in each group. Each leader receives a copy of the Joy in Jesus discussion guide, pencil and paper.

Joy in Jesus

1. What color do you think of when you hear the word joy? Why?

2. How would you define joy? Refer to the graffiti posters.

3. Where does joy come from? Make a list of the sources of joy. See Philippians 1:3-7; 2:2, 17-18, 28-29; 4:1, 10-13. What caused Paul to rejoice?

Have each group complete its list and share answers with the large group. Read Philippians 3:1 and 4:4. Ask, "Why do you think Paul commands joy?"

To make a distinction between joy and happiness, write "Happiness" on the chalkboard and write "Happen" below it. Explain that happiness depends on what happens, but joy does not depend on circumstances. Rather, joy depends on personal relationships to God. Happiness is a rollercoaster ride while joy continues regardless of circumstances. (Paul wrote the Philippian letter while in prison.)

Write on the blackboard, "Joy is an attitude."

Ask, how do you feel about that? What do you think it means? How, then, can we have joy when we're in the midst of troubles? Refer to Paul's life noting the importance of self-sacrifice, unselfishness, putting others first and the need to depend upon God as the source of joy.

Return to the groups and have the youth write a description of the joyous Christian's outlook on life. Have each group share its descriptions.

RESPONSE (OR CLOSING)

If time permits, give each youth a pencil and two 3 x 5 cards. Ask the participants to write on the left side of one card something that makes them happy and on the right side something that makes them unhappy. On the left side of the other card have them write "Joy comes from Jesus," and on the right side list the times they had the least joy.

When all are finished, have them tear the cards in half. Provide tape for them to put opposite sides together so the unhappy and happy sides are mixed.

Remind them that in Jesus, the happy and sad times flow together and have little effect on our Christian joy. The other card serves as a reminder during the difficult times that Jesus is the reason for and source of joy.

From the group lists of the joyous Christian's outlook ("Meat" of the Meeting), ask the youth to choose one characteristic they need in their lives. Have them write it on another 3 x 5 card, and how they will immediately utilize that characteristic in their lives. Allow time for volunteers to share their commitments with small groups.

Close with prayer in the groups. Encourage each person to pray for the person on his or her right.

A YOUTH-LED MEETING

by David Olshine

PURPOSE

To get away from adult-led youth ministries and instead to put the youth in charge. In so doing, the youth can develop responsibilities and maturity while strengthening their ability to serve God.

PREPARATION

Arrange for youth to assume the leadership roles in Bible studies and special events. Work with them and suggest study material and how they can obtain the items (see Resources for suggestions).

Help with the initial structure. Youth will have to be chosen to lead games, music, prayers, discussions and to make announcements. Make the necessary literature available.

Plan to meet weekly with the youth leaders to give guidance and keep updated. Emphasize you will be available to answer questions or to help with "snags" that might develop.

OPENING

The game leader plans about 15 minutes for activities, followed by 10 minutes of music led by the song leader (see the Resources for game and song ideas).

Follow this with the guidance leader who can give a brief outline of the meeting and explain its purpose.

THE "MEAT" OF THE MEETING

The study session should be the pivotal part of each meeting.

Your initial meeting should touch on the subject of spiritual gifts and how they will be used in this meeting series.

Romans 12:1-8 is a good study verse because it emphasizes the renewal and transformation of the mind and proper usage of these gifts. Emphasize that everyone has gifts. Some have the gift of teaching, others the ability to sing, still others the ability to relax people with crazy games. Encourage all youth to participate as leaders in upcoming meetings.

The study leader explains that as the weeks go by, each leader will attempt to experiment and expand spiritual gifts. The leader should encourage other youth to "step out" and to use spiritual gifts of mercy, faith, giving, exhortation and administration.

For example, the youth might plan a "help program" to involve all the group. Certain youth would decide who could use a helping hand such as elderly, poor or those with small children. Others would be in charge of working with these people and assigning youth to help. Examples include: Give an elderly person a ride to and from church, baby-sit for an afternoon with young children or have a food

200

drive for the needy. For this same program, other youth would be in charge of a study time to discuss the feelings the youth had while helping others and ways these emotions tie to the Bible.

The emphasis is to be on setting and living model standards.

RESPONSE (OR CLOSING)

The study leader can conclude by challenging the youth to "donate" their gifts. As the leader gets an idea of the attributes of the participants, he or she can write these down for reference and for planning of future projects.

The announcement leader gives notification of upcoming events and the next week's student-led meeting.

The prayer leader can close with a prayer that asks for maturity and perseverance to make the meetings worthwhile.

HELPFUL RESOURCES

Try This One, More Try This One and **Try This One . . . Too**, Group Books, P.O. Box 481, Loveland, CO 80539.

Insights for Living, Chuck Swindoll, P.O. Box 4444, Fullerton, CA 92634.

Songs, compiled by Yohann Anderson, Songs and Creation, P.O. Box 7, San Anselmo, CA 94960.

BE MY VALENTINE

by Dean Dammann

PURPOSE

To have the young people list characteristics of love as related to the love of God. To write a prayer asking help to better love Jesus, others and oneself.

PREPARATION

Provide paper, felt-tip markers or crayons, magazines with colorful pictures, scissors, glue or tape. You also will need a blackboard.

Prepare the Love handout in the "Meat" of the Meeting.

Note: Valentine's Day is an excellent occasion for this meeting. However, this design can be easily adapted for use any day of the year.

OPENING

Form groups of five to seven. The person with the darkest eyes serves as group leader.

If necessary, take a few minutes to get acquainted. Have the youth tell about a favorite party they attended when they were younger.

THE "MEAT" OF THE MEETING

In the small groups decide on a definition of love.

Distribute the art supplies and handout:

Love

Webster's New World Dictionary lists the following definitions of love:

- A deep and tender feeling of affection for or attachment or devotion to a person or persons.
- A strong, usually passionate, affection of one person for another, based in part on sexual attraction.
- A strong liking for or interest in something.
- A feeling of brotherhood and good will toward others.
- God's benevolent concern for humanity.
- Humanity's devout attachment to God.

Love has a different meaning for each of us. Which definition best defines the love you are most in tune with lately? Explain.

Valentine's Day is an occasion to show our care for others through messages of love. The Bible is filled with such messages. Pretend that you are one of God's angels with the task of choosing valentine texts. The valentines will be sent by God to his family on earth. Read 1 John 4:7-21 to find appropriate valentine messages. List messages for three valentines: one you think would be appropriate for yourself and two others for friends or family members. Use the art supplies to design the valentines.

Share your valentines with the group. Explain who the valentines are for and why you chose the recipients.

The last verse of 1 John 4 tells us to love others even as we love God. How are we to love? Read 1 Corinthians 13:4-8 and choose characteristics of love that apply to people you know. Choose at least two to rewrite or paraphrase as valentine messages and then design the new valentines.

Tell the group who you would send the valentines to and explain why.

If you were to receive a valentine, what would you want it to say? Share your selection with the group.

RESPONSE (OR CLOSING)

Gather in a large group. Read Matthew 22:35-40. Ask who is to be loved?

Use the chalkboard and explain:

The word JOY can be used to remind us of the command to love—
Jesus
Others
Yourself

Tell the youth to reflect on their love of Jesus, others and themselves, deciding which has been most neglected. Have the youth write a prayer asking for help in loving Jesus, others and themselves. The prayer should be as specific as possible. When everyone has written a prayer, have a period of quiet for each to silently pray. Close by praying together the Lord's Prayer.

WE LOVE YOU, GOD

by Ben Sharpton

PURPOSE

To lead young people to express an active love for God.

PREPARATION

Prepare copies of the Love worksheet and two copies of "The Unemployment Line" skit (both in the Opening section).

Gather Bibles, pencils, blackboard, chalk or newsprint and felt-tip markers.

In advance, ask two young people to perform "The Unemployment Line" skit. Help them gather props.

Become familiar with the scriptures used in this session. Work to determine what it says to you about loving God. Answer the questions used with John 21:15-19.

Prepare the room. Help the two youth ready for the skit.

Pray for guidance and assistance throughout the session.

OPENING

Begin this meeting in your traditional manner. Group singing or special music can be included at this time. Be certain to make announcements and to welcome guests.

Explain that the word "love" can be used in many ways. This session will concentrate on the action of love more than the feeling. Distribute copies of the Love worksheet to each member.

Ask each participant to list the names of three people they care about in the column on the left (can be anyone). Then in the second column the youth should jot specific things they do to show their love. After the members have had an opportunity to work through this section, have them write "God" after number four in the first column and then in the second column list specific actions they take to show their love. Ask for volunteers to name ways in which the love we show God differs from that which we show to others.

The two young people now can perform the skit:

The Unemployment Line

Scene: An unemployment office, with two or three lines of people waiting to see clerks seated behind a desk. God is dressed in everyday apparel.

Clerk (talking on the telephone): I don't care how many children you have, Mrs. Johnson, we've denied your request for aid. I don't have the power to give to every con artist who tries to take advantage of government funds. Who do you think I am, God? Why not get a job, for a change? ...Well, goodbye. Who's next? (Disgustedly looks toward God.)

God: I think I am. I'm a little confused, you see, I've never filed

Love Worksheet

PERSON	HOW DO YOU SHOW LOVE TO THIS PERSON?
1._____	_____
	_____
2._____	_____
	_____
3._____	_____
	_____
4._____	_____
	_____

for unemployment compensation before.

Clerk: Sure. That's what they all say. Well, what's your name?

God: God.

Clerk (gives questioning look): Where do you live?

God: Here. Everywhere.

Clerk: Is this some kind of joke? Am I on one of those hidden-camera television shows? Are you a television personality?

God: This is no joke. I'm as serious as sin. I am God.

Clerk: What are you doing here?

God: Well, I'm standing in an unemployment line, talking with you because, it seems, I am unemployed.

Clerk: Why don't you tell me about it. What was your job before you decided to file for unemployment?

God: I started out as the Creator. I made everything, even you. And it was good.

Clerk: I've heard that before.

God: Oh? You've read my book?

Clerk: Just parts of it. Continue.

God: Well, I went about my task of blessing man, loving him, giving to him, caring for him while he cared for the rest of my creation. Unfortunately, we were separated because man chose to do things his way, instead of mine.

Clerk: Really?

God: Yeah, but that's not all. I tried to guide my people. First through the prophets, but the people wouldn't listen. Then, I visited them in person through my Son, Jesus, but they killed him. Still, through it all, I have offered man an opportunity to share my love. Some accepted, but most just ignored my offer.

Clerk: So what's stopping you from continuing as you have since the beginning? You know, do a little creating, a little blessing, lots of loving.

God: That's a good question. Man is such an independent snob, he has tried to replace me with himself. Of course, that's been the problem all along. People seem bent on doing things their own way, regardless of what I say or what I do.

Clerk: Why don't you teach them a lesson. You know—really zap them. How about a flood?

God: I tried that.

205

Clerk: Well, why not fire and brimstone?

God: I've tried that. Remember Sodom and Gomorrah?

Clerk: How about miracles? Healings? Raise someone from the dead!

God: You haven't been doing your homework. I couldn't be with you today if I hadn't done that awhile back.

Clerk: Well, what's made you come here?

God: It's just gotten so bad. I took a real chance in putting people in charge. I gave them this beautiful world, and they've used and abused it, changed and rearranged it, ripped and stripped it, polluted and . . .

Clerk: I get the point.

God: No you don't. You see, for everything I offered, man came up with a counterfeit. I offered a beautiful natural world, and he came up with big air-conditioned glass buildings and little air-conditioned cars. I created compassion and concern, and he created cool and macho. I offered meaning and purpose in life, and he came up with sex appeal, popularity and fashions. I offered sexual intimacy in marriage and he created soap operas. How can I combat that? Let's face it. Television is powerful.

Clerk: It sure is.

God (clears his throat): Can I continue? You see, I'm out of a job. All that is pure, true and lasting which I have offered to man has been replaced with man's little plastic creations. Here's a prime example. I gave man the responsibility to love and care for the world—that includes other people. Man really finds purpose and meaning when he gives to others. But he's turned things around. He's always trying to find meaning by receiving instead of giving. If people really loved me, then they would love one another.

Clerk: That's a good point. I guess we have gotten things turned around a little bit. Why not give us a little more time. Maybe the church . . .

God: The church! It's sad, but so many churches are caught in the same endless race. They either build bigger buildings or go for bigger memberships. Even Christians seem ignorant of what it means to love others. What makes you think they love me?

Clerk: Perhaps you ought to wait just a little longer. Maybe Christians will come around and begin to show their love for you by loving others. Give us some time.

God: Well, I do feel a bit optimistic, after talking with you. Let's talk more often, okay?

Clerk: Don't worry, I'll be in touch. Thanks for dropping in.
(God walks away, smiling. Clerk picks up the telephone and dials.)

Clerk: Mrs. Johnson. I'm calling from the unemployment office. Something's come up and I think we might be able to give you some help. We'll begin by reconsidering your request for unemployment compensation. You will have to drop by to sign some forms. And, I know a couple of churches that . . . yes, churches. Well, they might be able to help you get some food until your checks come through. I also know where you might receive some clothes that are in pretty good condition. Can you come in this afternoon? Good. I'll see you then. Bye.

Next? (a little more sincerely.)

THE "MEAT" OF THE MEETING

Ask volunteers to read the folowing scripture passages. After each person reads a scripture, ask the group to suggest specific things that God wants people to do. List these on the blackboard or on newsprint: Psalms 15:1-4; 50:8-23; Matthew 19:16-21; John 14:15, 21; 15:8-14; 1 John 4:7-12.

Review the list and ask the youth to summarize it in a few words. The group members probably will say "love" or "obey." Challenge the young people to give specific answers as to how they can love and obey God.

Read together John 21:15-19. Use these questions to aid your discussion:

● Why do you think that Jesus called Peter (the name he gave him previously) "Simon" (his former name)?

● What did Jesus ask Simon in verse 15? If you were one of the disciples, would that have offended you? How did Simon respond? What did Jesus mean by "take care of my lambs"? Is there any significance to the fact that Jesus asked the same question three times? For example, Peter denied Jesus three times or because he wanted to emphasize the question. Note: For advice, confer with someone who can interpret the original Greek.

Again read John 14:15 and 15:9-12. Ask everyone to turn back to the worksheet used at the beginning of the session. Give the participants time to examine the names they listed in the left column and the actions they used to show love in the right column. Ask the young people to think of someone else they know who needs to receive the kinds of love they have shown in each of the three examples. For example, they might have said that they showed love for their fathers by doing chores or making good grades in school. Perhaps there is a teacher who needs that kind of love. Have the members write the name of each person they intend to show love to next to the names in the left column.

RESPONSE (OR CLOSING)

Close in prayer asking God for strength and guidance to love one another. Have each person take his or her worksheet home, and encourage the young people to pray daily for the people named on the sheet.

MODERN-DAY PARABLES

by Cindy S. Hansen

PURPOSE

To study the reasons Jesus taught with parables; to exercise creativity in making meaningful, up-to-date parables of our own.

PREPARATION

On 3 x 5 cards print the following parables: Matthew 13:2-12; 13:24-30; 13:31-32; 13:44; 13:47.

Gather props in a bag such as old shoes, scarves, hats, mirrors, dolls and tablecloths.

Collect enough paper, pencils and Bibles for everyone.

OPENING

The opening game is a variation of Forward and Backward.[1] Everyone sits in a circle of chairs and moves according to the answers of the following questions. Since not everyone answers the questions the same way . . . pileups on the chairs soon occur!

1. All those who have done a good deed today like the good Samaritan, move one chair to the right.

2. All who today feel like the man who was beaten and left to die, move three chairs to the left.

3. All who have read or heard a parable sometime in the past week, move two chairs to the right.

4. In the parable of the sower, all who feel like the seeds that fell along the path (hear the message but do not understand it) move three chairs to the right.

5. All who feel like the seeds that fell on rocky ground (hear the message gladly but it doesn't sink in and last long) move one chair to the left.

6. All who feel like the seeds fallen in the thorn bush (letting the worries of the world choke you) move one chair to the left.

7. All who feel like the seeds sown in good soil (hear and understand the message and bear fruit) move two chairs to the right.

8. All who are wearing yellow (the color of a mustard seed) move three chairs to the left.

THE "MEAT" OF THE MEETING

Read the parable of a sower (Matthew 13:3-13) to begin discussion. Ask the group members if they think parables are a good, effective way of teaching. What makes the parables powerful? Why do you think Jesus taught with parables? What must a story include before it is a parable?

Split into small groups and give each group a parable on a 3 x 5 card and a Bible. What are the facts brought out in the parable? Comparisons? What is the point of the parable? What people were involved? Think of a contemporary way to communicate the message of the parable.

An example of a contemporary

version of the parable of the sower is: A mother and father have four kids. One kid watches TV all the time and is oblivious to his surroundings—devoured in the world (as the seed that fell along the path and was devoured by birds). The second child watches TV and maybe picks up a magazine now and then (as the seed that fell on rocky ground with little soil). He has no depth and is oblivious to what is good for him. The third kid parties and hangs around with rough kids. Any good thoughts that he might have had are choked out of him (as the seed that fell among thorns). The fourth child listens to his parents, has many friends and helps all in times of trouble—he hears the word and bears fruit (as the seed that fell on good soil and brought forth grain). The parents love all their children and even though they are happy with their fourth child, they are sad that the first three didn't live up to expectations. Just as our heavenly father loves us all and hopes for the best from all his "seedlings."

A variation of pantomiming a parable is to use props. Instruct one member from each group to pick a prop (without looking) from the prepared bag. Each group now acts out the contemporary parable using the prop. For example, if the group that acted out the parable of the sower had a box of macaroni as a prop—child one might use it as a TV, child two could use it as a magazine, child three could use it as a radio and hold it to his ear and child four could use it as a Bible, etc.

Ask the entire group if the parables were more meaningful when translated to today's life. What new insights were gained? Are there any additional reasons you think that Jesus taught this way?

RESPONSE (OR CLOSING)

Now that you have worked with Jesus' parables and made a contemporary version of them, it is time to make up your own. It doesn't have to be a modern day variation of an old parable. It could be totally new, totally original, totally you.

Instruct each person to think of a favorite Bible verse. Then think of the things God has given such as nature, animals, the seasons, family and friends. Next, think of comparisons: This (a favorite Bible verse or phrase) is like this (something you are thankful for). Example:

The peace of God is like
The healing touch of a physician
The soothing hug of a mother
The comforting presence of a father
All rolled up in one.

Pass out paper and pencils and let the youth attempt to write their own parables. Share with the entire group. Pantomime these parables if time permits.

Close the meeting by giving thanks to God for stories to hear and lessons to learn.

An extra game to play is a variation of Scripture Hunt.[2]. Select a short parable and divide it into five parts. Write the first part onto a piece of paper with a clue which will lead the finder to the next words of the parable and the second clue. Example: using Matthew 13:33:

"He told them another parable . . ."
CLUE: Ashes to ashes.

The group would proceed to the fireplace and find the second piece of paper.

> "The Kingdom of heaven is like leaven . . ."
> CLUE: A book a day keeps the blahs away.

The group would proceed to the church library.

The last part of the parable will include a clue that will lead the group to refreshments.

> "... til it was all leavened."
> CLUE: Old Mother Hubbard.

This activity is done as a group with the first clue given by a group leader.

---

[1]Thom Schultz, ed., **More . . . Try This One** (Loveland, Colo.: Group Books, 1980), p. 29.

[2]Lee Sparks, ed., **Try This One . . . Too** (Loveland, Colo.: Group Books, 1982), p. 55.

PARABLES ON FILM

by Martin Doering

PURPOSE

To write and produce a film based on a parable. The participants will better understand the parable as a teaching tool and will be able to act out the importance of Jesus in their lives.

PREPARATION

Gather Bibles, paper, pencils, newsprint, felt-tip markers, film projector and screen, video camera with cassette recorder and play-back screen or home movie camera, blank film for 20 minutes, and a copy of a short Christian film. Suggestions for films include: **The Parable** (National Council of Churches); **The Fable** (F. Niles Communications); **The Music Box** (White Lion Pictograph). To order these write: ROA Films, 1696 N. Astor St., Milwaukee, WI 53202. Or check with your church office for a gospel film catalog.

When the time comes to make your film, you will need an adequate location. If you meet at night, consider artificial lighting. If you meet during the day, outside locations can be used if the sunlight permits.

If possible, borrow the equipment rather than renting or buying. Use individuals who are properly trained to operate the equipment. (You might want to arrange a learning session in the use of the equipment.)

If you are using a movie camera instead of video, find a photo lab that offers quick, reliable development.

Producing a movie can be a costly venture, so you'll want to have enough participating to make it worthwhile.

If cost is a factor, consider producing the film as a special Sunday school lesson or as an adult Bible study. Funds might be more easily justified when you can demonstrate continuing significance.

Arrange tables and chairs so all can easily view the screen. Ask the youth group members to sit at the tables as they enter the room.

Note: Allow two hours for the initial meeting (getting the idea for the movie, casting, rehearsal, etc.). Allow 30 minutes for filming and 30 minutes for viewing after the film is developed or the video is complete.

OPENING

Make certain all participants have a Bible, paper and pencil. Ask them to list their favorite television program and the reasons they like it. Have them briefly discuss the program with persons at their table.

THE "MEAT" OF THE MEETING

View a short Christian film and then discuss it.

Ask: What was the point of the film? How did the characters help develop the theme? How does the film tie in with the Gospels? How did it make you feel? Does it help you to better understand the Gospels?

Say to the group: "Stories are used to make a point. Even jokes have meanings that deal with human behavior. Jesus used stories to help his followers understand the power and meaning of the kingdom of God. Parables have been defined as earthly stories with a heavenly meaning. Parables are told to illustrate a central truth. Three of Jesus' parables are the good Samaritan, the prodigal son, and Lazarus and the rich man. Let's choose one of these parables: The good Samaritan is in Luke 10:25-37; the prodigal son is in Luke 15:11-31, and Lazarus and the rich man is in Luke 16:19-31. (After the participants have chosen a parable, read the text.)

Discuss the parable and manner in which it can be produced into a movie. Select the scriptwriter, actors, extras, technical crew, camera technician, director, and people to be in charge of costumes and makeup.

If the film equipment has sound capabilities, the technical crew will use the posterboard and felt-tip markers to write cue cards. If you are making a silent movie, the technical crew will be responsible for the title and cue cards.

After you have decided how to enact the parable, walk through the actions once or twice to determine camera angles, entrances, exits and rhythm.

Organize a time to meet again for the actual filming. When that day arrives, have everyone hold hands for a prayer asking God to bless the production of the film. Then, "Places everyone! Lights! Camera! Action!" Produce a movie!

RESPONSE (OR CLOSING)

When you have finished filming, ask the youth to re-evaluate their feelings regarding the parable and the manner in which it pertains to their lives.

After the video is completed or the film is developed, make arrangements for a premiere. Invite all involved in the production, church members, family and friends.

Close with a prayer of thanksgiving for the unique ways God makes his gospel known to us.

HELPFUL RESOURCES

TeleKETICS Films, Filmstrips and Slides, St. Francis Productions, 1229 S. Santee St., Los Angeles, CA 90015.

Concordia Film Rental Catalog, Concordia Film Service, 3558 S. Jefferson Ave., St. Louis, MO 63118.

THE PRAYER OF JESUS

by Christian Just

PURPOSE

To explore the Lord's Prayer in a new and meaningful way with youth, and to help the youth reflect upon their Christian life in relation to the Lord's Prayer.

PREPARATION

Type the questions listed in the "Meat" of the Meeting and make copies for each participant.

Note: If you want to be more creative for this meeting, produce these questions in an Encounter Booklet. Each booklet should measure 8½ × 2 inches and be fastened on the left side by a brad (so it can be fanned out). You can assemble the booklets by printing each page on a 2-inch section of 8½ × 14-inch paper (thus giving you seven pages per sheet), running them off (duplicating, copying or mimeographing), cutting into 2-inch strips and collating. You may want to add a front and back cover with heavier paper (such as cardstock). Each page has one phrase of the Lord's Prayer and all its open-end statements (see "Meat" of the Meeting).

Schedule a meeting area, preferably a place that affords privacy such as a gymnasium, sanctuary or park.

OPENING

This meeting is best initiated by getting to the task as quickly as possible, without lengthy introductions or explanations. You will need to explain a dyadic encounter and "walk through" the rules for this exercise.

Explain to the group members they will be sharing their faith in one-to-one (or dyadic) encounters.

Ask each youth to find a partner, preferably not a close friend. Distribute the encounter questions and send the pairs to areas where they can have some privacy. Inform them to return to the original gathering spot when they have finished their discussion.

THE "MEAT" OF THE MEETING

The meeting will center on the dyads in conversation, with the following material as a guide:

A Dyadic Encounter With the Lord's Prayer

You are invited to share with one other person, as honestly and openly as possible, your thoughts and feelings about each of these statements. Such one-to-one sharing is called a dyadic encounter. This experience is designed to help you get to know your partner and yourself more thoroughly. The discussion items, all based on the Lord's Prayer, are "sentence stems" that you are to complete. There are no right or wrong answers—just your own feelings.

The following rules should be

213

observed:

- Do not look ahead in this material.
- Anything you discuss with your partner must be kept confidential.
- Each partner responds to each statement before continuing. If either partner chooses, he or she may decline to respond to a statement.
- Listen attentively. Do not criticize or evaluate your partner's responses.
- Take this experience seriously, but not somberly.
- Answer each statement openly and honestly.

OUR FATHER

My relationship with my earthly father is . . .

The qualities I want in a father are . . .

When I think of God as my father, I think of . . .

WHO ART IN HEAVEN

If I were to describe my idea of heaven, I would say it is like . . .

My most "heavenly" experience so far has been . . .

I look forward to being with God in heaven because . . .

HALLOWED (HOLY)

To me, holiness means . . .

I think of myself as holy when . . .

When I consider God's holiness, I think of myself . . .

BE THY NAME

When I hear someone else abuse God's name, I feel . . .

If I abuse God's name, I feel . . .

THY KINGDOM COME

When I picture Jesus as a king, I see . . .

The idea of Jesus' kingship helps me to . . .

214

THY WILL BE DONE

The best way to discover God's will is . . .

Who, of the people you know, best understands God's will for his or her life?

ON EARTH

I believe God's will for me now is . . .

What I think is God's will for me right now makes me feel . . .

My biggest problem with doing God's will is . . .

AS IT IS IN HEAVEN

The person who best helped me grow in my Christian life is . . .

This person has helped me to . . .

Jesus' statement, "You must be perfect . . ." (Matthew 5:48) makes me feel . . .

GIVE US THIS DAY OUR DAILY BREAD

The one material thing I most desire right now is . . .

When I see the belongings of my friends, I feel . . .

The belongings I own are . . .

FORGIVE US OUR TRESPASSES

One time that I experienced forgiveness was . . .

I need forgiveness now for . . .

AS WE FORGIVE THOSE WHO TRESPASS AGAINST US

I have difficulty forgiving someone who . . .

I need to forgive . . .

For me to forgive this person, I must . . .

LEAD US NOT INTO TEMPTATION

My most frequent temptation is . . .

I usually deal with temptation by . . .

My "success" in dealing with temptation is . . .

BUT DELIVER US FROM EVIL

The greatest evil in the world today is . . .

If I had the power to change this, I would . . .

Sometimes I wonder why God allows . . .

FOR THINE IS THE KINGDOM

I want Jesus to be my king, but . . .

If Jesus were truly my king, I would . . .

AND THE POWER

I sense the power of God at work when . . .

I question God's power when . . .

AND THE GLORY

Christians can glorify God . . .

I think that I glorify God when I . . .

FOREVER AND EVER

The concept of "forever" makes me feel . . .

God is eternal. This statement makes me feel . . .

AMEN

Spend a short time in silence with your partner.

Join hands and pray with each other, for the hurts and doubts you've shared, for the joys you've discovered and for any questions you may have of the future.

RESPONSE (OR CLOSING)

The dyads will be ending their encounters at different times — some will finish quickly, some may want to spend a longer time together. If you have set maximum time limit, call "time" when that point is reached. Otherwise, let them continue as long as their conversations are productive. If you sense that any dyads have come to a point that their conversation is unproductive, invite them to conclude and move back to the central meeting point.

As the dyads begin to filter back to the starting place, gather them in groups of four to six. Give them 10 minutes to share answers to the following questions:

● What did you discover about yourself?

● What was the biggest surprise?

● Are there any changes you plan to make in your life?

● What new insights did you find in the Lord's Prayer?

● Will these make a difference in your prayer life?

After all the dyads have had the opportunity to discuss the above questions, gather into a circle for a chain prayer. The leader begins the prayer with a petition or thanksgiving and then squeezes the hand of the person to the left, who is thus invited to add his or her petitions and then squeezes the hand of the person to the left, and so on. When all have added their prayers, conclude with the whole group saying the Lord's Prayer.

THE RUNAWAY

by Robert C. Crosby

PURPOSE

To show the importance of recognizing responsibilities, to encourage youth to be faithful in fulfilling these duties, and to help youth set priorities in this area.

PREPARATION

Gather Bibles, nine 3 x 5 cards for each participant, felt-tip markers, paper, pencils, newsprint and posterboards.

About a month before the meeting, assign the monologue of Jonah to an adult. Provide any needed resources, including costume and makeup.

Study the book of Jonah and prepare the five Info Segments in the "Meat" of the Meeting.

Two or three weeks before the meeting, assign each of the chapters of the book of Jonah to four youth. Have them learn Jonah's life so well they'll be able to describe it to the group in their own words.

Prepare the impromptu Crew assignment sheets in the "Meat" of the Meeting and the Priorities Totem Pole sheets in the Closing.

On the posterboard, prepare a large version of the Priorities Totem Pole.

Note: This meeting lasts one to two hours.

OPENING

Have the adult present the monologue of Jonah.[1]

In sequential order have the four youth spend about four minutes for their presentations of the chapters of Jonah.

THE "MEAT" OF THE MEETING

Divide into five groups and appoint leaders to each. Each crew will be responsible for reading and dramatizing a part of Jonah's life. Allow 20 minutes for preparation.

The impromptu assignments are:

Crew 1:
Jonah Was "Religious"

Jonah was self-centered, jealous, blood-thirsty and lazy; he was a patriot and lover of Israel, but he didn't have the proper respect for God or his enemies (1:9).

Crew 2:
Jonah Was a Runaway

Jonah ran from the presence of the Lord (1:1-3).

Crew 3:
Jonah Was Reprimanded

Jonah directly disobeyed God. God didn't ask Jonah to go to Nineveh—God commanded Jonah. God then sent a storm and a huge fish to discipline Jonah (1:4-17).

Crew 4:
Jonah Repented

God forgave. Jonah regained his senses and returned to God's will (2:1-7).

Crew 5:
Jonah Fulfilled His Duty

Jonah took the message of God

to Nineveh (3:4).

After the impromptu preparation time, ask the participants to return to their seats. Begin the brief impromptus with crews 1 through 5 consecutively. After each impromptu, share a brief Info Segment.

Info Segments

How many times have we heard of the benefits of knowing God? In comparison, how often have we heard of the responsibilities of knowing him? The Bible speaks of God as Savior fewer than 40 times, but it refers to him as Lord about 2,000 times. This shows the benefits of salvation are secondary and the responsibilities of obedience are primary.

To further express this teaching, it is helpful to look at an individual who had to learn responsibility. Jonah was such a person.

Jonah Was "Religious"

Selfishness is at the foundation of sinfulness in man. The Bible commands us to avoid it (Philippians 2:3 and 2 Timothy 3:2) and instead to be selfless.

We need to make certain our faith remains pure through attitudes of humility and that we don't become self-righteous (1 Corinthians 13:1-3 and James 1:27).

Jonah Was a "Runaway"

Sometimes life can get very difficult and we feel we can't bear our responsibilities. Jonah felt the same way because he was working against God.

God didn't bring you to this point in your life and in your walk with Christ for you to run away. God has saved you and started you on the course, so you must try to finish. Revelation 3:21 says, "He who conquers, I will grant him to sit with me on my throne, as I myself conquered and sat down with my Father on his throne."

Jonah Was Reprimanded

Jonah already had made a vow to God (Jonah 2:9). God was holding him to that promise. How often do we make vows and promises to God and to friends, yet fail to carry through?

God disciplines us, as does our earthly father. God chastens us because we are dear to him and he wants us to learn to please him by doing his will.

Jonah Repented

God is loving, compassionate and slow to anger. The Bible proclaims that his faithfulness continues to all generations. Even when we fail and are faithless, he is ever faithful.

Jonah Fulfilled His Duty

Nineveh repented, but Jonah was indignant. He was more concerned that he be right and that Nineveh be punished. Initially, because of selfish reasons, Jonah resisted God's will. Then he did God's will, but still with selfish motivation. He was lacking the proper attitude. Where was the compassion (1 Peter 3:8)?

RESPONSE (OR CLOSING)

Distribute to each member a Priorities Totem Pole sheet. Instruct the youth to list their responsibilities by priority.

After a few minutes, put the large poster-sized Totem Pole in front of the group and explain they're now going to merge their priorities to try to choose the top 10 responsibilities of the sincere young Christian.

Try to get as many opinions as possible.

Lead in prayer reiterating the traits and qualities of a good friend and Christian.

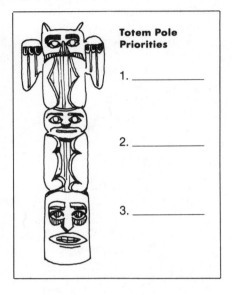

Totem Pole Priorities

1. _____

2. _____

3. _____

HELPFUL RESOURCES

The 12 Minor Prophets, by George L. Robinson, Baker, P.O. Box 6287, Grand Rapids, MI 49506.

The Victor Handbook of Bible Knowledge, 1825 College Ave., Wheaton, IL 60187.

The Zondervan Bible Dictionary, Zondervan, 1415 Lake Drive, S.E., Grand Rapids, MI 49506.

Suggested record album, **Vinyl Confessions**, by Kansas, Corn and Blood, CBS, 1801 Century Park W., Los Angeles, CA.

The Gift of Praise, Maranatha Music, Word, P.O. Box 1790, Waco, Texas 76796.

---

[1]**The Reluctant Missionary,** Downers Grove, Ill.: Contemporary Drama Service, n.d.)

LIFE IN PRISON

by Frank Zolvinski

PURPOSE

To inform students of prison conditions, the need for penal reform, and the importance of law and order. The youth will think of ways they can minister to those in prison.

PREPARATION

Invite an ex-convict to discuss his or her experiences. Ask one who is a Christian.

Before the talk, have the youth write questions they want to ask on 3 × 5 cards.

Questions can include:

Was it worth it to you to commit the crime? What motivated you to commit the crime? Were you innocent or guilty? How did you get caught?

How long did you serve? How did you spend your time in jail? What did you do for recreation? What else is there for an inmate to do? How were you treated? What were the conditions such as cleanliness, comfortableness?

Was it difficult to re-enter society? Do people view you differently as far as employment or family are concerned?

How can the system be improved? How can crime be prevented?

What is your family history? How old are you?

How did you become a Christian? How has your faith altered you?

OPENING

Open with the ex-convict sharing his or her life history and prison experiences.

THE "MEAT" OF THE MEETING

Give the speaker the questions and have him or her respond.

Possible follow-ups or alternatives to this might be to visit a penitentiary or jail, interview a criminal judge or lawyer, invite a news reporter who covers crime, or invite a police officer or sheriff.

RESPONSE (OR CLOSING)

Gather in a circle and discuss ways to minister to prisoners. For example, write to a state penitentiary or jail and ask for names and addresses of prisoners. Assign names of prisoners to the youth and have them correspond, using the church address. Ask the guest to share his or her prison ministry ideas, also.

Close by reading Matthew 25:34-40 and praying for the wisdom to know of ways to help those in need.

DISCOVERING
THE MISSING JEWEL

by Robert C. Crosby

PURPOSE

To help youth recognize their attitudes and opinions toward school, to challenge them with God's view of wisdom and learning and to help them make the best of their learning situations.

PREPARATION

Arrange three long tables and nine chairs for a panel discussion. Write on a huge poster or a banner-size sheet of paper "The Late Great (back to) School Debate."

Obtain several pieces of standard-size posterboard, three for signs to use on the table in the panel discussion and one for each of the five members. Also obtain ink markers, masking tape and Bibles for the entire group.

Contact three high school teachers, three teenagers, and three of their parents to be on the panel.

Arrange for a guitarist to attend the meeting to lead the songs. An assortment of enjoyable choruses can be found in **Communion**, Sparrow Records, 8025 Deering, Canoga Park, CA 91304.

Prepare the debate quiz list found in the "Meat" of the Meeting.

Assign two individuals to prepare refreshments and two people to be "survival agents" in a "survival sign-up." These agents arrive early to register youth for the giveaway and to list the main "survival tactics" they use to make it through high school. Example: "Every Friday my friends and I go to dinner and talk about the past week."

Consider giving gifts such as books to the panel participants.

OPENING

To set a warm mood for the meeting, you might want to play upbeat Christian music. Christian bookstores often have a good selection of music. As the young people arrive, the "survival agents" begin the "survival sign-up."

Open the meeting with praise songs. Then give the youth a few minutes to tell what they dislike most about school.

THE "MEAT" OF THE MEETING

Have the survival agents highlight some of the "survival tactics."

Seat the three teachers at one table, three parents at the second table, and three students at the third table. Try to get a good balance of responses from all three tables. Begin the panel discussion. Questions can be along the line of:

- Where would you place school on the "priorities totem pole"?
- How much time should be spent studying?
- What should a student look

for in a school friend?

- How involved should young Christian people be in extra-curricular activities?
- What are your goals for this school year?
- What are the biggest hassles of school?
- How would you change your school?
- What will motivate a student to study and learn?
- How can parents and teachers help a student's school life?
- How can a Christian student divide the wheat from the chaff in what is taught?
- Does school help you in the growth of your faith?
- What should be expected of a student by teachers and parents?

As you close the debate, distribute the gifts to the panel members. If you have time, there is a second part to this meeting—A Peek at Paul's Prayin'.

Divide into small groups and appoint group leaders. Provide each group with a piece of posterboard and ink markers. Then give the groups the following assignments: Your mission is to take a peek at the prayers of Paul. What was he asking God to do for the Christians in Ephesus, Philippi and Colossae? In single words, cover your board with Paul's requests. Study Ephesians 1:17-19; 3:14-19; Philippians 1:9-11; and Colossians 1:9-14.

Allow 20 minutes, then let everyone view the completed posters, and ask for explanations and discussion.

RESPONSE (OR CLOSING)

To "cap" the meeting, give a short teaching on the subject of wisdom. Consider God's teachings regarding students' attitudes toward teachers and school authorities. Apply Romans 13:1-5.

Discuss what God expects of students. Consider 2 Corinthians 8:7. Other verses to be included are Proverbs 1:5; Ecclesiastes 9:13-18; and James 3:17.

Select a student to close in prayer. Serve the refreshments.

HELPFUL RESOURCES

Education: A Christian View, by John W. Alexander, InterVarsity Christian Fellowship, 233 Langdon, Madison, WI 53703.

Shepherds and Sheep: A Biblical View of Leading and Following, by Jerram Barrs, InterVarsity Press, P.O. Box F, Downers Grove, IL 60515.

Walking in Wisdom, by William E. Mouser Jr., InterVarsity Press, P.O. Box F, Downers Grove, IL 60515.

Survive: The Art of Getting Through High School, Tyndale House, 336 Gunderson Drive, Wheaton, IL 60187.

CREATED IN GOD'S IMAGE

by Bob and Debbie Valleau

PURPOSE

To help young people realize that God made them the way they are and to help them to accept themselves.

PREPARATION

Gather Bibles, paper and pencils and prepare the I'm Okay handout on the next page.

Choose a group leader and assistant and prepare them by providing the following list of techniques to lead the study:

Leadership

● Provide an atmosphere of sharing.

● Stress honesty.

● Stay on the subject.

● Do not let any one person dominate the discussion.

● Do not let the discussion drag.

● Know what the Bible has to say on the subject.

● Ask questions and let everyone respond.

● Conclude with practical ways the Bible indicates should be used to apply what has been learned.

● Pray before and after the discussion.

OPENING

Begin with prayer asking God's guidance and presence.

Explain to the youth that this is a time of approval, not condemnation, and that they can't learn to like others until they first learn to like themselves.

Introduce the group leader and the assistant and let them lead the meeting.

THE "MEAT" OF THE MEETING

Distribute the I'm Okay guide and begin the discussion.

Read these scriptures one at a time: Psalm 139:14,16; Isaiah 45:9; Romans 9:20; 2 Corinthians 12:9; Ephesians 2:10; and Colossians 2:10. How do each of these apply to this study?

RESPONSE (OR CLOSING)

Distribute the paper and pencils and have each participant draw a picture that represents something that is making it difficult to be secure and happy. Discuss these.

Close with prayer, asking, "Lord, give me the guidance to know when to hold on and when to let go and the grace to make the right decision with dignity."

HELPFUL RESOURCES

Youth Aflame Manual, by Winkie Pratney, Spring Arbor Distributors, P.O. Box 985, Ann Arbor, MI 48106.

I'm Okay

The most crucial thing a person can do, other than accepting Christ, is to accept himself or herself.

Why is accepting yourself and learning to like yourself so important, both emotionally and spiritually?

What circumstances and situations make self-acceptance a struggle?

Describe a time you didn't like yourself very much and how it affected you.

How does a lack of feeling accepted and secure as a child affect a person for the rest of his or her life?

How does a lack of self-acceptance affect your relationship with Jesus? with others?

What are some outward signs that a person is having difficulties accepting his or her life?

Why are some people negative and fault-finding?

Why do some people find it difficult to accept affection and love? Do these people find it difficult to convey love?

What is indicated by constantly belittling oneself?

How can you feel secure and accept yourself?

Realizing that God made you just as you are, list your strengths and weaknesses.

Realizing that God is not yet finished with you, what changes do you hope to make in yourself?

Acting as a body of Christ, what can your group do to make itself more acceptable? What can be done to bring a new level of security to the group?

YOU ARE SPECIAL

by Cindy S. Hansen

PURPOSE

To take a closer look at the qualities that make each person a unique creation and to thank God for his originality. To also look at qualities that make each person similar and to thank God for his consideration.

PREPARATION

Gather paper, pens or pencils and Bibles for everyone.

Have yarn and scissors for the opening game.

OPENING

Pass a ball of yarn around with the scissors and have everyone cut a one- to 12-inch piece. Next, have everyone sit in a circle. One at a time, the youth wind the string around their fingers. With each wind they must give a fact of their lives.[1] This is a good game to get everyone acquainted.

Separate the youth members into groups of threes according to sock color—all reds in a group, light blues in another, dark blues in another, and so on. Instruct them to introduce themselves and to tell one recreational activity they like to do. After they have shared, instruct them to find one or two activities they have in common and make a singing commercial. The commercials should be informative so the others will learn more about that small group and

the things they have in common. All commercials can be sung to a familiar tune such as "Row, Row, Row Your Boat." Example:

Cindy, Joani and Lee
all like to ski
to the lodge from over the hills
for hot cider to warm their chills.

One at a time, each trio presents its singing commercial to the large group.

THE "MEAT" OF THE MEETING

Gather as a large group and discuss some of the things everyone has in common. Are these things the entire group enjoys? Point out that although we have many things in common, we are each unique.

Distribute pieces of paper and pencils to the participants. Instruct them to write their names down the side of the paper. By each letter of their first and last names, they are to write a word or phrase to describe themselves that begins with that letter. At the bottom of the paper they are to write the activities they would do in their most perfect morning. See the example at the top of the next page.

Discuss the personal descriptions. How is everyone unique? similar? What about the most perfect mornings? How are they different? Were any the same? How would life be if we all liked

224

> **J**-okes a lot
> **O**-nly sixteen
> **H**-onest
> **N**-ever a dull moment
> **S**-miley
> **M**-any friends
> **I**-ntelligent
> **T**-houghtful
> **H**-elpful
>
> I would get up at 10 on my most perfect morning. Breakfast would be made for me: an omelet with ham and cheddar cheese, pancakes and juice. Then my friends would pick me up to go sailing at a nearby lake.

the same things? looked the same? What would it be like if we were totally different? if we didn't enjoy any of the same activities?

Next, regroup in threes according to shirt colors so the small groups will include new members. Assign each small group one of the following verses: Genesis 1:26-31; John 3:16; 1 Corinthians 1:26-31; Ephesians 1:4-5; 2:4-9; and 1 Peter 2:9.[2]

Each small group answers two questions: What makes us special or unique according to the passage you were assigned? What makes us similar? Regroup and have each small group share its verse and its answer to the two questions.

What do these verses tell us about our uniqueness? What do the verses tell us about God's creativity? How does it make everyone feel to read these verses?

God in his creativity made each one of us special and unique, yet we are similar. We are made in his image and we live with the promise that whoever believes in his son will have eternal life.

RESPONSE (OR CLOSING)

Gather in a large circle for full viewing of the group. Take one minute to think of unique and similar qualities of the group members. Have the youth thank God for the qualities in a closing silent prayer.

Play a variation of the Lap Game.[3] Everyone stays in the circle and faces to the right so that each person is front to back with the next. On the count of three, everyone yells, "To all with these qualities . . . you now will sit on my knees!" Everyone sits on the knees of the person behind him or her and then attempts to walk in that position.

---

[1]Thom Schultz, ed., **More . . . Try This One** (Loveland, Colo.: Group Books, 1980), p.18.

[2]"You Are Special," GROUP (June/August 1981).

[3]Andrew Fluegelman, **The New Games Book** (New York: Doubleday, 1976).

SHYNESS SEMINAR

by Thom Schultz and John Shaw

PURPOSE

To confront shyness in your group. This experience is to help your members feel better about themselves and those around them.

PREPARATION

Gather enough paper, crayons or marking pens for everyone in the group and one roll of masking tape.

OPENING

On each youth's back, tape a blank sheet of paper. Distribute pencils or crayons and instruct the youth to mill about the room. Tell the youth to stop periodically and write on each other's paper a one- to four-word description of that person's best quality. Continue this activity until each person has many descriptions on his or her sheet. Then allow time for all members to remove their sheets and read them.

THE "MEAT" OF THE MEETING

To begin the Shyness Seminar, issue these directions:

On the back of the sheet, give yourself a shyness rating, from 1 to 10, indicating how shy you feel in the group. A score of 1 indicates no feelings of shyness in any situation—a very bold and self-confi-dent person. A score of 10 indicates very strong feelings of shyness in the group—a very in-turned, reclusive person.

Find a place where you can be alone. Underneath your rating number, write a short statement (three or four sentences) of the positive things about yourself that you could tell to others.

Now read your statement aloud. Work on saying it with energy and enthusiasm. Smile, with your head up. Lean forward as you speak. Practice as if you were with someone.

Again, gather as the total group. Pair off with someone sitting beside you. Practice saying that statement about yourself to your partner. Your partner then should give you *positive* feedback, pointing out the qualities in your voice tones, smile, posture and content of the statement itself. Then reverse, with you doing the listening and offering feedback.

Now invite another pair to join you. Then make your statement to the three people. They should then offer positive feedback to you. Follow the same procedure for each person in your foursome. Then talk about how your feelings may have differed in saying your statements to three people instead of one.

Merge your foursome with two or three other foursomes. Make your statement to the entire group. Then anyone who wants can respond with positive feedback. Repeat this procedure for each person in the group.

Now, re-examine your shyness rating. Do you still feel the same? Have your feelings changed? Give yourself another rating, based on your new feelings.

Volunteers now can share their feelings on their two shyness ratings. You may be surprised that some seemingly gregarious members have some significantly shy feelings.

RESPONSE (OR CLOSING)

To close the Shyness Seminar, join hands in a circle. Encourage all members to, in turn, voice a prayer for the person on their left, thanking God for that person's qualities and contributions to the group. Or, have a time of silent prayer in which each member offers a prayer for the person to the right and left. Squeeze the hands of the persons after you've prayed for them, indicating to them your prayerful concern.

IF I WERE A RICH MAN . . .

by Bill Pieper

PURPOSE

To let participants dream about their future needs and wants and also be creative about reality. To realize God as the giver of all and to praise and thank him for his gifts.

PREPARATION

Gather a Bible, pencils, play money or mock checks, and copies of the Dreams and Budget sheets for each person. Find songbooks with "Take My Life and Let It Be." Play The Game of Life or Monopoly at the end of the session if time permits.

OPENING

Ask the young people what they would do if they won $1,000,000 and give them a little time to dream about how they would utilize their winnings.

If the group is small, pass one of the large-denomination play bills from youth to youth. As each one holds the bill, he or she relates his or her money dream.

If the group is large, divide into smaller groups, give each group a play bill, and continue the same sharing process.

THE "MEAT" OF THE MEETING

Distribute the Dream and Budget sheets and the pencils.

Say to the group, "Throughout our lives we will be faced with the reality of living within the blessings which God has given us. We rarely will be given huge sums of money to do with as we please, rather we will have to do our best with what we are given. In this activity you will be given an opportunity to match your dreams to reality. Fill in the Budget sheet with your figures from the Dream sheet. Make your selections as you wish, but fill in all spaces and stay within your budget."

Allow 30 minutes for the participants to fill in the Budget sheet.

Afterward, discuss:

● How did your dreams match reality?

● What dreams were sacrificed?

● Do you think you can match your dreams to reality in the future?

● In what manner did this exercise alter your thinking or dreams?

Discuss Psalms 103:1-5; 116:12-14; and James 1:17. Ask how these passages show the source of all we have. What gifts do we have besides those that are earthly or monetary? What word best describes the way you feel toward the giver of all?

RESPONSE (OR CLOSING)

Sing "Take My Life and Let It Be" and then dwell briefly on the words and meaning of the hymn.

Have a closing prayer thanking

DREAM

Home:	2 Bd. Condo. (buy)	3 Bd. (buy)	4 Bd. (buy)	2 Bd. (rent)
Mortgage	$450	$600	$700	$375
Utilities	150	200	250	150
Furnishings	150	75	80	50
Insurance	25	25	30	20

Car:	Van	Sports car	Sedan	Econ- omy
New	$200	$250	$200	$200
Used	150	200	150	150
Insurance	35	50	25	20
Drive five to 10 miles	40	50	40	35
Drive 10-plus	80	80	65	50

Church: 10 percent or more
Clothing: 8 percent or more
Savings: your choice
Food (meals out each month):
$120 $150 $200

Other insurance:
Medical $50
Retirement $15
Life $20 per 10,000

Extras (select three or more)
Movies (each month)
$5 $10 $15 $20
Payment on a musical
instrument $50
Coffee/pop breaks $15
Boat $80
Cable TV $7
Skiing $150
Second car $150
Newspaper $5
Bowling $20
Golf $50
Credit card $15
Magazine $15
Recreational vehicle $300
Christmas account $25

BUDGET
Income per month $1,600

Home: Mortgage: _____
      Utilities: _____
      Furnishings: _____
      Insurance: _____   Total: _____

Car: Loan: _____
      Insurance: _____
      Gas: _____   Total: _____

Insurance: Medical/dental: _____
      Retirement: _____
      Life: _____   Total: _____
                               Church: _____
                               Clothing: _____
                               Savings: _____
                               Food: _____

Extras: _____   Total: _____

     Monthly expenses: _____

_____

God for his love and care and asking him to lead and guide each of the participants in utilizing the gifts they have received.

If time allows, play The Game of Life or Monopoly.

HELPFUL RESOURCES
Fun 'n Games, by Rice, Rydberg and Yaconelli, Zondervan, 1420 Robinson Rd., Grand Rapids, MI 49506.

"Take My Life and Let It Be," **The Lutheran Book of Worship**, Augsburg, 426 S. 5th St., Minneapolis, MN 55415. (Or borrow one from a Lutheran church near you.)

MATERIALISM—OUR GAIN OR LOSS?

by Peggy Frey

PURPOSE

To get young people to see that wanting and striving to accumulate items or riches can be a gain or loss in one's life. To look at some of the benefits as well as the consequences of seeking after a materialistic lifestyle.

PREPARATION

Attach each of the following to separate sheets of construction paper:

● A check for $10,000 and labeled "Savings account from parents." On this sheet write Luke 15:11-18.

● A mock deed labeled "'Deed for 260,000 acres of very rich, fertile land." Write Genesis 13:5-11.

● A savings account register book labeled "Large estate, valued at $900,000." List it in the register book as: "Estate, three houses, farm equipment, stables and animals, vineyards, barns, garages and storage buildings, woodlands, fields and crops." Write Luke 12:16-21 and Matthew 19:16-24.

● A picture of a sports car. You also can attach an old set of keys. Label this "Fast, shiny, new, racy sports car." Write Luke 12:31-34.

● Several travel brochures labeled "Traveling anywhere with all the money you need." Write Ecclesiastes 5:10.

● Several play money bills labeled "Job security, prestige, success and wealth." Write Luke 16:19-28.

You also will need Bibles, paper and pencils. Obtain 20 small items as prizes for the opening game.

OPENING

Explain the rules and play of the game Easy Come, Easy Go. Distribute pencils and papers.

Easy Come, Easy Go

Ask the participants to write 10 numbers between one and 75. The leader then rapidly calls out three numbers between one and 75. People who have written one of the numbers run to the table, grab a prize and return to their seats. This is repeated until all prizes have been claimed. When numbers are called, people with winning numbers may run to a person who already has a prize and claim it for themselves. Each time a new set of numbers is called, the prizes change hands. Those holding prizes at the last call get to keep them. Before the game begins, set a limit on numbers to be called.[1]

THE "MEAT" OF THE MEETING

After the game, explain the purpose of the meeting. Then have six of the participants each choose one of the construction paper items. If you have a large gathering, divide into smaller groups and give each group one of the items. (If you have a small group, you can eliminate one or two construction paper items.)

Explain that each group is to discuss benefits and hindrances to owning the object. Allow five to 10 minutes for this.

Have each group share its conclusions with the others. Give each group time to study the scripture reference. Gather in one large group to discuss these findings.

RESPONSE (OR CLOSING)

Explain: "Sometimes we tend to think and believe that the answer to any problem we have lies in material riches or possessions. We put our faith in material goods by thinking: If I had a good job and made lots of money, I'd be happy. If I had a fast sports car, I would be popular. If I had enough money to buy nice clothes, I'd attract friends. If I could travel the world, I'd have it made.

"On goes our list of 'if' or 'things' to make us happy, but Jesus says in Matthew 6:19-21: 'Do not lay up for yourselves treasures on earth where moth and rust consume and where thieves break in and steal, but lay up for yourselves treasures in heaven, where neither moss nor rust consumes and where thieves do not break in and steal. For where your treasure is, there will your heart be also.' "

Close with a circle prayer. Each person in the circle is invited to offer a request or thanksgiving.

---

[1]Bob Brewer, "Easy Come, Easy Go," GROUP Magazine (February 1980).

TITHES AND OFFERINGS, PART 1

by Douglas Karl

PURPOSE

To make young people aware of the role of finances in God's earthly work.

PREPARATION

Gather a bucket or offering plate, 100 to 200 pennies, two prizes (one of which can be a gag gift) and songbooks.

Note: This is session one of a two-part series.

OPENING

Open with songs, prayer, offering and announcements.

Play the game Give and Take. Begin by passing around a bucket of pennies. Tell the youth they can take as many or as few as they want.

After the coins have been distributed, have the youth mill about the room giving away or collecting as much money as possible. Instruct the youth to keep track of money they give or collect. When they run out of money, they keep playing by asking others for more.

Award prizes to the youth who gave away or collected the most pennies. Award the gag gift to the person with the least pennies.

Ask the following questions and allow time for discussion:

1. Did you feel any resentment toward those who took a lot of money?

2. How did you feel about the person who didn't get very much?

3. When I said you could take as much money as you wanted, what did you think?

4. Why did you take the amount of money you collected?

5. What types of feelings were you having as you were giving away money? collecting?

6. How did you feel about others having more money than you at the end of the game?

THE "MEAT" OF THE MEETING

Read the following material to the entire group:

"According to J.O. Atkinson, the crime of the ages has been the prostitution of money. Truly, money is one of the most powerful, yet dangerous forces in all the world. Perhaps this is why Jesus has more to say about the right use of possessions than any other subject. Someone figured there are 1,565 references to giving in the Bible, while there are only 523 references to praying. At least 20 of the 30 major parables by Jesus relate to attitudes toward property. It has been estimated that one verse out of every seven in the Gospels deals with money and the things money can buy."[1]

Allow time for questions and comments.

Read the next quote to the entire group, again allowing time for questions or comments:

"Modern man now has more money than ever before, but our wealth has brought us many strange and new problems. Never before have we had so much to live with and so little to live for. Never have we earned so much money with so little sweat. Never have we had so much time to waste and so much money with which to waste. Our money has brought us super-highways and jet planes and men in space, but it has left us without direction in life. It has brought us fine homes and left us with empty hearts. Instead of bringing us freedom, happiness and purpose, our prosperity has only increased our boredom and aimlessness. The free-spending practices of our fat-salaried society have corrupted us within. Our almighty dollar has given us a false security not unlike that which the Laodiceans had when they bragged about being rich—but heard God remind them that they were wretched, misera-ble, poor, blind and naked. Many of us have allowed our money to curse us instead of bless us. We are, in fact, being kicked to death by the golden calf. Maybe God is trying to say to us, 'Give account of thy stewardship.' "[2]

Break into four small groups and give each group a situation. They are to decide how they would act in the situation.

● Your church is experiencing a financial crisis. You are a board member. The church has been late in its building payments the past three months. Because of the lag-ging offerings, the church will be $1,000 short of its building pay-ment this month. You recently sold a large collection of wood-carved ducks for $3,000 so you could pave your driveway. Do you go ahead with this project or help the church in this time of need?

● You have just won $100 in a raffle. You are really excited about your win. The first thing you do is take the family to eat at a plush restaurant, attend a Christian con-cert and buy a good gospel record. A few weeks go by and you realize you forgot to give God 10 percent of your winnings. You say, "That's just $10, God won't miss it, be-sides I bought a good gospel rec-ord with it." Would you agree with the above or do something dif-ferently?

● You are taking a group of teenagers to visit your denomina-tional college. The church gives you $20 for your meals while on campus. You get to campus and find sponsors receive a free meal pass. What would you do with the money when you return home? Why?

● You and your wife decided that you were seeking more of God's blessing, so you have been double-tithing for 10 years. In that 10-year period you have seen your income triple and God bless you with three children. Through an ac-cident on a neighborhood play-ground one of your children loses sight in one eye. Two months later you find the bank is suing you for $150,000, the remainder of the bal-ance due the bank on your home. They are suing because the loan company you bought your home through went bankrupt. Finally, your wife is involved in a car acci-dent that does $4,000 damage to her car, yet she was not injured. You had forgotten to renew your car insurance policy and you were not insured. Do you stop double-tithing because you need the extra money and things aren't going your way or do you trust God for the future and continue in your giving?

RESPONSE (OR CLOSING)

One spokesman from each group shares the solution to its situation with the entire group and allows discussion. Do the rest of the group members agree or disagree with the solution?

Ask the youth to think about this session during the upcoming week and consider tithes for the next meeting.

Pray for God's guidance in finances and tithes.

HELPFUL RESOURCES

Scriptures to Sing, Lillenas, Box 527, Kansas City, MO 64141.

[1,2]F.C. Spruce, **You Can Be a Joyful Tither** (Kansas City, Mo.: Beacon Hill, 1966), pp. 14-15.

TITHES AND OFFERINGS, PART 2

by Douglas Karl

PURPOSE

To encourage young people to be joyful in their giving of tithes and talent.

PREPARATION

Gather Bibles, two chairs for the role play, paper, chalk and chalkboard, or newsprint and felt-tip marker.

Contact two youth to act in the role plays of the reluctant giver and the cheerful giver (see the Opening section).

Select two adults to share personal testimonies about tithing and giving. Be sure their views are in keeping with the church. Have one witness the importance of tithes, needs of the church and personal rewards. Have the other witness on the importance of giving offerings above tithes, the difference of this type of giving, personal rewards and other philosophies and beliefs.

On separate pieces of paper, type out these scripture verses: Leviticus 27:30-33; Deuteronomy 12:6; 14:22; and Nehemiah 10:38-39. Make copies for all participants.

Note: This is the second part of a two-part series.

OPENING

Include an offering in your opening and a prayer that the previous meeting on this subject will become a guide for the youth in their finances and tithes.

Have the youth present the role plays:

The Reluctant Giver—The first actor sits in a chair in front of the group pretending to be watching television. The second actor knocks on the door. The person inside greets the visitor and they both are seated. They begin to converse, and the visitor says the church is starting a new ministry and asks the other's involvement.

The first actor makes excuses of being too busy. The visitor says, "Well, if you think you're too busy to give of your time, would you consider helping support the ministry financially?"

The first actor makes various excuses about house and boat payments and the cost of bowling two nights a week. Reluctantly, however, the first actor makes a nominal contribution.

The Cheerful Giver—The role play is done just as it was the first time, only the first actor reacts positively when asked to donate time and money. With enthusiasm, the cheerful giver incorporates the teachings of 2 Corinthians 9:7.

THE "MEAT" OF THE MEETING

Discuss the role plays, asking:

• With which giver do you identify?

• Have you ever known someone like the reluctant giver? What were your thoughts toward that person?

• Why do you think some people are reluctant givers?

• Have you ever known someone like the cheerful giver? How did that person make you feel?

• Is tithing your time and talents as valuable as tithing money?

• Read aloud and discuss Matthew 5:42 and Luke 6:38.

• Which giver is more in tune with these scriptures? Why?

Have the two adults from the congregation share their views on tithing and giving. Afterward, allow the youth time to ask questions.

Explain tithing and giving were instituted by God at the time of Moses. The verses typed prior to this session describe tithing at the time of Moses. Distribute the verses and have the young people read them and keep the messages in mind as they discuss the seven statements in the Closing.

RESPONSE (OR CLOSING)

On the left side of the chalkboard or newsprint, number one through seven. Make two columns, one titled "agree" and the other "disagree." After each of the following statements are read, ask for a show of hands for those who agree of disagree and write the responses. Discuss each statement after voting.

• Because love should be spontaneous, we should not be systematic in giving.

• If I am in debt, I should tithe anyway.

• If I disagree with the way the church spends my money, I should withhold my tithe.

• Children, widows, housewives and others with small incomes should not tithe.

• It is bad for me to pay my tithe in one lump sum at the end of the year.

• If I sing in the choir, I don't have to tithe because I'm working for free.

• It's okay to give regularly to special projects and not to tithe.

Have each youth silently think of personal tithes. How can each one give to the church monetarily or in time commitments?

Thank the two adults who gave testimonies and ask them to close with a prayer on the importance of honoring and respecting God with tithes.

HELPFUL RESOURCES

Scriptures to Sing, Lillenas, Box 527, Kansas City, MO 64141.

IN GOD WE TRUST

by Beverly Hecht

PURPOSE

To help the youth learn about Christian stewardship by working on time and talent pledges and financial commitments. To study relevant scripture.

PREPARATION

Gather a candle, matches, pencils and envelopes. (Songbooks are optional.)

Print the scripture promise passages (found in the Opening Section) on cards or paper. For a creative touch, add artwork to the cards.

Make copies of the following for each member:

● The Discussion Guide, which is in the "Meat" of the Meeting section.

● The Monthly Budget Guide and the Youth Financial Goal Planner as described on the following page. Note: The budget guide and goal planner are optional.

● The Time and Talent Pledge and the Financial Commitment, which are also listed on the following page.

OPENING

Open with singing, then form groups of eight. Give each a different scripture promise card. Use these passages: Proverbs 19:17; Malachi 3:10; Luke 6:38; 12:24; 12:29-31; 2 Corinthians 9:7; 9:8; and Philippians 4:19.

THE "MEAT" OF THE MEETING

Have the oldest person in each group serve as its discussion leader and distribute the Discussion Guide.

Discussion Guide

● Read your scripture promise card and discuss its meaning within your group.

● Which promise brings you greatest comfort and assurance?

● Which promise most challenges you to return to the Lord a portion of what he has first given to you?

● What makes it so difficult to commit to giving God a specific portion of our time, talents and money?

● Does "If you give, you will get," mean the same as "You will get only if you give"? Why doesn't God's giving depend solely upon if or how much we give?

● How has God blessed you beyond your basic needs of survival? How will you respond to his goodness?

If you decide to use the Monthly Budget Guide and the Youth Financial Goal Planner, distribute them and the pencils to the groups as they finish their discussions. Be available for questions. Encourage the youth to discuss their plans with their parents.

Monthly Budget Guide

1. What do you receive monthly for your own use? $_____

2. What percentage have you promised to return to the Lord?
_____ % = $_____

3. Subtract the amount of your tithe from your monthly income for a subtotal. $_____

4. List your monthly expenses and their approximate amount. (Note if your parents help.)

school lunches	$_____
clothes	$_____
car expense	$_____
social events	$_____
miscellaneous events	$_____
Total	$_____

5. Subtract your monthly expenses from the subtotal in question 3 for a monthly savings goal. $_____.

Youth Financial Goal Planner

1. My long-range financial goal is (college, car, etc.): _____

2. Amount needed: $_____

3. Needed by (date): _____

4. Length of investment period (number of months from present until money is needed): _____

5. Monthly savings (estimate goal): $_____

RESPONSE (OR CLOSING)

Gather into one large group and distribute the Time and Talent Pledge and the Financial Commitment. The Time and Talent Pledge lists opportunities for youth to be involved in various ministries in both the congregation and the community. (Add to or delete from the list.)

Time and Talent Pledge

"All that I am and have is a gift from God. What I do with it is my gift to him."

In joyous response to God's many gifts to me, I will pledge myself to serve him in this manner:

_____usher
_____reader
_____office helper
_____banner maker
_____kitchen helper
_____yard worker
_____prayer chain
_____candy striper
_____greeter
_____worship assistant
_____communion preparer
_____baby sitter for Bible classes
_____elderly and shut-in visitation
_____peer counselor
_____assistant in vacation Bible school
_____youth-to-youth outreach

_____
(signed)

_____
(phone)

_____
(date)

Financial Commitment

Lord,

In response to the material blessings you have given me, I promise to return to you _____% of my income.

My offering will be $_____ per week.

_____
(signed)

_____
(date)

Ask the youth to read these statements and allow a moment

for silent prayer as each youth decides what his or her commitment will be. Promise the young people that their financial commitment will be kept between themselves and God and not even you will know what they have written.

Note: Some young people do not have jobs or allowances. Assure them that time is just as important to tithe as money. Do not make the youth feel guilty if they are not ready to pledge at this time. Simply encourage them to think about the subject of stewardship.

When everyone has finished, have the participants seal their financial commitments in the envelopes and self-address the envelopes. If they are not ready to pledge, have them write a prayer concerning their thoughts about this meeting. Nine to 12 months later, return their pledges to them as a reminder of their commitment or thoughts. Use the Time and Talent Pledge as a resource list and involve the group members in the ministries.

Lead the youth around the lighted candle in a darkened room. Ask for eight volunteers to each read one of the eight different scripture promise cards.

Then, give one person the candle, ask him or her to share what discovery or decision he or she has made as a result of this study. When finished, have the first youth place his or her envelope and pledge sheet in the center of the circle and then pass the candle to the next person.

When everyone has had an opportunity to share and all the envelopes and Time and Talent Pledges are in the center, replace the candle in their midst. Link arms and close with a prayer.

HELPFUL RESOURCES

Jesus Pocket Promise Book, Regal Books, 2300 Knoll Drive, Ventura, CA 93003.

Songs, Songs and Creations, P.O. Box 7, San Anselmo, CA 94960.

If a banker or investment consultant is a member of the congregation, ask him or her to be available to assist the youth with their Monthly Budget Guide and the Youth Financial Goal Planner.

TO ABUSE OR NOT TO ABUSE

by Ben Sharpton

PURPOSE

To lead young people to understand issues involved in substance abuse, and for the youth to formulate their own Christian views of substance use based on scripture and Christian traditions.

The issue of drug and alcohol abuse has been approached from many different perspectives. Varied approaches all have a place because young people respond to different emphases. Some youth need "black and white" arguments, while others may reject that format as another opportunity for adults to "preach" at youth. Other young people respond to personal testimonies of former drug users, though some may interpret such testimonies to indicate that people can abuse drugs for a time and still survive.

Other young people may be interested in a strictly educational approach, emphasizing physical effects of different chemicals. Some young people, however, may find that such a program piques their curiosity and interest instead of discouraging drug use.

This program approaches substance abuse education from the perspective of helping young people clarify and understand the issues and then to make their own decisions based on their understanding of scripture and Christian tradition. No one knows the needs of your situation better than you. Take time to structure this program around your group's needs. As in any curriculum, adapt this to your group. Add testimonies, a panel of experts, biblical preaching or whatever you feel would best minister to your youth group.

Above all, accept, affirm and support your young people. Many young people begin abusing drugs and alcohol because of personal feelings of inadequacy, and the church should not contribute to such anxieties.

PREPARATION

Gather Bibles, paper, pencils, blackboard and chalk or newsprint and felt-tip markers. On 3 × 5 cards write the "most desirable" and "least desirable" behavior (see the Closing). Prepare copies of the Anonymous Quiz in the Opening.

Become familiar with the passages of scripture. Discover what each says about use and abuse of alcohol and determine if they also speak to other substance abuses. You may want to ask your minister for personal advice about your church's views on substance abuse.

Study the procedure for the debate used in the "Meat" of the Meeting. Think through the anticipated views of each side.

Prepare the room.

Pray for guidance and assistance throughout the session.

OPENING

Distribute copies of the Anonymous Quiz to the members of the group.

Anonymous Quiz

Directions: Place a check by each of the following items that apply to you. Do not sign your name.

☐ I have never tasted an alcoholic drink.

☐ I have never been drunk.

☐ I have had a drink in the past two weeks.

☐ I easily could get marijuana.

☐ I have tried hallucinogens.

☐ Some of my closest friends have tried hallucinogens.

☐ I have spiked my dog's water dish.

☐ I have persuaded someone else to drink alcohol.

☐ I have successfully discouraged someone else from drinking or taking drugs.

☐ I think marijuana should be legalized.

☐ My parents drink quite often.

☐ The decision to use or abuse drugs or alcohol is up to the individual. What may be right for some may not be right for others.

☐ Christians should not hang around substance abusers.

☐ I think members of our youth group have a problem with drinking.

☐ People in our youth group abuse drugs.

☐ I once vowed never to drink, but have since broken that promise.

☐ The legal age for drinking should be lowered.

☐ Penalties for drunken driving should be stricter.

☐ Alcohol should be banned in our community.

☐ Substance use is okay as long as it is done in moderation.

Have them write yes or no by each item, indicating their opinions. Explain that they are not to sign their names, although you will study the findings together as a group. After everyone has finished the quiz, collect and redistribute the questionnaire to the group. Discuss each statement, asking the students to raise their hands if the sheet they are holding has a check by that item.

After a few of the statements, you can ask for volunteers to share responses to the quiz. Is the vote accurate? Do they agree?

Explain in your own words that this session will deal with the issue of substance abuse. Some people interpret this to mean illegal drug abuse, but most include alcohol abuse in their interpretation. Some people also include caffeine and chocolate. For the purpose of this session, we will include any substance that can be taken internally which will alter a person's physical or emotional state. This program will present them with the option of making their own decisions regarding substance abuse, and will give them a chance to take a stand on their decision.

THE "MEAT" OF THE MEETING

Take a few minutes to talk and list as many substances as the young people can which can be abused. List these substances on the blackboard or newsprint. Answers can include: marijuana, alcohol, tranquilizers, coffee, soft drinks, sleeping pills, cigarettes, aspirin, cocaine and chocolate.

Study the list and work as a group to identify those items which are discouraged or condemned by our society. Ask for volunteers to suggest reasons some are allowed and others are discouraged. Is this a double standard and if so, should it be challenged?

On another piece of newsprint or section of the blackboard, list reasons people abuse these substances. Reasons your group might suggest are: to feel better or happy, be accepted, escape from pain, satisfy one's curiosity, escape from stress, help "forget" and to control feelings and behaviors.

Examine each reason and take a group vote. Have the youth give a "thumbs-up" sign if they consider that reason is all right, and a "thumbs-down" sign if they disapprove of that reason. Don't dwell on the reasons, but do give individuals an opportunity to express reasons the item is acceptable or unacceptable.

Divide into two groups. (If you have more than 25 in attendance, you can divide into more groups.) Give each group one of the following tasks:

Group 1 should read the following verses and then prepare arguments for abstaining from substance abuse: Proverbs 20:1; Luke 21:34-35; Romans 13:11-14; 14:13-21; 1 Corinthians 6:9-11; Galatians 5:19-21.

Group 2 should take the following verses and work to find reasons that indicate some substance use is all right: Genesis 1:28-31; Matthew 11:16-19; John 2:1-11; Romans 14:14 and 1 Timothy 5:23.

After each group has compiled its arguments, re-form one large group. Place six chairs in the center of the room and ask each group to send three representatives to sit in their group's chairs and debate for their group's view. People can only talk if sitting in one of the chairs. If someone wants to talk, he or she may take the place of a debater, "tag-team style."

After the debate, discuss what transpired using the following questions:

● Do you think it is possible to prove through the use of biblical texts that using alcohol or drugs is right or wrong for Christians?

● Based on what you have studied, what guidelines would you recommend for Christians regarding alcohol and drug use?

● How difficult is it to change another's opinion regarding substance abuse? What seems to be the most convincing arguments?

RESPONSE (OR CLOSING)

Divide into small groups of six or eight and give each group a set of 3 x 5 cards on which you have written the following behaviors. Assign the task of placing the behaviors in order of most to least desirable.

You stayed home by yourself one night and got drunk.

You went out with non-Christian friends and got drunk.

Your nervous aunt abuses a prescription drug.

Your father takes tranquilizers.

You drank beer on the last youth retreat.

The minister of education went to a friend's party and had a couple of drinks.

After a recent illness, you find that you are addicted to the medication.

The chairman of your church board smokes cigarettes.

You are having a chocolate attack.

A counselor ordered beer at a youth party at a pizza parlor.

A youth counselor ordered a round of beers for youth while at a luncheon.

You had a glass of champagne at your sister's wedding.

After each group has created its ranking, have the members decide which of the behaviors are abuses. Why?

If time permits, have each group share the responses with the rest of the group.

As a total group, create a program on substance abuse for people at least three years younger than the members of your group. Decide what goals, methods and audio-visuals will be used.

After the group has had time to plan its program, arrange to present it to a Sunday school class or service club. Plan the presentation within two weeks of the session. Delegate responsibilities and assist in organization where necessary, but leave most of the work to the young people.

Note: If your group is fairly large, you may want to divide into smaller groups of eight to 15. Close in prayer asking that the youth depend only on God using his promises as strengths during times of need.

HELPFUL RESOURCES

Did I Have a Good Time?, by Marion Howard, Continuum, 815 Second Ave., New York, NY 10017.

"The Drinking Game," GROUP Magazine, Dec. 1978, Box 481, Loveland, CO 80539.

THE CARE AND PREVENTION OF SUICIDE

by Ben Lane

PURPOSE

To give youth practical guidelines on suicide prevention based upon biblical principles.

PREPARATION

Gather and print information about suicide prevention programs in your area. Make copies of these resources for each youth.

Prepare five skits based upon a suicide crisis as outlined in the Opening.

Make copies of the following which are listed in the "Meat" of the Meeting: biblical references to suicide, the Intervention—What Can We Do to Help guide, and the Care and Prevention of Suicide[1] handout.

OPENING

Divide the participants into five small groups. Assign each group one of the following "hints" or "cues" that people give when considering suicide.[2] Each group prepares a short skit using all its members.

In the verbally direct hint, one actor makes a blatant statement, "I want to kill myself."

In the verbally indirect cue, an actor says, "I don't care what happens to me."

In the sudden emotional change, the actor changes character—from an extrovert to an introvert.

In the severe behavioral change hint, the actor does something atypical, such as gives away a treasured collection.

The last one involves changes in appearance. The actor (usually neatly dressed) gives hints of suicidal thoughts by dressing slovenly.

The hints can be given in any order or melded. The dialogue needs to be terse and realistic. Each small group takes its turn performing for the large group.

Following the skits, lead a discussion using these questions:

● What were the five suicidal hints given in the skits?

● What would you do in these situations?

● How would you determine the seriousness of the hints? (Factors that affect suicidal risk include age, sex, race, marital status, employment situation, mental illness, previous suicide attempts and psychiatric disorders.)

● Why would someone want to commit suicide? (Causes of suicide include depression, loss of a relationship, guilt, hopelessness, sin, disappointment, low self-esteem, perceived or real failure, or unrealistic expectations.)

THE "MEAT" OF THE MEETING

Have the youth read the following biblical references regarding suicide: Judges 16:29-30; 1 Samuel 31:4-5; 2 Samuel 17:23; 1 Kings

16:18-19; and Matthew 27:5. In each passage, who was the person who committed suicide? What was the reason? Could you have prevented these suicides?

Read through and discuss the intervention handout. Give one to each person.

Intervention—What Can We Do to Help?

- Make the environment safe.
- Be willing to listen. A suicidal person needs to feel friendship, love, acceptance and a sense that somebody cares. Try to get the person to talk and express his or her feelings.
- Evaluate the seriousness of the situation. If the situation is too serious for you, consult community resources such as a suicide crisis telephone line, friends or your family. You also can turn to your church and its staff, youth leader or congregation for help. If the situation seems less serious, lend a listening ear and share scriptures dealing with hope such as: Psalms 23; 51; 55:22; 71:5; John 3:16; 15:9; Romans 5:8; Philippians 4:13; and 1 Peter 5:7.

Distribute and discuss the following handout:

Care and Prevention of Suicide

- A few facts and statistics can help you deal with people who are suicidal. For example, did you know females attempt suicide three times as often as males, although males are three times as likely to actually commit suicide. Furthermore, suicide is the second leading cause of death for adolescents.
- Suicides are more prevalent at the beginning and end of school semesters, on Mondays and Saturdays, during spring and Christmas, and during the late afternoon or early evening.
- Those who attempt suicide can be categorized into two groups, those who don't want to die and those who do want to die.
- Typical of those who don't want to die are statements used to manipulate others, such as, "If you don't marry me, I'll kill myself."
- Also, those who really don't want to die use the threat of suicide as a distress signal. These people often have drug-or alcohol-related problems.
- Those who really do want to commit suicide often want to punish someone. Other common factors among those seriously suicidal are the desire to join a loved one already dead, mental disorders, a seemingly unsolvable problem, or stress and depression.
- Of the people who are seriously suicidal, 71 percent are from broken homes.
- By intervening, you can save a life. To do so, look for warning signs and don't ignore any threats. Be willing to listen to the troubled person and then evaluate the seriousness of the situation. Certainly, don't be fooled if he or she says the crisis is over. Remember the parable of the good Samaritan who went "the extra mile," and do so, too. Refer the person to professional help as soon as possible.
- It's useful to know and re-

member these suicidal "cues" or "hints": verbally direct cue, verbally indirect cue, sudden emotional change, severe behavioral alteration, and changes in appearance.

RESPONSE (OR CLOSING)

To close, answer any questions the youth may have. Be certain they have the resource list for suicide prevention in your area. Make yourself open for counseling in case of a suicide crisis.

---

[1]Helen Hosier, **Suicide, A Call for Help** (Eugene, Ore.: Harvest House, 1978), p. 36.

[2]Frank B. Minirth and Paul Meier, **Happiness Is a Choice** (Grand Rapids, Mich.: Baker, 1978), p. 31.

SUICIDE

EXPLORING THE CHRISTIAN LIFESTYLE

by Peggy Frey

PURPOSE

To show there are many alternate lifestyles from which to choose; to show the difference between worldly lifestyles and true discipleship.

PREPARATION

Gather chalkboard and chalk or newsprint and felt-tip markers, paper, pencils and Bibles.

On small pieces of paper, list the following scripture verses: Matthew 16:24-25; 23:13-14; 23:25-28; Mark 7:6-9; Acts 8:3; 10:42-43; 2 Corinthians 13:5-6; Galatians 5:15; Ephesians 6:18-19; James 3:17; 1 Peter 3:3-4.

On 3 x 5 cards, write the tasks and alternate decisions. Gather the materials needed to do each task. Examples of cards are:

Task—Inflate a balloon and sit on it until it breaks.

Alternative—Stand up, turn in a circle and sit down five times.

Task—Get a small object (such as a fork, spoon or piece of chalk) and tie it around your neck for the rest of the meeting.

Alternative—Sit on the floor in the center of the meeting room for the remainder of the meeting.

Task—Get someone in the group to give you any amount of money.

Alternative—You give someone else some money and if you do not have any money with you, you must borrow some from someone else, promising to repay it.

Task—Borrow a pencil from someone and write one sentence describing your youth leader. Read the sentence to the group and return the pencil.

Alternative—Give the group your full name, address, telephone number, birth date, favorite color and television program.

Task—Get four other people in the group to do 10 jumping jacks.

Alternative—Tell the group three things about yourself, two of which are true and one that is a lie. Have them guess which one is the lie.

Task—Lead the group in a song of your choice.

Alternative—Stand in front of the group and recite your favorite nursery rhyme.

OPENING

Point out that throughout life there are many choices that will determine the kind of lifestyle to be lived. Explain you are going to play Alternate Choices, a game that involves making decisions.

Ask for as many volunteers as you have prepared task cards.

Give each participant one of the cards and explain they have a choice, they can either do what is on the card or they can trade it for an alternative card. If they trade their card, they must do the task

248

on the alternate card.

Proceed with the game until each participant has had a chance to perform the task. Ask what was difficult about the game. What makes some decisions difficult? Once a decision is made, is it difficult to follow through with the appropriate actions?

THE "MEAT" OF THE MEETING

Distribute papers and pencils and ask each individual to list some things that might turn people off to Christianity or prove to be hypocritical. Give the youth three to five minutes, then ask individuals to share with the group one thing from their list. Write the items on the chalkboard or newsprint under headings such as "Phony Christianity" or "Stumbling Blocks."

Then have the youth list on their individual papers some qualities or characteristics of a Christian or true disciple. Ask individuals to share one of these qualities with the rest of the group. List them on the chalkboard or newsprint under headings such as "True Discipleship" or "Real Christianity."

After you have completed the two lists and gone over them with the group, distribute the Bibles and the slips of paper with the scripture verses and explain you'll be studying about faith. Ask whether the scriptures depict qualities of a phony or true disciple. Which qualities should we display in our lifestyles? Which should we try to avoid?

RESPONSE (OR CLOSING)

Explain the first steps to becoming a true disciple of Jesus are to believe in him and to trust him.

Ask a youth to read John 3:16. Discuss the meaning of this verse. Explain: We can try to be "real Christians" and try to avoid "phoniness," but we are human and we can fail. Don't be discouraged by failures to be a true disciple. The main point to remember is God loves us and sent his son to die for us. All we have to do is believe. The rest falls in place according to his grace.

Close with a group prayer thanking God for giving us guidelines to live by and for his forgiveness when we fail.

PERSONALIZED PROVERBS

by Cindy S. Hansen

PURPOSE

To see the wisdom of proverbs by personalizing them and making them more meaningful and to apply the proverbs to a real-life situation.

PREPARATION

Print 3 x 5 cards with one of the following proverbs on each: Proverbs 1:8-9; 4:13; 4:26-27; 6:12-15; 6:20; 6:34; 9:13-15; 11:2; 11:9; 11:12-13; 12:25; 13:3; 13:20; 14:29; 15:1; 17:22; 22:6; 25:17.

Gather prizes, paper, pencils, Bibles for everyone and two signs. On one print: NEVER DO THIS. On the other print: ALWAYS DO THIS.

On slips of paper print well-known proverbs and then cut them in half for the opening game. Examples:

Silence	is golden
One good turn	deserves another
When in Rome	do as the Romans do
All that glistens	is not gold
The early bird	catches the worm
Birds of a feather	flock together
He who laughs last	laughs best
You can't have your cake	and eat it too
It takes two	to make a quarrel
People who live in glass houses	shouldn't throw stones
Two wrongs	don't make a right
A stitch in time	saves nine

A barking dog	never bites
A fool and his money	are soon parted
Every cloud	has a silver lining
It takes a thief	to catch a thief
All good things	must come to an end
A penny saved	is a penny earned
Honesty	is the best policy
Absence	makes the heart grow fonder
A watched pot	never boils
A rolling stone	gathers no moss
Rome	wasn't built in a day
An apple a day	keeps the doctor away
Brevity	is the soul of wit
Curiosity	killed the cat
Health	is better than wealth
A friend in need	is a friend indeed
Variety	is the spice of life

OPENING

Open with the game Fractured Proverbs. The proverbs that have been typed and cut in two are put in two separate piles. The idea is not to combine the original parts. Members should be encouraged to create their own new proverbs. For example: "An apple a day keeps the doctor away," would split down the middle as would, "A watched pot never boils." It would be acceptable if a member who chose "A watched pot" matched with a member who chose "keeps the doctor away." Award prizes for the most original proverbs.[1] Let the pairs share fractured proverbs with the entire group.

THE "MEAT" OF THE MEETING

Read sample proverbs to begin discussion: "The fear of the Lord is the beginning of wisdom, and the knowledge of the Holy One is insight" (Proverbs 9:10). "Pride goes before destruction, and a haughty spirit before a fall" (Proverbs 16:18).

Ask the group to define "proverb." What is included in a proverb? Are proverbs effective ways of teaching? Why or why not?

Divide into small groups of three to four and assign each two or three proverbs (written on 3×5 cards). Each group reads one proverb at a time and tries to think of a situation that has happened to its members that is similar to the proverb. What was the problem? What people were involved? Where did it happen? What was the outcome? How would you have liked it to end differently?

Choose one real-life situation per group and prepare a two-scene skit. Scene one shows how the event actually was in real life. One person will hold a NEVER DO THIS sign before it is shown. The second scene depicts a better ending

for the skit. A person holds the ALWAYS DO THIS sign before it is shown. One at a time, each small group presents its two scenes to the large group. The large group first tries to guess the proverb or the message—then a narrator reads the proverb on which the real-life situation was based.

Example: One person holds the NEVER DO THIS sign.

Scene one: A table is surrounded by gossips. One person stands close by and overhears the conversation and then runs and tells another person. That person then tells the people at the table who glare at the eavesdropper.

The ALWAYS DO THIS sign is shown.

Scene two: A table of gossips. One person overhears them, goes to the table and confronts their gossip.

The large group then tries to guess which proverb was depicted. Then a person reads, "Argue your case with your neighbor himself, and do not disclose another's secret; lest he who hears you bring shame upon you, and your ill repute have no end" (Proverbs 25:9-10).

RESPONSE (OR CLOSING)

Open a prayer time by asking for the wisdom of the proverbs and the judgment to know the best way to behave during difficult situations.

---

[1]Lee Sparks, ed., **Try This One . . . Too** (Loveland, Colo.: Group Books, 1982), p.12-13.

251

CONTRIBUTORS

Steve Allen

Tim Barnes

Lawrence Bauer

Dennis C. Benson

Karl Blaser

Karen Ceckowski

Paul Copeland

Robert C. Crosby

Dean Dammann

Roger Dill

Martin Doering

Peggy Frey

Cindy S. Hansen

Matthew E. Hartsell

Beverly Hecht

Christian Just

Douglas Karl

Larry Keefauver

Ben Lane

Joani Lillevold

Walter Mees, Jr.

Glen Miles

Gary Moran

Patrick M. Mulcahy

Mark Mustful

Bruce Nichols

David Olshine

Donald W. Palmore

Bill Pieper

Dave Pearce

Mark Reed

James P. Reeves

Arlo R. Reichter

Maryellen Reidy

Gary Richardson

Ed Rush

Thom Schultz

Ben Sharpton

John Shaw

Rickey Short

Lee Sparks

Tammy Spigelmire

Wesley Taylor

Paul M. Thompson

Denise Turner

Margaret Tyree

Bob and Debbie Valleau

Michael Walcheski

Linda Webster

Sandra Wilmoth

Bill Wolfe

Frank Zolvinski

ABOUT THE AUTHOR

Mr. Richard W. Bimler is the executive secretary for the Board for Youth Services, Lutheran Church—Missouri Synod. Before joining the synodical national staff, Mr. Bimler was assistant to the president of the Minnesota South District, LCMS, in the areas of youth ministry, evangelism and social ministry. While in the district, he also taught part time at Concordia College (St. Paul, Minnesota). He has served in various positions for major Lutheran youth gatherings and has been a speaker and leader for various groups throughout the country.

Mr. Bimler was born and raised in Illinois. He was graduated from the Youth Leadership Training Program of Valparaiso University with a bachelor's degree in theology. He earned his master of arts degree in counseling and guidance from the University of Missouri, and has done further graduate work at Concordia College (River Forest, Illinois) and the University of Houston.

Mr. Bimler has written many books, articles, tracts and other educational youth ministry materials. His previous books are **Pray, Praise, and Hooray!**; **77 Ways to Involve Youth in the Church**; **Lord, I Want to Celebrate** and **The New You** (all published by Concordia Publishing House) and **Grand Opening—Prayers From the Empty Tomb** (C.S.S. Publishing). He also has written articles for various publications such as Resources for Youth Ministry, GROUP Magazine and the Lutheran Education Journal.

Richard Bimler and his wife Hazel have three children: Diane, Bob and Mike.

OTHER YOUTH MINISTRY RESOURCES FROM

COUNSELING TEENAGERS, BY DR. G. KEITH OLSON. The authoritative, complete and practical reference for understanding and helping today's adolescents. Hardbound, 528 pages. $19.95.

THE BASIC ENCYCLOPEDIA FOR YOUTH MINISTRY, BY DENNIS BENSON AND BILL WOLFE. Answers, ideas, encouragement, and inspiration for 230 youth ministry questions and problems. A handy reference. Hardbound. $15.95.

THE GROUP RETREAT BOOK, BY ARLO REICHTER. This is *the* resource for start-to-finish retreat planning, execution and evaluation . . . plus 34 ready-to-use retreat outlines. 400 pages. $15.95.

HARD TIMES CATALOG FOR YOUTH MINISTRY, BY MARILYN AND DENNIS BENSON. Hundreds of low-cost and no-cost ideas for programs, projects, meetings and activities. $14.95.

THE YOUTH GROUP HOW-TO-BOOK. Detailed instructions and models for 66 practical projects and programs to help you build a better group. $14.95.

CLOWN MINISTRY, BY FLOYD SHAFFER AND PENNE SEWALL. Everything you need to know to begin a clown ministry or enhance your present ministry. Includes 30 detailed skits and over 50 short clowning ideas. $7.95.

YEARBOOK: UNTOLD STORIES, BY BILL WOLFE AND JANITA WOLFE. Each page of this book shares experiences from the viewpoint of a person looking back on his or her high school years. The readers will examine their own struggles and feelings in their search for self-identity, friends, acceptance and God. $5.95.

LEADERS GUIDE FOR YEARBOOK: UNTOLD STORIES, BY BILL AND MARTHA WOLFE. This leaders guide is a *must* for youth group use of **Yearbook: Untold Stories**. Over 70 meeting outlines, a retreat outline and a large-group event outline. $6.95.

THE BEST OF TRY THIS ONE (Volume 1). A fun collection of games, crowd-breakers and programs from GROUP Magazine's "Try This One" section. $5.95.

MORE . . . TRY THIS ONE (Volume 2). A bonanza of youth group ideas—crowd-breakers, stunts, games, discussions and fund raisers. $5.95.

TRY THIS ONE . . . TOO (Volume 3). The newest in this popular series. Scores of creative youth ministry ideas. $5.95.

STARTING A YOUTH MINISTRY, BY DR. LARRY KEEFAUVER. An insightful book with tips on starting a youth ministry program or revitalizing an existing program. $5.95.

FRIEND TO FRIEND, BY J. DAVID STONE AND LARRY KEEFAUVER. Provides a simple yet powerful method for helping a friend sort through thoughts, feelings and behaviors of life problems. $4.95.

Available at Christian bookstores or directly from the publisher: Group Books, P.O. Box 481, Loveland, CO 80539. Enclose $2 for postage and handling with each order from the publisher.